INTERCOLLEGIATE FORENSICS

A Project of the Northern California Forensics Association

Edited by

T. C. Winebrenner

California Polytechnic State University
San Luis Obipso

KENDALL/HUNT PUBLISHING COMPANY
4050 Westmark Drive   Dubuque, Iowa 52002

This edition has been printed directly from camera-ready copy.

ISBN 0-8403-9749-6

Printed in the United States of America
10 9 8 7 6 5 4 3

Table of Contents

Part III: The Oral Interpretation Events

Part IV: The Debate Events

Preface

This book was born in 1983 as a project of the Northern California Forensics Association, a professional organization of community college, college and university forensics programs in Northern California, Southern Oregon and Nevada. In its first incarnation, distributed as the *NCFA Handbook*, the manuscript was little more than a mimeographed collection of handouts from various forensics classes. The initial idea was that students could profit from access to the collective experience and wisdom of the NCFA coaching community. For seven years, under the capable guidance of Allan McKissick, then Director of Forensics at Modesto Junior College, the manuscript evolved into a more complete volume of forensics instructional materials.

The second phase of development began in 1990, when the Association decided to reframe the manuscript as a comprehensive introductory forensics textbook. Although the *NCFA Handbook* was originally intended as a resource for member programs, the Association began to receive requests to make the volume available to forensics programs outside the area. While the manuscript had served members well as an *ad hoc* handbook of tips and advice, it was ill-suited for distribution as a textbook — too much of the material remained in handout form, and there were gaping holes in the contents. Phase two involved replacing handouts with instructional articles, commissioning articles on the many standard forensics events missing from the phase one manuscript, and seeking critical feedback from forensics educators outside the Northern California region. To symbolize the new direction the project was taking, the revamped manuscript was distributed under the title *Intercollegiate Forensics: A Participant's Handbook.*

This textbook represents the final phase of the project. It now contains instructional articles on each of the platform speaking, oral interpretation and debate events commonly offered at intercollegiate forensics tournaments. Several new articles were commissioned for this phase, including an introductory essay on "The Values of Forensics Participation," and the remaining articles were revised in order that the final product would reflect the cohesion and sense of purpose necessary for an introductory textbook. To reflect the final transition from handbook to textbook, the manuscript now is called simply *Intercollegiate Forensics.*

I would like to thank my friends and colleagues in the Northern California Forensics Association for encouraging, supporting, and contributing to this project. I particularly would like to thank Allan McKissick and Jan McKissick for initiating the project, as well as Diana Crossman, Mark Crossman, Steve Hunt and Brenda Logue, who read and critiqued the phase two manuscript.

Finally, I would like to thank the scores of forensics students with whom I have had the pleasure of working over the past twenty-three years. In their own way, they each have contributed substantially to my philosophy of forensics education, and helped sustain my belief in the value of forensics competition.

The Values of Forensics Participation
Steve Hunt

Self-expression is truly an art, and its successful development requires steady practice and determination. To articulate one's thoughts in a lucid and expressive manner — to capture and maintain the interest of an audience, whether it be in the classroom or in the United Nations General Assembly Hall — is strongly supported by the skill and knowledge one acquires from a forensic education.
— Donald F. McHenry, U.S. Representative to the United Nations

What are intercollegiate forensic activities, and why should you participate? These are questions constantly asked of forensics teachers, questions that probe to the very essence of the values of forensics participation. My purpose is to briefly answer these questions. I am a firm advocate of forensics participation — classroom and co-curricular work in debate, public platform speaking, and oral interpretation practice — and I believe that forensics experiences, solidly grounded in an educational forensics philosophy, cannot help but enhance a liberal arts education. While I admit that forensic activities have some drawbacks in terms of too much competitiveness and the promulgating overly stylized debate and speech, my focus will be unapologetically positive.

To answer these interrelated questions, I will first examine the ancient and honorable history of forensics in philosophy, rhetoric, dialectic, public address, and speech communication. Second, I will give my own interpretation of what forensics is today. Third, I will discuss the potential knowledge and skills you can glean through forensics participation. Fourth, I will comment on the relationship between forensics and career preparation. Finally, I will analyze the potential role of forensics participation in gaining personal self-actualization, satisfaction, and enjoyment.

Forensics: An Ancient and Honorable History

Forensics started as the study of courtroom speaking and public deliberation around 450 B.C. in Greece. That is why many people, when they think of forensics, think of forensics pathology or lab work — they too derive their origins from the study of legal events. Forensics in the Western Intellectual Tradition has come to encompass the study and practice of argumentation (especially debate in its many forms), of public platform speaking or deliberative address, and of public dramatic reading (most often called oral interpretation).

Dr. Hunt is currently Director of Forensics at Lewis and Clark College.

The Greek study of forensics began with the Sophists, itinerant teachers who taught wealthy citizens to speak in the law courts or other public forums. Protagoras, the Father of Debate, was one of the earliest of the Sophists. The most famous Sophist was Isocrates, from whose school came many of the most famous and distinguished Athenian statesmen, leaders, and orators. Plato, the famous philosopher and teacher, opposed the Sophists as men who taught merely emotional appeals and style thus making "the worse appear the better cause." Aristotle was a student of both the Sophists and of Plato. He presented the world with its first fairly complete rhetoric in his works *The Organon*, a study of logic, and in *The Rhetoric*. Aristotle declared that there were three available means of persuasion, **ethos**, personal charismatic credibility appeals, **pathos**, emotional appeals, and **logos**, the appeal of evidence and logical reasoning.

The Romans continued most of the Greek rhetorical tradition, and expanded upon it. The two greatest Roman rhetoricians were Cicero and Quintillian. Cicero honored rhetoric as both a practitioner and a theorist. He called the study of oratory the highest of the arts, the culmination of a cultured man's education. He claimed in *De Oratore*:

> But the truth is that this oratory is a greater thing, and has its sources in more arts and branches of study, than people suppose. . . .
>
> To begin with, a knowledge of very many matters must be grasped, without which oratory is but an empty and ridiculous swirl of verbiage; and the distinctive style has to be formed, not only by the choice of words, but also by the arrangement of the same; and all the mental emotions, with which nature has endowed the human race, are to be intimately understood, because it is in calming, or kindling the feelings of the audience that the full power and science of oratory are to be brought into play. To this there should be added a certain humour, flashes of wit, the culture befitting a gentleman, and readiness and terseness alike in repelling and in delivering the attack, the whole being combined with a delicate charm and urbanity. Further, the complete history of the past and a store of precedents must be retained in the memory, nor may a knowledge of statute law and our national law in general be omitted.[1]

Quintillian was the quintessential Roman teacher. He tried to summarize Greek and Roman knowledge of rhetoric in his *Institutes of Oratory*. He presented the world with a series of *controversiae*, Latin argumentation exercises, focusing on the five canons of rhetoric: invention, disposition, style, delivery, and memory. Invention had to do with thinking about topics for discussion or debate, and thoroughly researching them. Disposition concerned organization, or the outlining and layout of ideas. Style encompassed grammar, language usage, and the overall impression of language as well as the study of figures of speech. The study of delivery was the

---

1 Cicero, *De Oratore* Book I, F. W. Sutton and H. Rackham, trans. (Cambridge: Loeb Classical Library, 1942), 17-18.

study of voice, gestures, posture and carriage, and appropriate adjustment to the audience. Memory, the study of mnemonic devices, was necessary since print and its reproduction did not yet exist, and a speaker had to memorize and deliver as much as several hours of material with few or no notes.

The study of rhetoric, dialectic, and public address continued through the Middle Ages and to the Renaissance, largely because St. Augustine had been a classically trained rhetorician who thought that, though God might well inspire his ministers and apostles, it would be good if they also were trained to give good sermons and to defend themselves in disputations with heathens and the pious alike. The fortunately few who were educated according to the Western tradition during the one-thousand years between 400-1400 A.D. studied the **trivium** and the **quadrivium**. The **trivium** was the essence of a liberal arts humane education consisting of the study of grammar, logic, and rhetoric. The **quadrivium** concerned more practical arts: arithmetic, geometry, astronomy, and music. Catholic priests, royal clerks, educated nobles, and lawyers took their basic instruction in these arts, and practiced their work with disputations in Rome, Florence, Paris, and Madrid, and at Oxford, Cambridge, and Edinburgh in Great Britain.

Forensics was a particularly important subject in British education because of the nation's violent religious disputes, the development of parliamentary government, and the creation of common law. Kings, lords involved in land disputes, parliamentarians, and lawyers all had great need for the techniques of argumentation and persuasion, and plenty of opportunity for their usage. Francis Bacon, Chatman, Pitt the Elder, Pitt the Younger, Edmund Burke, and a long list of others prominent in English history, studied rhetoric, logic, and evidence and practiced disputation. Many were barristers trained exclusively for advocacy at the famous London Inns of the Court.

Forensics disputations came through the Western Intellectual Tradition, from Greece and Rome, though the Catholic Church, through Great Britain and its schools, to the United States. Disputations were an essential part of basic education at such universities as Harvard, Yale, William and Mary, and the University of Virginia from their earliest days. Seniors did not write a thesis, rather they gave a senior speech. Besides formal work in classes on rhetoric, students formed literary and debating societies. The Spy Club at Harvard and the Linonian Society at Yale, among others, debated issues, studied controversial current events, and invited speakers to their activities. This kind of education was essential in developing the minds of American Founding Fathers like George Washington, Thomas Jefferson, James Madison, James Monroe, Benjamin Franklin, John Jay, and Alexander Hamilton. The kind of thinking and rhetorical skills this type education produced can be seen in the expressions of The Federalist Papers, The Declaration of Independence, and the U.S. Constitution.

The study of rhetoric and public address, the use of disputations and declamations, and literary and debating societies continued in the nineteenth century. Late in the century, formal interscholastic debates developed with schools challenging one another to debates — Harvard versus Yale, Northwestern versus Iowa, Michigan versus Wisconsin, etc. Frequently large audiences attended these debates with the crowds cheering for their team. Also late in the century, oratory contests began with the creation of the Old Line Oratory Contest and The Interstate Oratory Association.

Early in the twentieth century, Departments of Speech broke away from Departments of Rhetoric and Departments of English, taking took with them the study of speech theory and rhetoric and public address through classes such as Classical Rhetoric, Public Speaking, Discussion, Argumentation and Debate, Persuasion, British and American Public Address, and Rhetorical Criticism. Soon, speaking/debating societies were commonly associated with the study of speech and rhetoric and public address. Forensics honoraries were founded, starting with Delta Sigma in 1906, followed by Tau Kappa Alpha in 1908, Pi Kappa Delta in 1912, and Phi Rho Pi in 1928. To save time and money the multi-school invitational tournament was created, the first of which probably took place in 1923 at Southwestern College in Winfield, Kansas. Debate was the primary activity of these tournaments, although sometimes platform speaking events (oratory, informative speaking, extemporaneous speaking) and oral interpretation were included.

The modern pattern for intercollegiate forensics developed mostly after World War II. Individual colleges now sponsor forensics tournaments with debate, individual speaking events, or both. Usually at least five colleges or universities attend such tournaments, although sometimes as many as eighty might attend a very large tournament. Toward the end of the year, various forensics organizations sponsor national championships. The American Forensics Association sponsors the National Debate Tournament (NDT), a national championship in policy debate, and the National Individual Events Tournament (NIET), a championship in individual speaking and oral interpretation. The National Forensics Association (NFA) also sponsors a national championship tournament in individual speaking and oral interpretation. The Cross Examination Debate Association (CEDA) sponsors a national championship in non-policy debate. Various national forensics honoraries, Pi Kappa Delta, Delta Sigma Rho Tau Kappa Alpha and Phi Rho Pi also sponsor championships for member schools in debate, platform speaking, and oral interpretation. Various regional associations, such as the Eastern Forensics Association, The Northwest Forensics Association, Western Forensics Association, Northern California Forensics Association, and the Pacific Southwest Collegiate Forensics Association also sponsor championship tournaments.

Today, speech communication departments have grown to encompass interpersonal communication, communication theory, intercultural communication, organizational communication, quantitative and qualitative research methodology, and mass communication, but most departments still pay significant attention to rhetoric and public address, the "speech" part of speech communication. Classes and activities are still offered in classical rhetoric, rhetorical theory, argumentation and debate, persuasion, listening, discussion, British and American Public Address, rhetorical criticism, and oral interpretation. Forensic activities serve as the applied or laboratory experience for many of these classes. The theories of invention and disposition are implemented in the structuring of a persuasive or informative speech or in a debate case. The criticism of speakers of speeches is practiced in rhetorical criticism. The forensics tournament hones the skills of student advocates as they put theories of rhetoric and public address into practice, spurred on by the stimulus of competition.

Forensics Today: A Diverse Arena

Forensics has an ancient and honorable twenty-five hundred year history as the heart of The Western Intellectual Tradition. But, what is it today? Forensics, broadly construed, is many things. It is an intellectual tradition and perspective. It is a series of curricular and co-curricular activities. And, it is a great intellectual game like bridge or chess, but infinitely more complicated and pertinent to the managing of society. It is a game played both for contest and in reality.

Forensics is concerned with deliberative and forensic speaking; in modern terms, public forum decision making and legal communication. It is concerned with rational decision making, which is at the heart of democracy. Wherever there is healthy democracy there are public forums with public debate and discussion of controversial issues. Essential to the democratic "marketplace of ideas" is freedom of expression, free press and free speech. In this marketplace, those who would assert must prove. The advocacy system demands that the proponents of fact, value, or policy be prepared to back up their statements with logic/reasoning and evidence, and be prepared to refute the attacks of informed opponents. This requires dialectical skills — skills in analyzing and evaluating theories and data. It also requires rhetorical skills — skills in manipulating language so as to adjust ideas to people and people to ideas. Effective advocacy skills also play a prominent role in legal communication. At the very heart of the American legal system is advocacy, with attorneys attempting to prove their cases and persuade with written briefs and supplementary oral argumentation.

David Zarefsky, a former debater, forensics educator, and President of the Speech Communication Association of America, states the essence of this tradition well: "Our common interest is in promoting reasoned controversy in making public decisions and in teaching this art to future citizens."[2] This position is also articulated in what has become the most often repeated rationale for forensics from the first national conference on forensics:

> Forensics is an educational activity primarily concerned with using an argumentative perspective in examining problems and communicating with people. An argumentative perspective on communication involves the study of reason giving by people as justification for

---

2 David Zarefsky, "Keynote Address," *Dialogue inthe Forensic Community: Proceedings of the Conference on Forensic Education,* Jack Kay and Julie Lee, eds. (Kansas City: National Federation of State High School Associations, 1990) 20.

acts, beliefs, attitudes, and values. From this perspective, forensics activities, including debate and individual events, are laboratories for helping students to understand and communicate various forms of argument more effectively in a variety of contexts with a variety of audiences.[3]

Forensics is an intellectual tradition and perspective — the tradition and perspective of dialectic and rhetoric in intellectual discourse, a tradition and perspective associated with democracy, the marketplace of ideas, freedom of expression, rational decision making, and the advocacy system.

Forensics is a series of curricular and co-curricular activities. Some educators call forensics a liberal art, because its traditions encompass a broad range of disciplines. Others prefer to call forensics an educational laboratory in speech communication, because many of the classes in speech communication departments, usually classes in rhetoric and public address and oral interpretation, draw upon the same traditions as forensics. A list of such classes would include, but not be limited to: Public Speaking, Rhetoric, Classical Rhetoric, Argumentation and Debate, Discussion, Rhetorical Criticism, Oral Interpretation, Listening, Persuasion, Legal Communication, Political Communication, and British and American Public Address. A number of co-curricular activities are used to enhance this education, including mock negotiation, Model U.N., mock trial, moot court, group discussions, and public debates and speakers' bureaus. The most visible and widespread of these activities is intercollegiate forensics. First and foremost of the forensic events is debate in its many formats: policy or non-policy debate, parliamentary debate, Lincoln-Douglas debate, etc. Second are the public platform events: oratory or persuasion, informative or expository speaking, speaking to entertain (sometimes called after dinner speaking), rhetorical criticism or communication analysis, impromptu and extemporaneous speaking, and radio speaking and editorial commentary events. Finally, there are the many oral interpretation events: Readers' Theater, dramatic interpretation, prose, poetry, duo interpretation, program oral interpretation, differentiated by format, style or genre of literature.Forensics is also a game, a very sophisticated, complicated, perplexing, fascinating game. It is a game played by intercollegiate debaters, speakers, and interpreters in practice and competition, and a game played by advocates, politicians, lawyers, ministers, and teachers in the course of their professions. Some people play bridge, chess, or computer games diligently and seriously. Debaters, speakers, and interpreters play the game of forensics. They learn a great deal as they participate in forensics, but they also participate for fun. The various strategies and tactics employed in forensics are wondrously ambiguous and complex, ever evolving, and continuously fascinating. Later in life, the gaming strategies and tactics of language usage, creative

---

3 James McBath, ed., *Forensics as Communication: The Argumentative Perspective* (Skokie: National Textbook, 1975), 11.

and critical thinking, research, case construction and destruction, are employed by lawyers, politicians, ministers, teachers, and others in real life decision making in a variety of contexts and before a variety of audiences.

Knowledge and Skills from Forensics

There are many lists of the values of forensics. Most of these lists apply to the values of debate, but reasonably can be extended to the values of forensics as a whole. Any single list is likely to be incomplete, but the following is fairly thorough. Keep in mind that knowledge and skills are only gained with good intentions, good instruction, good practices, good experiences, and the whole-hearted effort of participants. Given that, here is what you might expect to learn from participating in intercollegiate forensics.

First, you should learn more about the functioning of democratic societies and to become a better citizen and potential leader. Russell R. Windes noted:

> One cannot study the history of argumentation without becoming aware of a striking fact. Wherever free societies have existed, there also debate has abounded. Debate, or advocacy if you will, is an intrinsic part of democracy's decision making, and the making of decisions through democratic means is vital if free people are to govern themselves wisely.[4]

Forensics deals with rational decision making. It assumes the advocacy system, a marketplace of ideas, and free expression. Through participating in the marketplace of ideas, you will learn that people have a very broad variety of religious, political, economic, and social ideas. You will learn that the same data can be interpreted in a variety of ways, that people of good will and great capacity can come to opposing viewpoints. All this breeds a certain skepticism for easy conclusions and unexamined opinions, and a tolerance for diversity and respect for civil public discourse. Forensics helps you understand how democracy works, how critical the marketplace of ideas really is, and helps you gain the self-confidence and rhetorical proficiency necessary to become a better citizen and better potential civic leader.

Second, forensics helps hone your critical, reflective, and creative thinking capacities. Though there has been recent doubt cast on particular studies of forensics and critical thinking, most forensic educators and alumni still believe that debaters have critical thinking abilities significantly more developed than those of non-debaters. As a forensics student, through invention (the discovery, research, and analysis process), you must discover the critical lines of argument which support your opinions. You must analyze problems, select and examine evidence, interpret data, determine logical relationships, test reasoning, and reach conclusions. All this helps develop your critical, reflective, and creative thinking capacities.

---

4 Russel R. Windes, Jr., "Competitive Debating: The Speech Program, The Individual, and Society," *The Speech Teacher* IX (1960): 99.

Third, you learn research methods as you learn to support your advocacy. You will learn to use the library and all its resources. You will learn to find books, articles, government documents, and special studies. You will learn to utilize every sort of index, both print indexes and computerized indexes. You also will learn both quantitative and qualitative research methodologies as you begin to examine and criticize the research you read. Good forensics students have to be familiar with humane, social scientific, and scientific methodologies and with case studies, surveys, and statistics. Without such knowledge, you cannot separate good logic, good reasoning, and good evidence from mediocre or poor logic, reasoning, and evidence.

Fourth, you will learn a great deal about proof. Proof consists of logic, reasoning and evidence in support of a position. You will learn logical reasoning and its counterpart, fallacious reasoning, as you construct your own arguments and attempt to find flaws in your opponents' arguments. The Western Intellectual Tradition is a tradition of rationalism, at least in so far as we can prove things in those arenas where only probabilities exist and where controversy continuously swirls, the arenas of ethics, values, politics, religion, public policy, and law. Forensics teaches you to attempt to prove your conclusions, to support your opinions with the best case you can construct and with the best defenses or refutation you can come up with.

Fifth, you will learn more about and become more skilled in organization and arrangement. You will learn to outline your positions. You will learn how to select main ideas and to subordinate lesser ideas in support of these main concepts. You will learn to coordinate your main points. You will learn to preview your positions, to provide transitions, to give internal summaries, and to summarize your points. Most of all, you will learn that content cannot be disconnected from context and style. You must not only have a good case, you must lay it out clearly and cogently.

Sixth, you will learn about language usage and style. You will learn the power of the word, to appreciate the symbolic power of expression. You will learn the impact of metaphor, the simile, and other figures of speech. You will learn how important style is, and how oral style differs from written style, even though both must be clear, concise, correct, and colorful to be powerful and effective. By analyzing and evaluating, conceptualizing and utilizing, language in every way possible, you will become keenly aware that it is not only what you say that counts but also how you say it.

Seventh, forensics participation will help you develop listening and note taking skills. You have to listen to yourself, to your fellow squad members, and your opponents. You will learn to be an accurate, critical listener. You will learn to take notes quickly, efficiently, and effectively. Advocates who are not good listeners and note takers usually are not effective advocates. The essential counterpart of good presentation skills is good listening skills.

Eighth, you will vastly improve your public speaking skills. While there are many examples of forensics students failing to attain the best possible public speaking skills, generally forensics makes you more aware of what you ought to be doing, and will help you improve your oral style.

Debaters, public speakers, and interpreters learn that dress and posture, the very way they nonverbally handle themselves through eye contact, gestures, projections of attitude, can powerfully affect their judges. All public speakers learn the potential powers of the human voice when used in various pitches, tones, volumes, resonances, and inflections. And, whether you do it effectively or not, you will learn that you should at least attempt to analyze your audiences and to adjust your presentations to those audiences while still staying true to your own substance and style.

Ninth, you will learn about the ethics of advocacy. You will learn that evidence has to be properly cited, evaluated, and entered into the argumentative process. You will learn that arguments should be supported with sound reasoning. You will learn respect for your opponents and for the dialectical/rhetorical process of public discourse. You will learn that truth and probability are discovered by sound advocacy and the thorough testing of arguments in the marketplace of ideas. You will learn that arguing should be an honest, civil process of humane public discourse.

Finally, by participating in forensic events, you will become much more familiar with current events and controversies. As a debater, extemporaneous speaker, orator, or interpreter, you will become familiar with social, religious, economic, and political theories. You will learn the cross-disciplinary connections of many disputes. You will learn that in-depth analysis and research is necessary to understand current issues. Of necessity, you will become familiar with contemporary disputes about science, social science, and the humanities. You should become more open minded and tolerant about the opinions of others, and should have a better grasp of the issues which affect your life.

To sum up, by participating in intercollegiate forensics, with the proper educational perspective, through individual hard work, and with good instruction, practices, and experiences, you should gain considerably in knowledge and skill.

Empirical evidence supporting the values of forensics participation is sparse, but anecdotal evidence attested to by forensics participants past and present is overwhelming. Most students who participate in forensics consider those experiences to be amongst the most valuable of their collegiate careers.

Forensics as Career Preparation

A Forensics education is a microcosm of the Western Intellectual Tradition and of the liberal arts. The fundamental knowledge and skills potentially gleaned in forensics reads like a list taken from Mortimer Adler's *The Paideia Proposal,* the U.S. Department of Education's *A Nation at Risk,* or any of a number of recent documents about fundamentals and excellence in higher education. Forensics helps you learn how to learn, to be able to think clearly and adapt to rapid change. "At its essence, forensics is an educational activity which provides students with the opportunity to develop a high level of proficiency in writing, thinking, reading, speaking, and listening."[5] These are skills most employers list as the fundamentals they seek when hiring and skills fundamental to living a life in the modern information age. Forensics is an excellent preparation for any career and for life.

Forensics participation you learn about grammar and language. It helps you learn to analyze complex written materials quickly and efficiently. These abilities are of inestimable value when you take the Graduate Record Exam or Law School Aptitude Test. Graduate professors and law deans appreciate a forensics record. When they note membership in forensic honoraries, or forensics participation and success on a vita, it gives you a leg up on entry to graduate or law school. The record of previous forensics students has been outstanding, thus forensics participation is at least one indicator of potential graduate or law school success.

Forensics is not only great preparation for graduate or law school, it is great preparation for professional careers. It is especially valuable for careers dealing extensively with advocacy and persuasion. Law is an obvious example. Thousands of attorneys and judges have found their forensics experiences directly relevant and helpful in their profession. Politics is another career much enhanced by forensics participation. Many surveys of presidents, cabinet members, governors, and members of the U.S. Congress have shown that successful politicians have forensics backgrounds. One such survey showed that "over 80% of all current members of Congress were on their schools forensics teams."[6] Sales and business administration are also enhanced by forensics participation. Sales people must advocate all the time. Persuasion is their business. Business administrators are constantly dictating memos, making reports, and participating in meetings where their research skills and persuasive powers will decide which of several options should be taken. Forensics also aids in the development of good teachers. Teachers and professors must constantly speak and write in order to educate. The art of persuasion is at the heart of the teaching profession and of a free educational system. Finally, forensics helps those who are ministers, rabbis, priests, or imams. The uninitiated are not likely to hear the call unless it is persuasively made. The faithful must be reenlightened, heartened, and rededicated through the power of the word.

All professions demand skills in language — speaking, listening, reading and writing. As such, all professions demand the very same skills you must develop to succeed in forensics competition. If you aspire to a career in business, law, or politics, to be a doctor, a preacher, or a teacher, you need to develop the skills honed by a forensics education.

---

5 James H. McBath, "Toward a Rational for Forensics," *American Forensics in Perspective,* Donn Parson, ed. (Annandale: Speech Communication Association, 1984), 10.

6 Don R. Swanson and Raymond F. Zeuschner, *Participating in Collegiate Forensics* (Dubuque: Gorsuch Scarisbrick, 1983), 2.

Forensics, Fun and Self-Actualization

Forensics is more than an ancient and honorable tradition, an intellectual perspective, a way to gain knowledge and develop rhetorical skills, and a great way to prepare for careers. Forensics is also an enjoyable route to self-actualization. Forensics competitors tend to be some of the best and brightest students in the university. As you do your forensics work, you naturally come into contact with other forensics students, both at your own school and at other colleges and universities. Competing in intercollegiate forensics contributes to a perpetual striving for excellence. Only those meeting the highest standards of thinking, research, organization, presentation, and persuasion triumph. Through forensics competition, you can learn the standards of real, enduring excellence, and begin to grow more confident in yourself and in your critical abilities.

Forensics participation contributes to personal sophistication. You will travel to forensics tournaments throughout your region, perhaps throughout the nation, seeing new places and meeting new people. You will learn about other ways of seeing things, other ways of advocacy, and how to act in varying public forums.

You also play advocacy games. You will learn about advocacy strategy and tactics. You will learn the packaging methods of the rhetorical marketplace. Forensics is about real issues, with real world connections and effects. But, as a student advocate, you will get to experiment with advocacy as an intellectual game before applying forensics strategies and tactics in other arenas of life.

Finally, forensics makes for fast friendships. Any number of marriages and life-long friendships have come from forensics contacts. Forensics students learn to work together, putting in long hours, sometimes under trying conditions. Debate partners and forensics team members, learn teamwork, cooperation, and develop esprit de corps.

All of this is great fun at the same time it helps you become more enlightened in and better at the art of persuasion. Forensics helps you learn what you can become, helps you set goals for yourself, and take strides toward self-actualization. Thus, it is little wonder that so many thousands have spent so much time and effort on forensics activities, and proclaimed afterwards that they loved every minute of it.

Conclusion

So, what is forensics? It is an ancient and honorable intellectual tradition, encompassing argumentation and rationality as examined in the disciplines of dialectic and rhetoric, and as practiced in democracies where the marketplace of ideas seeks relative truth through free expression. Forensics involves classes in speech communication, in rhetoric and public address, and includes co-curricular activities such as public debates, discussions and commentaries, as well as competitive intercollegiate debate, public speaking, and oral interpretation. Forensics is a sophisticated intellectual game.

Why participate? Because forensics students gain knowledge and develop skills integral to the functioning of democratic societies, learn to think creatively critically, and reflectively, learn about research methods, methods of proof, organization, language, listening and note taking, public speaking and communication, the ethics of advocacy, and the cross-disciplinary examination of current events. Forensics students become more open-minded, tolerant of intellectual diversity, and appreciative of civil public discourse. Intercollegiate forensics is also great preparation for a number of careers, particularly law, politics, business, education and the ministry, which focus on advocacy and the use of language to persuade. Last and far from least, forensics competition is fun and self-fulfilling. Forensics students make great friends, become more sophisticated, travel, and learn how to participate actively, intelligently, and civilly in purposive problem solving, policy making, public discourse.

Selected Testimony from Forensics Alumni

"I think debating in high school and college a most valuable training, whether for politics, the law, business, or for service on community committees such as the PTA and the League of Women Voters. A good debater must not only study material in support of his own case, but he must also, of course, thoroughly analyze the expected arguments of his opponents. . . . The give and take of debating, the testing of ideas, is essential to democracy. I wish we had a good deal more debating in our institutions than we do now."

—John F. Kennedy, former President of the United States

"There are few other activities in high school or college that are as important as speech and debate. Regardless of an individual's academic or career goals, the ability to research a complex question, marshal arguments and present them in a persuasive and compelling way, are skills that will serve you well all your life. Both my wife and I debated in high school and college. Before I entered public life, I taught debate and speech at Dakota Wesleyan University in Mitchell, S.D. I attribute whatever political success I may have enjoyed, in large part, to the training I received as a participant in debate and speech activities."

—George McGovern, former U.S. Senator and Democratic candidate for President

"The development of leadership in a democratic society has a very direct relationship to the art of debate. One becomes a leader by molding public opinion to support a given course of action, not by dictating such an action. This involves the ability to pinpoint the critical issues of the day, and the willingness to apply oneself to the task of research in order to assemble all considerations bearing upon those issues. It requires the ability to apply logic, rather than emotion and prejudice, to the assembled data, the courage to accept the decisions thus indicated, and the ability to present the opinions thus developed in such a way as to persuade others to a like point of view."

—Edmund S. Muskie, former U.S. Senator and Democratic candidate for Vice President

---

Testimony compiled from: Austin J. Freeley, "An Anthology of Commentary on Debate," *The Speech Teacher* IX (1960): 121-126; James H. McBath, ed., *Forensics as Communication: The Argumentative Perspective* (Skokie: National Textbook, 1975); National Forensic League, *Golden Anniversary Tournament Booklet* (Ripon: National Forensic League, 1980); Kent R. Colbert and Thompson Biggers, "Why Should We Support Debate?" *Journal of the American Forensic Association* XXI (1985): 237-240; and Austin J. Freeley, *Argumentation and Debate: Critical Thinking for Reasoned Decision Making* 8th Edition (Belmont: Wadsworth, 1993). These comments represent only a small sample of the published testimony from former forensics students.

"Debating is one of the most valuable academic exercises in which I have ever engaged. It taught me to speak on my feet, to organize my thoughts, and to defend and refute a point. All of these abilities have stood me in good stead during my career as an attorney, as a judge, and now, as a U.S. Senator."

— Howell Hefling, U.S. Senator from Alabama

"As a U.S. Senator, my principal responsibilities are threefold: First, a Senator must do his best to reach logical policy conclusions about the issues with which our nation is confronted. Second, a Senator should be able to effectively translate technical aspects of a position into language that will clearly communicate it to the public. Third, to be effective, a Senator must have the ability to persuade others to accept his policy conclusions. No aspects of my education was more useful in preparing me to meet these responsibilities than my training in speech and debate."

— David Boren, U.S. Senator from Oklahoma

"One of the most important decisions in my life was when the student body of Warren Central High School in Indianapolis decided I should not be a varsity cheerleader. It meant my weekends were free. For the next three years, I spent most Saturdays on the road with the largest National Forensic League chapter in the country.

"While a fifteen-year-old girl inside me still mourns the lost letter sweater, the adult Jane is grateful to NFL for something much more important a — career."

— Jane Pauley, NBC television journalist

"No college freshman can project 25 years to decide what he needs to learn — subject matter is easily forgotten and in today's world, the knowledge explosion makes constant learning an inevitability. But all adults today need to be able to communicate with clarity, to articulate ideas, to reason, to separate key facts from the barrage of ideas we all are exposed to every day. No single activity can prepare one better than debating — the ability to think on one's feet, to form conclusions rapidly, to answer questions logically and with clarity, to summarize ideas are all processes which forensics activity develop and develop well."

— Helen M. Wise, former President, National Education Association

"My debate experience at Bates was helpful in my postgraduate study at Oxford. At all times, the necessity of organizing ideas and presenting them vigorously has been pertinent to newspaper writing. Asking questions at press conferences or interviewing statesmen was aided by my public speaking experience."

— Erwin D. Canham, editor of *The Christian Science Monitor*

"Forensics has influenced my personal and professional development more than any other activity or experience. Those who have participated in forensics often share this view. A survey of Governors, Senators, and other leaders across the country conducted by the Bicentennial Youth Debates found a high level of agreement about this key role of debate and speech activities.

"Debate teaches so many things — the complexity of issues, the importance of research, techniques of gathering and organizing information, analytic and verbal skills, respect for opposing views, the interaction of evidence and values, and a variety of frameworks for evaluating arguments and reaching decisions. At the heart of this is something crucial to our society — the open testing of ideas."

— James Luck, Executive Director, Battelle Memorial Institute Foundation

"I have deep and abiding faith in the personal value and social utility of courses in debate and forensic events, which are something more than games in which to score points. Training and practice in debate enhance the indispensable resources of intellectual rigor, orderly analysis, rational and emotional discipline, sense of structure, and effective expression. A course in debate provides — at least it should — both a method and an ethic for a person's management of private and public discourse in a free society."

— Lester Thonssen, former President, Speech Communication Association of America

"Years of observing high school and college students in forensics have convinced me that this is one of the major contributions we in speech communication can make to the education of youngsters. It is our various forensics activities, more than in any other of our programs, that most of what we believe in and study can be brought together and passed on to each generation of students. It is in our various forensics activities that we can most effectively communicate the values that form the base of speech communication. And it is these activities that can best help our students to develop their capacities for leadership. It is no accident that such a large percentage of the outstanding leaders in our country have been high school or college debaters."

— Sam Becker, former President, Speech Communication Association of America

"My speech and debate experience and training at Pennsylvania State was the most important single educational experience of my life. . . .

"Dialectical and communicative competencies and insights are the major educational values which result from participating extensively in forensics and debate. From my experience as a participant, coach and teacher, I believe those competencies and insights are better developed through forensic and debate experiences than any other educational experience."

— Jerry M. Anderson, President, Ball State University

"As I look back upon my own experiences, when I try to single out from among the long line of college students some one group which shall stand forth as intellectually the best — best in college work and best in promise of future intellectual achievement — I cannot draw the line around my own favorite students of philosophy, nor the leaders in mathematics, nor those successful in biology; nor could I fairly award the palm to the Phi Beta Kappa men who have excelled in all their subjects.

"It seems to me that stronger than any other group, tougher in intellectual fiber, keener in intellectual interests, better equipped to battle the coming problems are the college debaters — the students who apart from their regular studies, band together for intellectual controversy with each other and with their friends from other colleges."

— Alexander Meiklejohn, former President, Amherst College

"Among the marks of an educated person are the abilities to think intelligently, to hold convictions, and to speak clearly and persuasively on public issues. We at Harvard are committed to the high standard of education represented by these marks, and one measure of these indicators is formal debate. We are happy, therefore, to have so many representatives of other academic institutions join us in this activity."

— Derek Bok, former President, Harvard University

"The group developed fellowship and team camaraderie which had important by-products for personal growth. The visits to other schools, and travel experience, the living and working together — all under the high expectations of the 'Coach' and his most gently administered but ever firm supervision — made for an individual development which has remained for me a high point in my educational experience.

"The meaning of scholarship, the 'feel' for the handling of ideas, the fellowship of professional service were for me but some of the outcomes of my debate experience."

— David B. Henry, President, University of Illinois

"If I were to choose any single activity in college which has contributed most to my career, I would certainly choose debating."

— Samuel B. Gould, President, Antioch College

For Additional Reading

Aden, Roger C. "Reconsidering the Laboratory Metaphor: Forensics as Liberal Art." *National Forensics Journal* IX (1991): 97-108.

Andersen, Kenneth E. "A Critical Review of the Behavioral Research in Argumentation and Forensics." *Journal of the American Forensics Association* X (1974): 147-155.

Bartanen, Michael. *Teaching and Directing Forensics.* Scottsdale: Gorsuch Scarisbrick, 1994.

Bennett, William H. "The Role of Debate in Speech Communication." *The Speech Teacher* XXXIX (1972): 281-288.

Bradley, Bert E., Jr. "Debate: A Practical Training for Gifted Students." *The Speech Teacher* VII (1959): 134-138.

Cardot, Joseph. "Coaching and Directing Forensics: The Battle Between Curricular and Cocurricular Activity." *Proceedings of the 1991 Pi Kappa Delta Professional Development Conference.* Ed. Sally Roden. (N.p.: University of Central Arkansas, 1991. 79-86.

Colbert, Kent R. "The Effects of CEDA and NDT Debate Training on Critical Thinking Ability." *Journal of the American Forensic Association* XIII (1987): 194-201.

_________ and Thompson Biggers. "Why Should We Support Debate?" *JAFA* XXI (1985): 237-240.

DeLancey, Charles A. "The Values of Forensic Activities to Speech Communication Programs in Liberal Arts Colleges." *ACA Bulletin* XLCII (1984): 56-57.

Faules, Don F., Richard D. Rieke, and Jack Rhodes, eds. *Directing Forensics: Contest and Debate Speaking* 2nd Edition. Denver: Morton Publishing, 1976.

Freeley, Austin J. "An Anthology of Commentary on Debate." *The Speech Teacher* IX (1960): 121-126.

Greenstreet, Robert. "Academic Debate and Critical Thinking: A Look at the Evidence." *National Forensic Journal* XI (1993): 13-28.

Hill, Bill. "Intercollegiate Debate: Why Do Students Bother?" *The Southern Communication Journal* XLVIII (Fall, 1982): 77-88.

_________. "The Value of Competitive Debate as a Vehicle for Promoting Development of Critical Thinking Ability." *CEDA Yearbook* XIV (1993): 1-22.

Hunt, Steven B. "A Philosophic and Pragmatic Rationale for Individual Events" *Perspectives on Individual Events: Proceedings of the First Developmental Conference on Individual Events.* Eds. Larry Schnoor and Vicki Karns. Mankato: Mankato State University, 1989. 33-36.

_________. "Forensic Education Curriculum on the Undergraduate and Graduate Levels: A Response." *Proceedings to the 1991 Pi Kappa Delta Professional Development Conference.* Ed. Sally Roden. N.p.: University of Central Arkansas, 1991. 187-195.

Huseman, Richard, Glenn Ware, and Charles Gruner. "Critical Thinking, Reflective Thinking, and the Ability to Organize Ideas: A Multivariate Approach." *Journal of the American Forensic Association* IX (1972): 261-265.

__________ and Davis Goodman. "The Editor's Corner: BYD Congressional Questionnaire." *JAFA* XII (1976): 225-228.

Johnson, John R. and Nancy Szczupakiewicz. "The Public Speaking Course: Is It Preparing Students with Work Related Public Speaking Skills?" *Communication Education* XXXVI (1987): 131-137.

Kaplan, Stuart J. and G. P. Mohrmann. "Reader, Text, Audience: Oral Interpretation and Cognitive Tuning." *The Quarterly Journal of Speech* LXIII (1977): 59-65.

Logue, Brenda and B. Christine Shea. "Individual Events Research: A Review and Criticism." *National Forensic Journal* VIII (1990): 17-29.

Matlon, Ron and Lucy M. Keele. "A Survey of Participants in the National Debate Tournament 1947-1980." *JAFA* XX (1984): 194-205.

McBath, James H., ed. *Forensics as Communication: The Argumentative Perspective.* Skokie: National Textbook Co., 1975.

__________. "Toward a Rationale for Forensics." *American Forensics in Perspective.* Ed. Donn Parson. Annandale: Speech Communication Association, 1984: 5-11.

McGlone, Edward L. "The Behavioral Effects of Forensics Participation." *Journal of the American Forensic Association* X (1974): 140-146.

McMillan, Janet Kay and R. Todd Mancillas. "An Assessment of the Value of Individual Events in Forensics Competition from Students' Perspectives." *National Forensics Journal* IX (1991): 1-17.

Mohrmann, G. P. and Stuart J. Kaplan. "The Effect of Training on the Oral Interpreter's Perception of a Text." *Central States Speech Journal* XXI (1980): 137-142.

National Forensics League. *Golden Anniversary Tournament Booklet.* Ripon: National Forensics League, 1980.

Nichols, E. R. "A Historical Sketch of Intercollegiate Debating." *Quarterly Journal of Speech* XXII (1936): 213-220, 591-602.

Norton, Larry. "Nature and Benefits of Academic Debate." *Introduction to Debate.* Eds. Carolyn Keefe, Thomas B. Harte, and Laurence E. Norton. New York: Macmillan, 1982: 24-40.

Rohrer, Dan M. "Debate as a Liberal Art." *Advanced Debate: Readings in Theory, Practice, and Teaching* 3rd Edition. Eds. David A. Thomas and Jack Hart. Lincolnwood: National Textbook Co., 1987: 7-14.

Swanson, Don R. and Raymond F. Zeuschner. *Participating in Collegiate Forensics.* Dubuque, Iowa: Gorsuch Scarisbrick, 1983.

Thomas, David A. "Forensics Shock: Making Forensics Relevant to Tomorrow's Higher Education." *The Speech Teacher* XXIII (1974): 235-241.

_________. "Sedalia Plus Five: Forensics as Laboratory." *Proceedings of the Summer Conference on Argumentation*. Eds. Jack Rhodes and Sarah Newell. Annandale: Speech Communication Association, 1979: 245-257.

_________ and Stephen C. Wood. *CEDA: Twentieth Anniversary Assessment Conference Proceedings*. Dubuque: Kendall Hunt, 1993.

Wallace, Karl, ed. *A History of Speech Education in America.* New York: Appleton Century Crofts, 1954.

Windes, Russel R., Jr. "Competitive Debating: The Speech Program, The Individual, and Society." *The Speech Teacher* IX (1960): 99-108.

Zarefsky, David. "Keynote Address." *Dialogue in the Forensic Community: Proceedings of the Conference on Forensic Education.* Eds. Jack Kay and Julie Lee. Kansas City: National Federation of State High School Associations, 1990.

Attending Forensics Tournaments

Raymond "Bud" Zeuschner

Forensics tournaments defy linguistic descriptions. They must be experienced to be comprehended fully, but they might be partially described. With this in mind, this is what happens at most tournaments. A tournament is usually (but not always):

- A competition involving many colleges and universities (from 5 to 100).
- Held at a college campus using classrooms for speaking.
- Broken into several patterns, events and divisions.
- Seldom on time (although you must always be on time).
- Plagued by lousy food.
- A jovial, exhilarating, depressing, inspiring, exasperating, tiring, up-lifting experience.

Most tournaments operate according to the same basic procedures. The following is intended to prepare you for the way tournaments normally operate, and make your first tournament experience a little less intimidating. You will almost always have "experienced" team mates who will be happy to answer your questions and point you in the right direction, but here are some things it is nice to know about in advance.

Posting Area. There is a great deal of information you will need in order to participate in a forensics tournament. Much of it you will know in advance — which events you are competing in, which divisions, the number of rounds of competition, etc. Some information, however, is not available until you arrive at the tournament. Some of what you knew in advance is easy to forget in the anxiety of competition. Tournaments will always designate a central location as the "posting area," or the place where the information you need will be posted. The posting area doubles as a general meeting place; if you are trying to find a team mate or coach, the posting area is the place to look. The first thing to ask when you arrive on campus is, "Where are the postings?"

Tournament Schedules. Tournaments post schedules so you will know when the events you have entered will be taking place. Figure 1 illustrates the "look and feel" of a typical tournament schedule. Notice that the events have been divided into *conflict patterns,* groups of events which will take place at the same time — Poetry Interpretation and Impromptu Speaking are scheduled in Pattern A, Persuasive Speaking and Informative Speaking are scheduled in Pattern B, and Debate and Readers' Theatre are scheduled in Pattern C. In this schedule, each event has two rounds. (In individual events there are often three rounds, and in debate there are normally

---

Dr. Zeuschner is a former Director of Forensics at California Polytechnic State University, San Luis Obispo. An earlier version of this chapter appeared in Don R. Swanson and Raymond F. Zeuschner, Participating in Intercollegiate Forensics *(Dubuque: Gorsuch Scarisbrick, 1983) 11-15.*

six.) If you were entered in Poetry, you would speak twice — at 9:00 and at 4:00 — mostly against different opponents, usually with different judges, and often in different rooms. Check the appropriate postings to find out where to go and when. Persuasive and Informative are both in Pattern B — this is a conflict, so you may be entered in only one of these events. However, you might enter Persuasive *and* Informative to give yourself two events, even though they are scheduled to take place at the same time. Entering conflicting events, called *double-entering,* is allowed by most tournaments. If you are double-entered, it is your responsibility to move quickly and quietly between events so you do not delay or disrupt the tournament.

Figure 1

Schedule — Saturday

9:00 am	**A-I**	**Poetry, Impromptu**
10:00 am	**B-I**	**Persuasive, Informative**
11:00 am	**C-I**	**Debate, Readers Theatre**
1:00 pm	**C-II**	**Debate, Readers Theatre**
2:45 pm	**B-II**	**Persuasive, Informative**
4:00 pm	**A-II**	**Poetry, Impromptu**

Code Lists. Contestants are usually assigned a code to facilitate tournament administration. Codes normally have two parts — a *school code* and a *contestant code.* Your personal code will be a combination of the two. Figures 2 and 3 illustrate the most common code assignment schemes for individual events:

Figure 2

AA = Midstate Junior College
- **AA-100 = Van Dern**
- **AA-101 = Tammi Tyler**
- **AA-102 = Steve Jones**

BB = Western State University
- **BB-100 = Marvin Crumby**
- **BB-101 = Melody Sweet**

Figure 3

1 = Midstate Junior College
- **1-A = Van Dern**
- **1-B = Tammi Tyler**
- **1-C = Steve Jones**

2 = Western State University
- **2-A = Marvin Crumby**
- **2-B = Melody Sweet**

In Figure 2, Midstate Junior College has been assigned code AA. Van Dern is coded AA-100, Tammi Tyler is AA-101, and Steve Jones is AA-102. Western State University has been assigned code BB, making Marvin Crumby BB-100, and Melody Sweet BB-101. In Figure 3, schools have been assigned numeric codes, and contestants alpha codes. Van Dern is thus contestant 1-A, and Marvin Crumby is contestant 2-A. If you are entered in more than one individual event, you normally will have the same personal code for each event.

In team events (duo interpretation and debate), codes are assigned in several ways. You may have a code using the same system as individual events. Since there are two contestants to a team, your code for a team event will be different than your code for your individual events (should you be entered in both). School code "A" and team code "21" would make you team A-21. Sometimes, team codes just combine individual codes. If Van Dern and Tammi Tyler were entered as a debate team, they might be coded AA-100/101. Sometimes, school names are used rather than codes. Sometimes team codes are drawn from the initials of the contestants. For instance, Dern and Tyler might be coded Midstate DT.

Tournaments generally post code lists so you can find out what personal code you have been assigned. If not, your coach will have been given a code list. In any case, you are responsible for checking your code — if you are entered in a team event, help your partner by double-checking.

Posting Sheets. Once everyone has been assigned a code, contestants in each event are separated into *divisions* (your coach decides when entering the tournament the division which is appropriate for your level of experience). For individual events, it might be "Novice Persuasive" or "Junior Prose," etc. You will know the divisions and events in which you are entered. Each division of each event is divided into *panels* consisting of 5 or 6 speakers — this is your competition for a particular round. The panels are posted on sheets which list the code numbers of the contestants assigned to a panel, the room in which they will compete, the order in which they are expected to speak, and (normally) the name of the judge. There are generally several rounds of competition in each division of each event, and you will be assigned to a different panel for each round. When you check a posting sheet to see when and where you will speak, make sure you are checking the sheet for the right event, the right division, and the right round. Once you find where you are to speak, be sure to make a note of it. Never assume you will remember the room number as you walk across campus. Debate events are likewise separated into divisions. However, only two teams are assigned to a room. The debate posting sheet will not only indicate round, room and judge, it will indicate which team is assigned to be on the affirmative, and which is assigned to be on the negative.

Figure 4 illustrates a typical individual events posting sheet. It tells you the room in which you will speak, the order in which you will speak, and who your competition will be. Notice that Steve Jones (AA-102) should go to room BH 414, and he will be the first speaker. Professor Maslow will be the judge. The round is scheduled to begin at 1:45 pm, so Steve should leave for the room in plenty of time to make it there *before* 1:45. How about your new friend Marvin from Western State University? The code list indicates that his code is BB-100, and you know he is also entered in Persuasive. However, you cannot find his code on the posting sheet. Oops, this is *Novice* Persuasive, and he is entered in *Open* Persuasive. Always double-check that you are looking at the right posting sheet!

Figure 4
Novice Persuasive
Round II — 1:45 pm

Panel: A	**Panel: B**
Room: BH 414	**Room: ADM 212**
Judge: Maslow	**Judge: Katz**
1. AA-102	**1. M-21**
2. R-71	**2. SS-34**
3. Q-44	**3. BB-6**
4. J-14	**4. K-21**
5. CC-11	**5. RR-67**

A debate posting sheet looks somewhat similar. Figure 5 is a typical debate posting sheet. Since you and your partner are team 6-MB, the posting indicates that you will be on the affirmative, debating against team 19-RM (you can check the code list to see who that is), at 3:00 in BSU 112. The judge will be Professor Freeley. You friends, Samantha Gearheart and Alfie Firradeaux (6-GF) will be on the negative this round against a team from school 18, with Professor Perella judging.

Figure 5
Novice CEDA Debate
Round II — 3:00 pm

Aff.	**Neg.**	**Room**	**Judge**
6-MB	**19-RM**	**BSU 112**	**Freeley**
22-AN	**14-PS**	**ADM 222**	**Zarefsky**
4-EC	**8-UH**	**SS 233**	**Ziegelmeuller**
18-BN	**6-GF**	**ADM 211**	**Perella**

It is your responsibility to check the correct posting for your event and division, and to know in advance how many rounds there will be and when they will be. But what if your code is not posted? You will not be dropped from an event halfway through the tournament, so if you do not see your code posted, something is wrong. Immediately, do the following:

- Double-check. Have someone else double-check with you. Correct event? Correct round? Correct division? Correct time? Correct day? Correct code number? If careful double-checking fails to reveal your number . . .
- Try to find your coach. Tell him or her your number, event, category, division and round. "I'm BB-32 and I'm not posted for round 2 of Novice Impromptu for today. What should I do?"

- If you cannot find your coach, go to tournament headquarters, give them the above information, and tell them that you have double-checked and still cannot find your code. (Do not be miffed if they re-check the postings.) They will try to find out where the mistake is and put you in a panel. Do not give up until you are placed in a panel in the correct event, division, and category.

Most posting "errors" occur when you look at the wrong posting sheet, or just do not see your code even though it is listed. However, posting sheets are sometimes incorrect, so when you are certain that you have not made a mistake, find a coach or a tournament administrator.

Tournaments often use multiple buildings. Sometimes tournaments provide campus maps for all contestants, and almost every tournament posts a campus map in the posting area. Before you leave for your round, make sure you know where you are going. If you cannot find a room, ask for help from anyone — janitors, students, contestants. If the room is locked, check the room number you have written down. If it is the same, go back to the postings and check what you wrote down. If you wrote down the right room, report the locked room to tournament headquarters and wait for instructions on where to go or where to wait.

If a judge fails to show up after 10 or 15 minutes, again check your room number, check the posting sheet, then report to headquarters for further instructions. They may tell you to go back to the correct room and wait — they will send someone.

Locked rooms and missing judges, like missing codes, are generally attributable to misreading, miscopying, or misremembering. But, the correct room is sometimes locked, and judges are sometimes late. Always check first to make sure that you are not mistaken, and then report to tournament headquarters.

Rounds. When you arrive *on time* at the room, check before entering to make sure that you are not interrupting a late speaker from the previous round. Under no circumstances do you ever enter or leave a room while another contestant is speaking! And do not just open the door and look — listen first. Assuming all is quiet when you put your ear to the door, open the door carefully, and you may see any or all of the following:

- An empty room. Have a seat. Take one near the middle of the room, and wait for the judge and other contestants to arrive.
- A room with one or two contestants. Smile and take a seat near the middle, but not right next to someone else (this is not a good time to be invading personal space). You might be friendly and converse if you wish, but keep it light — do not list your past victories to others.
- A judge (they are sometimes quite young, so do not be fooled). Smile politely and take a seat quietly. The judge may ask for your code. Be polite, but not aggressively friendly. Do not ask them where they are from or try to initiate small talk.
- A judge and some contestants. Smile, take a seat, and when asked, give your code.

In some areas, it is traditional for students to "sign-in" on the chalk board so judges know who is in the room and ready to speak. You can tell whether this is expected of you by looking at the chalk board — if there is a numbered list of codes, you are expected to add your code to the list. Usually, the first contestant to arrive erases the board and starts a new list, indicating the round and event at the top of the list. *If you enter an empty room, check to see if the list which is already on the board is from this round. If it is, do not erase it; just add your code to the list. Sometimes, a contestant will arrive first, start the list, and leave the room for some reason. You do not want to erase their name from the board.*

If you are double-entered, check to see when you are scheduled to speak in each event. Go first to the room for the event in which you have the *later* speaking position, and tell the judge that you are double-entered, leave a message (including round, event, division and your code) indicating that you are double-entered, or add your code to the list and write "double-entered" beside it. Once you have taken care of this, go to the event in which you have the earlier speaking position. When you have finished with your performance, explain to the judge that you are double-entered, and excuse yourself. Go *immediately* to your second round. Remember, it is your responsibility to get to both rounds without delaying the tournament.

You are not penalized if you are late because a previous round made you late. When you get to your next round, tell the judge (after you've waited, listened, and not interrupted another speaker) that your previous round was late getting finished. Then sit quietly and proceed as normal. *If you have any questions, problems, or doubts, please* see your coach before you panic. If you cannot find your coach go to headquarters and find someone with a sympathetic ear. Always *ask* — do not assume something until your coach has verified it, and *do not* passively let your chance at competition pass you by.

You are expected to speak in the order listed on the posting sheet. However, the logistics of people moving around campus and the problems caused by double-entering mean that the judge may ask you to speak out-of-order. If you are double-entered, you might politely ask the judge in your first event if you can speak earlier so you can get to your second event. The only individual event in which speaking order must be maintained is Extemporaneous Speaking. If you are entered in this event, make sure you draw and speak on time. Other events have to give way.

When the round starts, give each speaker your full attention. A positive audience member will likely generate a positive audience in return. If you wish, you may applaud each speaker. A judge also notes if you are a good listener as well as a good speaker. Do not flip through your manuscript or distract the speaker or judge in any way. When your turn is called, calmly, with strength, dignity, courage, and fortitude, walk to the front, wait for a moment until you have everyone's attention (wait for the judge to stop writing), and then begin.

"Do well" by remembering that you are there to learn. If you make a small error or slip, do not let it throw you — continue on as well as you can under any circumstances — we do not apologize, we give speeches.

When all speeches in your panel have finished judges will usually say, "Thank you," or something to tell you to leave. They may have some suggestions or comments to tell you right then. If so, wait for them, and just listen. We judges are all different, and we all have individual preferences which can vary widely. Do not argue with the judges if they tell you something — just listen, make a note of it, and tell your coach afterwards but *before* you change your speech. If the judges do not want to, they do not need to give you an oral critique — so do not press for one. *Never* ask how well you did. They will write comments on the ballots which are given to you at the *end* of the tournament.

If you feel like it, you may compliment another contestant after you are out of range of the judge. Never offer negative comments about a speaker, even if you are trying to help — that is why coaches and judges get paid. Never make a negative comment *about* anyone *to* anyone during a tournament. Save your gripes for private airing later. Return quickly to the posting area after the round and check the posting for your next round.

Final Rounds. Most tournaments use "finals" or "elimination rounds" to determine award winners. During the course of the tournament, a tabulations staff records the results of individual panels and debates. At the end of a pre-determined number of preliminary rounds (usually two or three rounds of individual events and six rounds of debate events), the tabulations staff computes the results of the preliminary competition in each division of each event. Several contestants, based upon performance in the preliminaries, will be selected to compete in the finals. In individual events, there usually will be a single final round; in debate, there will be a series of rounds in which the division champions may have to survive two or more elimination debates. Tournaments use finals to determine award winners because the size of divisions often means that top contestants do not get to compete against each other in preliminary rounds. In final rounds (with the exception of extemporaneous and impromptu), you start with a clean slate; it is your performance in this one round (or series of rounds) which determines whether or not you win the tournament.

Sometime prior to the scheduled starting time for the finals, the tournament will post a list of the contestants who will be competing. Final round posting sheets contain the same information as preliminary round posting sheets. Only a few contestants make it into finals. Do not be disappointed if your code is not posted for a final round. That is what you are working to accomplish, and it may take time, experience and hard work to make it to your first final round. It is always a good idea to sit in the audience for the final rounds in your events. This is your chance to see the best performances in your events, and you can learn a great deal from watching the way the top contestants perform.

Awards Assemblies. The final activity of a tournament is the awards assembly. It is often a team's custom to sit together and enthusiastically applaud all the winners in all the events from all the schools. First place winners as well as the sweepstakes schools usually deserve a bit of extra recognition. However, do not carry your enthusiasm to extremes. Side conversations, whispered comments about the winners and general inattentiveness are rude and reflect badly on your school. Applaud others as you would have them applaud you.

How to Dress. Forensics is not a fashion contest, but try to look neat. As a general rule, contestants wear casual clothes. For men, slacks and a sweater or sport shirt are acceptable, but a jacket and tie would also be appropriate. For women, slack and sweater outfits, pant suits, blouse and skirt ensembles, or casual dresses are all appropriate. For both men and women, jeans have become more common as public casual wear. However, there is a world of difference between neat-and-clean blue jeans with a nice shirt, blouse or sweater, and ratty jeans and T-shirts. Forensics is not a formal dress affair, but your clothing should connote respect for yourself and for the activity. You do not need to dress as if you were interviewing for a job, going to church, or dining in an expensive restaurant. On the other hand, your typical school outfits are probably too casual for the situation. Your team may well have a dress code, so ask your coach or "seasoned" team mates how your team dresses. After one or two tournaments you will get the feel and be fine. Remember, you are representing your school, your coaches, your team, and yourself.

Miscellaneous. There are still lots of things you will want to know about attending tournaments. Much of this information must come from your coach. When will you leave for the tournament? When will you return? Who provides the transportation? Do you have to provide your own meal money, or does the school give you a meal allowance? Will you be commuting or staying overnight? If you are not commuting, where will you be staying? Will the school be responsible for fees and housing costs? Will you miss classes? What kind of arrangements do students normally make about missed classes and school work? Sometimes coaches forget that new students do not know the "system," so do not be embarrassed to ask questions; it is always better to ask than to assume incorrectly.

This is just a start so that you can get to your first tournament and concentrate on doing your events and enjoying the competition. While it sounds like a lot to keep track of, you usually are an "old hand " by the second day. The events, numbers, postings, maps, codes, schedules, etc., are all designed so that you can have the best competitive experience possible. Like all human systems, mistakes happen from time to time, but if you know how the tournament is set up, it is easier to spot a mistake quickly, take care of it, and go on, than if you do not understand how the tournament is supposed to operate. Forensics participation is typically mentioned in survey after survey of successful people in all walks of life as their single most significant learning experience. All of us involved in forensics education hope the same will be true for you as well!

Basic Research: Sources and Strategies

Allan McKissick, Randy Siefkin and Steve Collins

When you enter forensics competition you may suddenly find yourself with a greater need for quick access to up-to-date, accurate information in very specific subject areas than ever before, and your research skills suddenly seem inadequate. Your coach tells you that the easy-to-research topics (or your favorite pieces of literature) are "overdone." The quick and obvious material takes up very, very little space in the debate evidence file. What follows is a partial remedy made up of indexes, guides, abstracts, catalogs, etc., geared to forensics students' needs, but useful far beyond speech competition. This guide will conclude with a chart illustrating the political or philosophical bias of several major publications, and our Top Ten Hints for Effective Research.

Books (In and Beyond Your Library)

You are probably familiar with your library's card catalog (author, title, and subject indexes), but do not give up too quickly when you do not immediately find what you need. First, you might check the *Library of Congress Subject Headings* to make sure you have not missed relevant subject headings. Second, use your library to locate books beyond your library through the following indexes:

- *Books in Print* indexes by author and title all books currently in print in the U.S. — available on CD ROM.
- *Cumulative Book Index: A World List of Books in the English Language* lists books published in the English language throughout the world; frequently updated.
- *Subject Guide to Books in Print* is a subject index supplementing the above — available on CD ROM.

Periodicals (Magazines, Newspapers and Scholarly Journals)

There are a number of guides enabling you to locate the periodicals you need in or beyond your library. Some of the more popular guides are:

- *Ayers Directory of Newspapers and Periodicals* lists American newspapers and periodicals.

Professors McKissick and Collins are former Directors of Forensics at Modesto Junior College. Professor Siefkin is a Political Science instructor at Modesto Junior Colege.

- *Magazines for Libraries* is a subject guide with useful descriptions and evaluations of magazines listed.
- *Standard Periodical Directory* contains subject listings of U.S. and Canadian periodicals.
- *Ulrich's International Periodicals Directory* is an annual guide to thousands of foreign and domestic periodicals — available on CD ROM.

Popular magazine indexes like these will help you locate articles on current events and topics of current interest:

- *Access: The Supplementary Index to Periodicals* lists articles in magazines not covered in the *Readers' Guide.*
- *Alternative Press Index* covers over 150 newspapers, magazines and journals; mostly "alternative," politically progressive and radical publications)
- *California Periodicals Index* is a subject index to articles in "selected magazines published in and about the State of California" — covers about 60 periodicals with emphasis on government, politics, legal issues, and the environment.
- *Consumers Index* is a guide to magazine articles and government resources that provide information on consumer and health related topics and on specific products and services" — covers over 110 periodicals and services.
- *Popular Periodical Index* also covers magazines not listed in the *Readers' Guide.* Some focus on special interest and regional magazines.
- *Reader's Guide to Periodical Literature* is probably the most familiar. This highly useful reference indexes articles in over 180 magazines dating from 1890 to the present — it is very good but it is not complete. Use the following to supplement.

These magazine indexes are computerized:

- *Academic Index* is a computerized index covering popular periodicals but with more emphasis on scholarly journal articles than the above two.
- *Dialog* (see Current Events section).
- *Magazine Article Summaries* is another computerized index with broad coverage of periodicals and an abstract for every citation.
- *Magazine Index Plus* is a computerized index to articles in over 400 popular and general interest periodicals. Also includes some article summaries.

Standard newspaper indexes include the following:

- *Christian Science Monitor Index*

- *The Los Angeles Times Index*
- *New York Times Index*
- *Official Washington Post Index*
- *The San Francisco Chronicle Index*
- *The Times (of London) Index*
- *Wall Street Journal Index*

These newspaper databases are for computerized searches. Most of the newspaper indexes listed above are contained in one or more the these databases:

- *National Newspaper Index* provides an "on-line" index to *Christian Science Monitor, New York Times, Wall Street Journal, Los Angeles Times, and the Washington Post*; also available in microfilm.
- *Newsearch* is an "on-line" daily update of *National Newspaper Index and Magazine Index.*
- *Newsbank* (index and service) provides microfiche copies of major articles from approximately 150 newspapers around the U.S. There is an annual cumulative index with monthly updates. Most powerful newspaper database available and easy to use.
- *Papers* is a collection of newspapers available in the *Dialog* database containing over 2 million records, updated daily. Full text of many major U.S. newspapers.

These indexes focus on professional and scholarly journals — the "second level" of periodicals — and are considered excellent sources for relatively recent articles covering a wide range of subjects. Most of these indexes are devoted to scholarly work in particular academic disciplines. If you do not see what you need here, do not give up — ask librarians and members of the field in question about additional indexes.

- *Applied Science and Technology Index*
- *Art Index*
- *Biography Index*
- *Biological and Agricultural Index*
- *Business Periodicals Index*
- *Cumulative Index to Nursing and Allied Health Literature*
- *Education Index*
- *General Science Index* (also indexes popular magazine articles)
- *Humanities Index*
- *Index of Economic Journals*
- *Index to Journals in Communication Studies*
- *Index to Legal Periodicals*

- *Index Medicus* (medicine and health professions journals)
- *Management Index*
- *Music Index*
- *Physical Education Index*
- *Public Affairs Information Service*
- *Social Sciences Index*

The following resources contain abstracts (summaries) of professional and scholarly journal articles on various subjects. Like the preceding indexes, the collections of abstracts are devoted to particular academic disciplines:

- *Abstracts in Anthropology*
- *Biological Abstracts*
- *Book Review Digest*
- *Child Development Abstracts*
- *Communication Abstracts*
- *Dissertation Abstracts International*
- *Economic Abstracts*
- *Language and Language Behavior Abstracts*
- *Psychological Abstracts*
- *Sociological Abstracts*
- *Women's Studies Abstracts*

Quick Access to Current Events

These resources focus on broad coverage of current events:

- *Congressional Quarterly (CQ) Researcher* (formerly *Editorial Research Reports*) provides more in-depth coverage of some contemporary issues.
- *Dialog* provides on-line access to some hundreds different databases ranging from popular magazines, to specialized technical databases, to a database that tracks coffee prices. Many of the indexes listed elsewhere in this chapter are available for computerized research through this resource.
- *Facts on File* provides a brief, broad scope, chronological account of news events; assembled in annual volumes and supplemented weekly.
- *Kessings Contemporary Archives* is along the same lines as *Facts on File*, but more internationally oriented.
- *Knowledge Index* is a limited collection of the *Dialog* databases available for after-hours use for personal computer users.

- *Lexis* provides an on-line library of legal documents. Includes citations, abstracts and full-text documents.
- *Nexis* provides on-line access to Associated Press, United Press International and Reuters wire services along with many regional, national and international newspapers, scholarly journals and popular magazines. Includes citations, abstracts and full-text documents.
- *Public Affairs Information Service* is an index, but it provides weekly coverage of books, documents, pamphlets, and selected articles from over 1000 periodicals - primarily focused on political science, government, economics, and legislation.

Government and Politics

These resources provide general information about United States government structure and operation, and national politics:

- *Almanac of American Politics* contains profiles of every Senator, Representative and Governor including election results, voting records, ratings by liberal and conservative interest groups and information about campaign contributions and expenditures; updated annually.
- *Congressional Information Service Index: Index to the Publications of the United States Congress* contains abstracts and index of congressional publications including from House and Senate committee hearings — available "on-line."
- *Congressional Record* contains an edited transcript of activities on the floor of the House and the Senate, and is published each day Congress is in session; index updated biweekly.
- *Congressional Quarterly Weekly Report* contains current information on congressional activities, progress of major bills, background information on major policy issues; indexed quarterly and annually.
- *Congressional Quarterly Almanac* is an annual compendium of the weekly reports and more.
- *Digest of Public General Bills and Resolutions* summarizes essential features of public bills and resolutions and their changes).
- *Gavel to Gavel* (see Television section).
- *Government Publications Index* is a computerized index covering "much the same" information as the *Monthly Catalogue of United States Government Publications.*
- *Information U.S.A.* is a guide to direct access to U.S. Government experts and information services, containing thousands of names, addresses, and phone numbers providing access to an extraordinary diversity of information at little or no cost

- *Major Legislation of the U.S. Congress* contains summaries of selected relevant major legislation and related background on important issues.
- *Monthly Catalogue of United States Government Publications* lists documents issued by all branches of the Federal Government; has monthly and annual indexes — available on CD ROM.
- *National Journal* provides information on important executive branch and congressional actions.
- *Supreme Court Reporter* describes selected Supreme Court cases and provides full text of judicial opinions.
- *United States Law Week* contains complete transcripts of current Supreme Court decisions, summaries of lower federal court decisions and other legal matters.
- *United States Government Manual* is the official handbook of the U.S. government, containing details on structure and operation.
- *Weekly Compilation of Presidential Documents* contains statements, messages, etc., released by the White House during the preceding week; has weekly, quarterly, and annual indexes.

These resources focus on California government and politics. Most states have similar resources devoted to the structure and operation of state government:

- *California Almanac* is a unique publication covering political and economic as well as some cultural data.
- *California Government and Politics Annual* contains candid profiles of state's politicians, constituencies, voting records on key issues, ratings by liberal and conservative special interest groups; published annually.
- *California Handbook* is a compendium of organizations and publications covering a wide variety of subject areas. For each subject, the *Handbook* lists and sometimes describes the principal sources of information, the government and private organizations involved and pertinent books, articles and reports.
- *California Journal* provides a monthly analysis of current state issues.
- *California Roster* is a directory of federal, state, county and city officials in California.
- *California Statistical Abstract* is compiled and published annually by the State Department of Finance. The data covers a wide variety of areas, including population, income and cost of living, health and welfare, manufacturing and construction, and public finance.
- *A Guide to California Government* is a publication of the League of Women Voters. Provides basic information on the structure and function of state and local government in California.

Almanacs (And Other Fast-Fact Annuals)

Almanacs are published yearly with the intent of creating the "foremost single-volume reference work" containing current event summations, various facts and figures, etc. Some of the more prominent almanacs are:

- *Europa Yearbook* focuses on Europe.
- *Information Please Almanac* is another good U.S. oriented almanac.
- *Statesman's Yearbook* emphasizes British and world-wide orientation, including a statistical and historical summary of important world events of the previous year.
- *Statistical Abstract of the United States* is prepared by the U.S. Bureau of the Census; has a wealth of statistical data collected from government and non government agencies - considered the definitive work of this nature.
- *The World Almanac* is considered to be the standard; somewhat oriented to the U.S.

These annuals are less general in scope than almanacs, but nonetheless contain yearly updates on a diverse scope of valuable and easily accessible information:

- *Guiness Book of World Records* lists a wide variety of records and extremes; updated yearly.
- *Political Handbook of the World* is an annual publication which contains brief descriptions of foreign nations, emphasizes government, political situation and economy.
- *State of the World (Worldwatch Institute Report on Progress Toward a Sustainable Society)* is published annually; provides extensive coverage of major social and environmental trends and problems.
- *U.N. Yearbook* covers contemporary world issues, especially problem areas, especially ones relating to the activities of the U.N. and its agencies.

Associations (People to Contact)

There is some kind of professional or promotional organization related to most topics, and on either side of most important contemporary issues. The trick is to locate the organization you need and to contact it for information. Do not neglect your local phone book, but the following can be very helpful:

- *Encyclopedia of Associations* is national in scope; lists by interests and titles many public and private organizations concerned with various political, social, and cultural concerns.
- *National Directory of Addresses and Telephone Numbers* contains over 50,000 of the "most wanted" addresses and phone numbers indexed by type of interest.

- *Washington Information Directory* is a similar directory but focuses on public and private agencies with offices in the Washington D.C. area — better describes nature and purpose of each organization.

Television (Transcripts, etc.)

Many news broadcasts, current events programs, and educational programs offer transcripts. The program itself will often indicate how to get a tape or transcript. Listed below are two valuable indexes:

- *CBS News* provides full text transcripts of all daily news broadcasts and public affairs broadcasts, including "60 Minutes," available from CBS News Television Broadcasts in microform. Also, when a particular segment is needed, it can be obtained free of charge by writing CBS News, 524 West 57th St., New York, NY. The *CBS News Index* can be very helpful in locating individual items.)
- *1990 Transcript/Video Index by Journal Graphics* distributes transcripts and some videos of 50 nationally broadcast television shows and specials, including "Nightline," "20/20," "60 Minutes" and "Donahue." DONAHUE. Write to 1535 Grant St., Denver, Colorado, 80203 or order by calling 1-800-TALK-SHO.

With cable television service, you can watch live, unedited debates in the House and Senate, as well as speeches, media events, sessions of the British House of Commons, etc. These resources will help you find out what is being broadcast, where, and when:

- *CSPAN Update* a weekly program guide for CSPAN cable network. Subscriptions are available from CSPAN, P.O. Box 75298, Washington, DC 20013. CSPAN also maintains a schedule update telephone "hotline" (202-628-2205).
- *Gavel to Gavel* explains what's happening on and off the Senate and House floors during televised proceedings in both bodies. Also contains glossary of key congressional terms. Available from CSPAN (see above).
- *Public Affairs Video Archives* catalogs all CSPAN programming. Write to Purdue University, Stewart Center G-39, West Lafayette, IN 47907.

Literature (Prose, Poetry, Plays, Essays, Speeches and Quotable Comments)

There are many excellent indexes and guides to literature. Some of the more generally useful are listed below:

- *Essay and General Literature Index* lists essays in periodicals and collection of essays; updated semi-annually.

- *Fiction Index* a general index to works of fiction; published annually.
- *Fiction Catalog* is an index published every five years; now in its 10th edition.
- *Genreflecting: A Guide to Reading Interests in Genre Fiction* is edited by Betty Rosenberg (Littleton, Colorado: Libraries Unlimited, 1982). Focuses on various fiction genres. It's also useful to know that many genres of fiction — science fiction, mystery/detective, romance, historical, etc. have their own indexes. Consult your librarian.
- *Granger's Index to Poetry* indexes poems by author, subject and first line.
- *Humanities Index* this quarterly index includes lists stories, plays and poetry published in periodicals.
- *Reader's Guide to Periodical Literature* (see Periodicals Section) also provides index to short stories, poetry, plays, published in current periodicals.
- *Short Story Index* lists stories in anthologies and periodicals.
- *Speech Index* is an index to important speeches which is updated every five years.
- *Vital Speeches of the Day* is a periodical containing the texts of recent important speeches.

The standard references for quotations and literary references are the *Oxford Dictionary of Quotations* and *Bartlett's Familiar Quotations*. *Peter's Quotations: Ideas for Our Time* is newer, somewhat more oriented toward contemporary figures, easier to use, and places more emphasis on the witty and irreverent. Many students find it quite useful.

The standard play indexes (*Play Index*, *Index to Full Length Plays* and *Ottemiller's Index to Plays in Collections*) are quite useful, but not as up-to-date as you might wish. The *Humanities Index* (see above) also can be helpful. The following play service catalogs come most highly recommended:

- *Basic Catalog of Plays by Samuel French, Inc.* is an often updated catalog describes a wide variety of plays, musicals, television dramas, etc., available from Samuel French, Inc. The catalog is rather extensive and lists plays by type, length, number of characters, etc. Contains a synopsis of each play and review excerpts. The inexpensive catalog and the plays - relatively inexpensive for single copies — listed therein can be purchased by contacting: Samuel French, Inc., 7623 Sunset Blvd., Hollywood, CA 90046 (213-876-0570). Another possible route to getting a look at this catalog is to contact a Theatre instructor
- Dramatist's Play Service, Inc., *Complete Catalogue of Plays* is very similar to French's; its collection is not as extensive but considered excellent for catalog and plays. Purchase by contacting: Dramatists Play Service, Inc., 440 Park Avenue South, New York, NY 10016 (212-683-8960).

- The Dramatic Publishing Company's *Complete Catalog* is smaller and less prestigious than French's or Dramatist's Play Service, but can still be quite useful. Purchase by contacting: The Dramatic Publishing Company, P. O. Box 109, Woodstock, IL 60098 (815-338-7170).

Media Bias

The effects of bias in the mass media range widely from selective coverage (in some publications or broadcasts, topics simply will not be mentioned at all) to coverage that is incomplete or otherwise distorted. Good research requires such strategies as discovering the general bias of sources and taking it into account, and comparing the coverage of a topic by a number of sources with different biases. Below are several media criticism resources which might help you come to grips with media bias. Following that is a chart reflecting our "reading" of left/right slant of some major publications.

- *Extra* is a monthly newsletter published by Fairness and Accuracy in Media (666 Broadway, Suite 400, New York, NY 10012). It seeks to counter what it considers the center-right bias of the media in coverage of such issues as minorities, national defense and the environment.
- *Aim* is a semi-monthly newsletter published by Accuracy in Media (1341 G Street, NW, Suite 312, Washington, DC 20005). It seeks to bring pressure on the news media to provide more balanced programming content; claims that news reporting is skewed to the left, especially on issues like national defense and internal security.
- *Columbia Journalism Review* critiques the journalism profession, especially its coverage of government.

Political Spectrum of Major Periodicals

LEFT-WING	POLITICAL MIDDLE	RIGHT-WING
Daily World	Christian Science Monitor	
New York Times		Wall Street Journal
Mother Jones		National Review
Los Angeles Times		Spectator
Progressive		U.S. News
Washington Post		Economist
Newsweek		Human Events
Time		Reader's Digest
	San Francisco Chronicle	
Rolling Stone		

Editor's Note: This chart reflects the way Professors McKissick, Siefkin and Collins interpret the traditional philosophical slant of several major periodicals. It is not intended to describe official editorial policies or the political affiliation of publications, editors or publishers.

Top Ten Hints for Effective Research

1. **Make friends with a librarian.** A person who has spent his of her life learning how to organize and store the accumulated wisdom of the human race likes nothing better than to meet someone who truly wants to use that accumulation. Let a librarian know you are interested in learning to use the facility they love and you will never regret it.

2. **Become familiar with the reference resources in your library.** It is astounding how few student researchers know that there are valuable reference sources beyond the basic indexes. Spend some time browsing through the reference section of your library and learning what's there. You'll be amazed at what you find.

3. **Browse the periodicals section of your library.** Learn the incredible richness of current periodicals. Every element of the global economy, every perspective on politics, every trade, every profession or interest group is reaching out to the market place of ideas. Superb informative and persuasive speaking topics, along with unique debate case, ideas fill the pages of an enormous range of publications. Don't neglect them.

4. **Learn about government documents.** The U.S. government documents virtually every discussion, decision, piece of legislation and executive and administrative decision. Most university libraries are government document depositories, which means that they receive a copy of all government documents designated for general deposit. Somebody in the federal government has had something to say about almost any topic you can think of, and those comments are probably in print and on deposit in your library. Learn what the various agencies, committees and subcommittees do, and where their reports are shelved in your library.

5. **Read footnotes.** As you research, pay particular attention to footnotes. Not only will they refer you to other vital research documents, but often commentary footnotes will give you new or unique perspectives on the subject under study.

6. **Don't forget about personal interviews.** Interviews can be a source of ideas, facts and references to other sources of information.

7. **Make friends with aides or representatives for local congress people.** Few sources of information are richer for speakers than House or Senate hearings. The testimony, governmental research, and article reprints found in transcripts are invaluable. A friendly Congress person or aide can help you get these documents quickly.

8. **Make friends with local experts.** Find a faculty member or community based authority on the subject matter of the resolution or your speech. Make an appointment. Carefully plan an interview. If you convey a genuine interest in a topic which fascinates your authority, you may discover you not only have a new friend, you also have a guide to great information and a valuable critic for your ideas. Don't be bashful! It is amazing how many famous college faculty members spend their office hours alone because undergraduates assume that professors are swamped with visitors.

9. **Take advantage of public relations officers.** Every major, and not so major, corporation and non-profit group related to your topic has a public relations or information office anxious to communicate its information or perspective. Get a copy of the *National Directory of Addresses and Telephone Numbers*, select ten possible sources and write them requesting information. You'll be surprised at the results.

10. **Do research about how to do research.** Set out on your own to improve your research techniques and increase your knowledge about reference works. It is sad that you do not have to travel very far down that path to leave most of your fellow competitors behind. A few starting points are listed below. These works are helpful, but do not forget about the experts around you — instructors, librarians, and local experts — who can guide you in researching particular topics.

Todd, Allen. *Finding Facts Fast.* Berkeley: Ten Speed Press, 1979. (A concise classic on reference works and "basic" "intermediate" and "advanced" research techniques.)

Bell, Marion V., and Swidan, Eleanor A. *Reference Books: A Brief Guide.* Baltimore, Maryland.: Enoch Pratt Free Library, n.d. (A handy and inexpensive paperback guide that is a good place to begin before tackling the more comprehensive librarian's guides.)

Hillar, James M. *Where to Find What: A Handbook to Reference Services.* Rev. updated. Metuchen, New Jersey: Scarecrow Press, 1984. (Another good beginning point)

Sheehy, Eugene P. *Guide to Reference Works*, 10th ed. Chicago: American Library Association, 1986. (A well-established and more comprehensive guide to reference works in almost all subjects.)

Nine Principles of Practice

Allan McKissick and Jan McKissick

These guidelines apply to practice for many kinds of skills — not just Forensics Speaking.

1. **Practice.** Some practice (even a once-through) is much better than no practice at all.

2. **Practice what you have.** You do not need a finished product to practice. Practice the part or parts that are done. It need not be "Part One" either (and sometimes, it should not be).

3. **Practice frequently.** It may be theoretically possible to over-practice, but it is not likely to be a problem. The more the better.

4. **Practice with purpose.** Practicing is much better than not practicing, but practice does not automatically make perfect — you could be practicing the wrong things. Have specific improvement goals in mind, and strive to come closer and closer to meeting those goals.

5. **Practice with focus.** Do not try to improve too many factors at once. Usually it is better to concentrate on one or two things at a time — later practice can focus on something else.

6. **Practice with feedback.** If you must practice by yourself, use a mirror, a tape recorder, or a video camera. However, it is better to have someone else's observations and suggestions. Expert feedback is best of all — but even an amateur critic could be told what to look for.

7. **Practice realistically.** Avoid Murphy's Law. Make your practice sessions simulate the real thing as closely as possible. If you are not yet skillful or confident enough to approximate the real thing, approach it, step by step, more realistically each time.

8. **Practice efficiently.** Avoid the Law of Diminishing Returns. Educational research indicates that it is generally better to spread out a number of practice sessions rather than concentrate a large amount of practice time together.

9. **Practice systematically.** A practice plan with special attention to *scheduling* can make all the difference in accomplishing your goals.

Professor Allan McKissick is a former Director of Forensics at Modesto Junior College. Professor Jan McKissick is currently Director of Forensics at Butte College.

Argument Analysis

Suzanne Larson and Joe Corcoran

What Is Argument Analysis?

Argument analysis has been offered for a number of years as an individual event at Northern California Forensic Association tournaments, and is now beginning to appear on an experimental basis at tournaments in other regions. The event can best be described as a cross between Communication Analysis and Extemporaneous Speaking — the event expects an analytical substance (a kind of "gut-level" argument criticism) in a limited preparation setting. The format of Argument Analysis reflects this unique blend. A significant period before the round (preparation time varies from tournament to tournament), you are given an example of argumentative discourse, which you must critically analyze. The performance dimension of the event comes from the seven minute speech you deliver in which you identify, explain and justify your analysis. The relatively lengthy preparation period allows time for you to choose an appropriate analytical tool and go into some depth in your analysis, yet it preserves the limited preparation quality of an extemporaneous event.

Argument Analysis topics may be editorials, short speeches, advertisements, cartoons, or any communication which is in some way argumentative in nature. Some recent topics have included a letter to the editor of a school newspaper questioning the effects of the feminist movement on campus, an advertisement placed in *Newsweek* by the Chrysler Corporation justifying the company's need for federal aid, and a synopsis of an actual small claims court case between a renter and a landlord. The topics are intended to encompass a wide variety of argumentative forms and fields, and to encourage diverse analytic approaches.

All of the contestants in the event analyze the same topic in a given round, so you are not allowed to enter the room before you speak. After speaking, however, you are encouraged to stay and listen to the remaining contestants.

Choosing a Critical Method

You are free to select any critical tool to analyze the topic. Some popular approaches include analyzing the form of the argument, identifying examples of fallacious reasoning, evaluating the strength of the evidence presented, identifying the implicit target audience, recasting the argument using the Toulmin model. Some speakers combine dimensions of several analytic approaches to construct a unique method of analysis appropriate for a particular topic.

Dr. Larson is currently Director of Forensics at Southern Utah University. Professor Corcoran is currently Director of Forensics at California State University, Chico.

Many resources are available to you. Check textbooks you have used in persuasion and argumentation courses. Some excellent places to start would be:

Ehninger, Douglas and Wayne Brockreide. *Decision by Debate.* New York: Harper and Row, 1978.

Freely, Austin J. *Argumentation and Debate: Critical Thinking for Reasoned Decision Making* 7th ed. Belmont: Wadsworth, 1990.

Miller, Clyde R. "How to Detect Propaganda." *Language in Uniform: A Reader on Propaganda.* Ed., Nick Aaron Ford. New York: Bobbs Merrill, 1967.

Rieke, Richard D. and Malcolm O. Sillars. *Argumentation and the Decision Making Process*, 4th ed. Belmont: Wadsworth, 1971.

Simon, Herbert W. *Persuasion: Understanding, Practice, and Analysis.* Reading, Massachusetts: Addison-Wesley Publishing Company, 1976.

Sproule, J. Michael. *Argument: Language and Its Influence.* New York: McGraw-Hill. 1980.

Toulmin, Stephen, Richard Rieke and Allan Janik. *An Introduction to Reasoning.* New York: MacMillan, 1979.

Ziegelmueller, George W. and Charles A. Dause. *Argumentation: Inquiry and Advocacy.* Englewood Cliffs: Prentice Hall, 1975.

Analyzing the Argument

After your receive your topic, examine it carefully. Identify the central argument it makes, and locate any supporting arguments. Isolate the strengths and weaknesses of the argument. Look at the overall form of the message to determine what it is like. Look for examples in the message that reflect its overall tone. Look closely at supporting materials in the argument. Reconstruct arguments for the purpose of discovering patterns of consistency and inconsistency. Isolate the elements of the argument that get treated ambiguously or might not have been stated explicitly. Compare the arguments, appeals and evidence in the message with those that might have been used. Look for exceptional or unusual elements in the argument.

In analyzing the argument you might use any of the following approaches to help you understand the argument.

- Evaluate the data in the speech using the standard tests of evidence (recency, completeness, etc.).
- Classify the type of proof (logical, ethical, emotional).
- Identify the underlying values in the argument.
- Isolate the claim (point of the argument) then evaluate the data (evidence) supporting the claim.
- Summarize the effects of the argument.

- Evaluate the argument to see if the stock issues have been fulfilled (ill, blame, cure, cost).
- Isolate any fallacies in the argument.
- Identify the message targets in the argument (e.g., Maslow's hierarchy of needs).

Preparing Your Speech

Once you have analyzed the argument and decided what you want to say about it, you must begin to prepare your speech. From this point on, you will prepare much as you would for any other public address event. There are three things you must keep in mind as you prepare: First, your speech must be carefully arranged. You should have an introduction which both attracts the audience to your topic and makes your thesis clear. The body of the speech should be logically arranged, and the points you make should be generously supported by examples drawn from the topic. And, you should make sure that you prepare a conclusion which reiterates the points you have made and emphasizes the inferences you have made about the topic. Second, the speech should quickly summarize the topic (judges will have seen the topic but are unlikely to have thought much about it), identify the way you went about your analysis, and clearly explain and support the conclusions you reached in your analysis. Finally, the speech should be proficiently delivered. Every public address event expects that you demonstrate basic public speaking skills. Mull over the speech in your mind. Give thought to how you could best express complicated or delicate matters. The fact that your speech will be presented extemporaneously is not an excuse for inattention to matters of style. You are unlikely to provide an impressive performance if you first begin considering matters of expression as you walk to the front of the room.

Here are some tips that might help you prepare an Argument Analysis speech:

Introduction. Address the overall importance of the argument and the reasons for analyzing it. Furthermore, explain to the audience why your particular critical approach is an appropriate way of analyzing this particular argument. Besides this justification, as in all introductions, preview the speech. Basically, this means indicating what you will talk about in the speech, and the order in which you will talk about it. You may also choose to reveal the conclusions you have reached about the argument. While this may make the speech seem anti-climatic, it actually facilitates explaining your analysis. If you do not reveal your conclusions in the introduction, you must do as you conclude the speech. This is not an event where you leave your audience to draw their own conclusions, you are supposed to be revealing to the audience the results of *your* analysis.

Body. There are three steps you must go through to make your analysis clear to your audience. First, briefly summarize the topic, paying special attention to those elements of the argument which will be important to your analysis. Be wary of spending too much time describing the argument — this step is merely to assist you in making sure that the audience knows what you understood the argument to be. Second, explain your critical method and how you went about applying it to the topic. Again, be wary of spending too much time setting-up your analysis. Finally, methodically go through the critical process, sharing your insights with the audience and generously illustrating your points with examples from the argument. Approached this way, your audience will know what you saw as the substance of the argument, how you went about analyzing it, and what you found when you examined it carefully. Thoughtfully done, this approach will make the conclusions you reach about the argument seem clear, intelligent, and insightful.

Conclusion. *Briefly* review your speech — the conclusion is a time for summary, not a time to revisit your speech. Draw out of the body of your speech only what it takes to reiterate the inferences you made and to reinforce your general assessment. As with any public speech, the conclusion of an Argument Analysis speech is intended more as a graceful way to bringing closure to the experience than to deliver final insights.

Summary

Argument Analysis is a special forensic event which combines the analytic dimension of Communication Analysis with the situational constraints of Extemporaneous Speaking. You are expected to intelligently criticize an example of argumentative discourse, constrained by the pressure of a limited amount of time to prepare, and to present the product of your analysis as an extemporaneous public speech. The event provides an excellent opportunity to discover how well you understand the dynamics of public argument, how effectively you can analyze arguments under severe time constraints, and how persuasively you can explain your thoughts in an extemporaneous setting. In this way, Argument Analysis is unique among individual events.

NOW and the ERA

Last summer the Equal Rights Amendment died and with it died the pro-ERA rhetoric of those seeking its passage. One example of rhetoric used to try to win passage of ERA was a 1980 to 1982 advertising campaign sponsored by the National Organization for Women's (NOW) Legal Education and Defense Fund. NOW's rhetoric seemed to be typical of pro-ERA rhetoric. In essence, this rhetoric, as used by NOW and others, seemed to include, to some degree, an implied rebuttal against common anti-ERA claims. Anti-ERA literature at that time espoused the belief that the ERA was an unneeded dangerous amendment, solving nothing and threatening the family. A commonly held pro-family belief included the notion that the Equal Pay Act already provided enough protection for working women, and ERA would only serve to create unisex bathrooms and establish a women's combat force.

The NOW campaign attempted to refute these claims by showing that women fall behind men as far as pay is concerned. But why did rhetoric such as NOW's fail in obtaining passage of the ERA? Could it be that there are flaws in the argumentation?

An analysis of the structure of thier argument, and NOW's view of their audience, reveals some flaws which could have contributed to the failure of this campaign, and similar arguments made by other individuals and groups, to promote passage of the Equal Rights Amendment.

Structural analysis can come through use of Stephen Toulmin's model of argument. Toulmin's model is an appropriate tool for analysis because employing his model can reveal structural flaws the NOW Legal Education and Defense Fund advertisements contain. Also, Herbert Simon's discussion of meta-communication can help us determine whether NOW's rhetoric properly accounted for its audience.

First, Toulmin's model can provide the structural analysis needed. Toulmin outlines his model this way: he explains that there is a claim, data to support the claim, and a warrant to tie the data to the claim. The claim that the NOW Legal Education and Defense Fund seems to be making is that certain jobs are low paying because women predominantly hold them. The data that NOW uses to justify the claim are outlined in the advertisement. Women make only 58 cents to every dollar that a man makes. Women consist of a high percentage of those employed in low-pay, highly-qualified positions. And, on the average, women make $8,000 per year. The warrant that NOW seems to use is that the data are sufficient to justify the claim.

This sample was constructed by Professor Corcoran to illustrate an Argument Analysis. The topic used was a National Organization for Women persuasive campaign supporting the Equal Rights Amendment.

On the surface, it appears that NOW has justified its claim that certain jobs are low-paying because women hold them. However, a clearer look at the warrant may reveal some flaws in the argumentation. The warrant claims that the data are sufficient. But are they? Was the data really sufficient and complete enough to justify the claim?

In order to determine whether a claim has sufficient data, one can look at negative instances that deny the claim. Some argumentation scholars feel that negative instances provide insight into Toulmin's model that would be unattainable otherwise. The most obvious claim-denial would be to show that certain mid-to-high-paying occupations merely employ women. According to the 1981 *Statistical Abstract of the United States*, such is indeed the case. A high percentage of women are nurses and accountants. Women comprise 81% of all librarians, 70% of all primary and secondary teachers, 66% of office managers, 55% vocational and education counselors, and 50% of editors and reporters. Consequently, it becomes rather obvious that the presence of women in certain jobs does not necessarily result in wage depression. Clearly, these exceptions to NOW's claim reveal a major flaw in their argumentation.

A second negative instance refuting NOW's claim can be found by examining the number of men in low-paying jobs. In actuality, men hold by far the highest percentage of laborer and menial factory jobs, according to a Bureau of Census Report. Again, it seems that what NOW claims are true only of women can also be applied to men. In such a claim, NOW has failed to show how the problem is uniquely one of sex. Perhaps, the problem the office workers face is not one of gender, but one of a lack of unionization. According to an AFL-CIO Report, the second least populated union listed was the Office Workers Union.

So what Toulmin's model and some negative circumstances have shown us is that NOW's argumentation obviously lacks perfection. NOW tried to propose a claim that simply seems untrue.

Furthermore, NOW did not really address the crux of the ERA issue. An analysis of NOW's argument via meta-communication shows that NOW misanalyzed its audience and the issue. Herbert Simons delineates his method by posing a number of piercing questions. One question seems to be most revealing: Simons asks one to look for "communications about how the communicator perceives his (or her) audience. . . ." NOW seemingly believed its audience to be unaware of the ERA per se. In order to be effective, NOW needed to have addressed the concerns of its audience. NOW's audience-perception is revealed not so much by what it advertised but by what it did not.

First, those reading the ads were concerned about the vagueness of the Equal Rights Amendment. If enacted, the vague amendment could force unwilling women into combat or support unisex bathrooms. NOW needed to address this concern if its ads were to convince skeptical readers. Furthermore, NOW needed to show that women, working in the same jobs as men, were making less money. All NOW showed were atypical examples of women making low wages. In actuality, though, according to a Bureau of Labor report, women holding equal jobs do make less than men. That is the statistic that NOW should have revealed. Along with this statistic, NOW and other pro-ERA groups needed to show that the ERA could solve the equal pay problem. Many people believed, however, that if the Equal Pay Act was not solving the problem, neither could the ERA — all we would get from ERA would be women combat soldiers and sit-down urinals, and women would still make 58% of what men make in comarable job.

While NOW did attempt to refute certain anti-ERA claims, it did not refute the most relevant claims. The stubborn state legislators, that pro-ERA rhetoric attempted to sway, could not be swayed by incomplete refutation. The arguments against the ERA were too strong for weak rebuttals. And, perhaps NOW and other ERA advocates suffered the casualty of the ERA because their rhetoric failed to respond to the critical issues in the debate.

The argument Mr. Sames analyzed took the form of a two-page advertisement which began with a banner headline screaming ***ENRICHMENT*** *and ended with a discretely placed General Foods USA logo. One page was devoted to a picture of two Black youths intently studying a computer screen, one while typing on the computer keyboard, the other while eating a bowl of cereal. The second page had large, prominently placed boxes of Post brand Super Golden Crisp and Natural Raisin Bran. A small inset pictured a professional-looking Black man sitting at a breakfast table reading a scholarly-looking magazine while eating cereal, ostensibly from the box of Super Golden Crisp discretely placed in the background. The visual images are accompanied by the following text: "Nothing feels better than knowing you're improving yourself. Whether you're broadening your mind by satisfying a hunger for knowledge, or strengthening your body by selecting the good, nutritious foods you've always known. Choosing to attend a Black college means you're striving to improve yourself, too. Because a Black college provides an environment that places no limits on how far you can go. And Black colleges produce 40% of Black college graduates. So while you're away at school exercising your mind and your body, exercise good judgement (sic) by sticking with some of the wholesome foods you were raised on — like the great taste and nutrition of Post Cereals. General Foods, makers of these and many other family traditions you grew up with, wants to remind you that we've always been there for you . . . and we're still with you. All the way."*

In the past year, the trend in advertising has been the targeting of minority audiences, specifically Blacks. The "Mickey-D" commercials for McDonalds, the Flintstone "pushups" ice cream treats done in rap format, and even commercials with Barney Rubble dressed as MC Hammer have been used with varying degrees of effectiveness.

However, Post Cereals' parent company, General Foods, has taken this approach one step further — they put an ad linking Black colleges and Post cereals in Ebony Magazine's August 1990 issue. In it, they discuss success and how to get there. Today, we are going to analyze this ad and see if it really holds true under closer scrutiny. To do this, we will use the tests of opinion evidence, as these tests not only cover the important points of an assertion, but they also directly relate to this ad, for the tests were designed to see whether or not the ad's originator knew what he was talking about.

This recreates an extemporaneous Argument Analysis speech presented by Gerald R. Sames when he was an undergraduate student at Fresno City College.

The first test of opinion evidence is source expertise. Examples of this are expert witnesses, professionals in a certain field, or people with enough background, either through education or training, to be credible sources. Because there are no source citations for this ad, we must assume that Post cereals is the source. Post knows a lot about cereals, it is their specialty after all, and thus we can believe them when they claim that their cereals are wholesome and nutritious. They can, after all, pull out a box of Grape Nuts and show us the nutritional information, so we can accept that claim. However, as to their claim that you can "exercise good judgment by sticking with some of the wholesome foods you were raised on — like the great taste and nutrition of Post Cereals," we get a suspicious. Exercise good judgment by buying Post cereal? It sounds a little opinionated. Furthermore, the picture of the smiling Black man in the suit and tie, probably a successful professional we assume, reading a magazine and eating a bowl of cereal seems to say that Post cereals are at least partly responsible for his success. This subliminal message is furthered with the picture of the two Black girls eating cereal while working on the computer. So, while Post knows cereal, the link between their cereal and the people in these pictures is slim.

The next text is the source bias. Here, we check to see if the material is slanted toward one point of view in such a way that the truth is distorted. Obviously, a little bias is to be found here, it is an ad for Post cereals, and this is shown in the last paragraph where they claim to have made family traditions and that they've "always been there for you . . . [and are] still with you. All the way." Whether or not Post has always been there for us is a little unclear. Right now, this statement is simply a plug for their product, and thus biased.

Unfortunately, they lose all credibility on the third test, the factual basis of the opinion. For starters, what does Post know about colleges, especially Black ones? So, when they state that you are striving to improve yourself by attending a Black college, their claim doesn't ring true. The women at Mills College say they're attending that school because they can't get fair treatment at traditional schools. That seems like a better reason to go to a Black college than, for example, MIT. Furthermore, they cite a figure which says that 40% of Black college graduates come from traditional colleges where Blacks compete with students of other racial backgrounds. When you analyze this figure, it really serves only to cloud the issue. Where are these colleges? What about post-graduate education? What scholarships are offered at Black colleges? Without answers to these questions, we can't begin to understand Post's intent in including this. The remainder of the ad is just conjecture about how Black colleges *and* Post cereals help Blacks better themselves. No other evidence about Black colleges, Post cereals, or what link exists between the two appears in the ad.

In conclusion, this ad has failed all three tests of opinion evidence. Post overstepped its boundaries on the test of source expertise when it tried to tell us that good judgment involved buying Post cereals. Furthermore, the pictures in the ad had no link to Post cereals other than the subliminal suggestion that Pose makes you a success. The second test, that of source bias, was acceptable from the standpoint that a certain amount of bias was needed to sell the product. Unfortunately, other statements were made which cannot be excused through advertising necessity, and it fails this test, too. The final test was the factual basis of the opinion. This test was failed miserably as Post attempted to show us a link between Black colleges, Post cereals and success. This was not accomplished, and Post's ad therefore does not meet the requirements for the tests of opinion evidence. After analyzing this ad, we see it for what it really is — a clever attempt to direct advertising toward a minority group.

Communication Analysis

T. C. Winebrenner

What is Communication Analysis?

This event generally is defined as an original public speech in which you identify, describe and critique a communication event of social, political or academic significance. In its relatively short history, the event has gone through a number of different names. The contemporary title "Communication Analysis" has grown in popularity because it emphasizes two important dimensions of the event: *Communication* is a reminder that you may examine the wide range of communication experiences — public speakers and speeches, movements and campaigns, literature, films, songs, cartoons, posters, etc. *Analysis* is a reminder that your commentary need not be negative — your objective is to analyze, to dig beneath the surface of human communication in order to come to a greater understanding about what it means or how it works in a given circumstance.

As this description suggests, the Communication Analysis event has a split personality. On the one hand, it involves public speaking competition. You prepare an original text in a style conducive to persuasive oral expression, and are required to present it as a public speech. On the other hand, the event involves competition in rhetorical criticism.[1] One recent examination of more than 1,400 comments gleaned from Communication Analysis ballots found that 54% of the judges' comments focused on public speaking skills, while the remaining 46% focused on rhetorical critical skills.[2] Other studies of judges' reported expectations and actual ballot comments have likewise found that in Communication Analysis you will be judged both as a

---

Dr. Winebrenner is currently Director of Forensics at California Polytechnic State University, San Luis Obispo.

1 In this context, the terms *communication analysis* and *rhetorical criticism* are used interchangeably. Some forensics coaches and judges imagine that the forensic event *communication analysis* is substantively different than academic *rhetorical criticism.* However, the forensic event was modeled after the academic activity. When the forensic event was introduced by the National Forensic Association in 1974, it was called *rhetorical criticism,* a name the NFA event retains. While *communication analysis* is now the more popular name, the goals of the event are unchanged. Even today, tournaments sometimes call the event rhetorical criticism, communication criticism or rhetorical analysis.

2 Kevin W. Dean and William L. Benoit, "A Categorical Content Analysis of Rhetorical Criticism Ballots," *National Forensic Journal* (Fall 1984): 101.

public speaker and on your insight as a rhetorical critic.[3] I will not address the public speaking dimension of the event. Principles of argument, organization, style and delivery do not vary substantially between the numerous public speaking events, and helpful comments about public speaking in the forensics tournament setting can be found elsewhere in this book. Instead, I will focus on the substantive dimension of the event in an attempt to introduce you to the world of rhetorical criticism, as well as provide some normative comments about what it takes to produce a successful Communication Analysis speech.

As practiced in forensics tournaments, the term "communication analysis" has a dual meaning. First, it signifies that communication is the *object* of analysis in the sense that you analyze communication experiences. Such experiences are embodied in *rhetorical acts* in which messengers interact with audiences — a public speech, an artistic performance, or a televised advertising campaign, for example. These experiences generally produce *rhetorical artifacts* as tangible evidence of the experience — a printed text of the speech, a recording of the performance, video-recordings of the commercials in the campaign, etc. As a rhetorical critic, you most likely will be analyzing artifacts as representations of communication experiences in which you did not participate personally.

The term also signifies that communication is the *subject* of analysis in the sense that the reason for analyzing particular experiences is to better understand human communication as a psychological, social and political force. Thus, you are guided in your critique by the unique perspective of the communication discipline. A speech text, for instance, can be examined in any number of ways. As a rhetorical act it is a historical event, and it would be wholly appropriate to analyze it as would a historian, e.g., to determine its causative role in history. As a rhetorical artifact it is a piece of literature, and it would be likewise appropriate to analyze it as would a literary critic, e.g., to judge its aesthetic value. As act or artifact, it remains a *communication* experience and can be analyzed from the perspective of the communication scholar, e.g., to critique its rhetorical properties. Often, the distinctions between perspectives seem blurred, as when you undertake a feminist critique of product advertising or a sociological analysis of popular fiction. What distinguishes rhetorical criticism from historical, philosophical, literary criticism, etc., is your interest in the experience *as* communication and its implications *about* communication. Thus, while you may borrow *method* from other disciplines, your *application* is guided by an intrinsic interest in human communication. As a rhetorical critic, you are engaged in the process of generating a deeper understanding of human communication. You examine a particular persuasive campaign, for example, in order to better understand why it made the

---

3 See Suzanne Larson, "Communication Analysis: A Survey Research Report," *National Forensic Journal* (Fall 1985): 140-153, and Edward J. Harris, Jr., "Rhetorical Criticism: Judges' Expectations and Contest Standards," *National Forensic Journal* (Spring 1987): 21-25.

appeals it made, and how those appeals influenced the campaign's audience and affected its immediate history.

Not to be obscured by the forensics term "communication analysis" is the essential *critical* nature of the event. *Critical* analysis does not necessarily equate with negative commentary, for criticism can as easily produce positive comments as negative. Rather, critical analysis equates with *evaluative* commentary — your role is to evaluate, to make an *assessment* of the rhetorical act which is the object of criticism. Rhetorical criticism inherently involves judgment. In some way or another, you are judging a communication experience to be effective or ineffective, productive or unproductive, appropriate or inappropriate, significant or insignificant. The standard rules for Communication Analysis are quite clear in reinforcing the essential critical nature of the event. While the American Forensic Association rules indicate that the speech should be "designed to offer an explanation and/or evaluation of a communication event," you should not be misled by the phrasing. In a rhetorical critical context, *explanation* is not synonymous with *mere description.* The Phi Rho Pi rules make this clear: "The analysis should be critical rather than descriptive in nature — strictly historical or biographical analysis is not acceptable." To rhetorical critics, explanation aspires to *understanding.* An inability to produce a meaningful critique is a common shortcoming of Communication Analysis speeches. According to the previously mentioned examination of judges' ballots, one of the ten most common comments relates to competitors' failure to *assess*, by whatever standards, the object of their analysis.[4] It should be clear that criticism demands, the event requires and judges expect analysis to culminate in relevant assessment.

How do you analyze a communication experience?

Despite the rather limiting sound to the phrase "communication perspective," the interests of rhetorical critics are quite broad. Not only have communication theorists and practicing critics produced any number of popular analytic methods, it is quite common for critics to borrow method from sister disciplines. In fact, the search for tools to guide systematic analysis is limited not nearly so much by perspective as it is by *curiosity* — what you hope to learn from the act of criticism. The significance of any rhetorical act is manifested in many levels of meaning, any of which may spark curiosity about the act and give focus to, or *center,* critical analysis. Criticism is *message-centered* when it is motivated by curiosity about a particular message and/or its implications about similar messages, *messenger-centered* when motivated by curiosity about the person, persons or institutions which produced the message, *audience-centered* when motivated by curiosity about what the act reveals about its audience, and *situation-centered* when motivated by curiosity about the synergism of exigence, message and effect.

---

4 Dean and Benoit 106.

Once you decide what you want to better understand about a particular rhetorical act, your search for an appropriate method may take one of three directions. First, you may choose to use a standard critical method. Rhetorical criticism involves a systematic application of the communication perspective to rhetorical acts. Often, similar ground has been trod by professional critics who have developed, refined and described a standard method of analysis. When appropriate, such a method provides you with a ready-made procedure for interpreting and evaluating a communication event. Second, you may choose to adapt a standard method. Sometimes, a standard critical method maintains a perspective appropriate for the act but involves procedures which are inappropriate for the artifact studied. In such cases, you may decide to modify the procedures to produce a better fit between artifact and method. Finally, you may choose to devise an original critical method which breaks new theoretic ground or introduces new critical procedures. However, such an endeavor normally is beyond the skills of undergraduate students, and should be left to professional critics. You are likely to find that a standard critical method is best suited for your purpose. If you are an advanced student of rhetorical criticism, you may be prepared to adapt methods to the requirements of a particular artifact, but even that course should be pursued cautiously.

What follows are brief descriptions of eight popular schools of criticism. The list is by no means exhaustive, nor is it intended as a series of "how-to" statements regarding standard critical methods. It is intended merely as a starting point for your venture into Communication Analysis. At the end of this article you will find a select bibliography of resources more complete in substance and directive in nature.

Argument Criticism examines the interaction of message, messenger and audience in an argumentative situation, or one in which messengers use reasoned discourse to persuade or dissuade audiences. Such criticism is generally message-centered in that its purpose is to better understand how argument functions in interpersonal and social discourse, and often offers normative statements about what constitutes effective and/or ethical argument. A wide number of methods are available to the critic, most notable of which are those derived from the works of Chaim Perelman, Stephen Toulmin and Richard Weaver.

Burkeian Criticism has grown out of Kenneth Burke's philosophy of rhetoric. Burke argues that men are naturally divided into communities of interests or insights, and that this divisiveness is an invitation to rhetoric. Unlike traditional critics, Burke is only indirectly interested in what was said and how it was said. Instead, he seeks to understand *why* it was said, and why it was said the *way it was said.* Three elements of Burke's philosophy have made significant contributions to critical practice — his theory of identification and the search for consubstantiality; his dramatistic hierarchy of acceptance/rejection, guilt, and purification/redemption; and his pentad of act, scene, agent, agency and purpose.

Fantasy Theme Criticism is grounded in Ernest Bormann's notion that people cope with their here-and-now condition by constructing subjective interpretations of their past, present and future in the form of *fantasies* fulfilling psychological or rhetorical needs. When these fantasies are publicly expressed they are likely to converge with the fantasies of others and form a shared *vision* of reality. Like Burkeian criticism, fantasy theme criticism is dramatistic in nature, but it focuses on the drama *within* discourse rather than the drama *of* discourse in order to understand persuasiveness.

Genre Criticism appears audience-centered in the sense that it has grown out of a notion of audience as constraint, but it is really message-centered in that it seeks out normative statements about messages, presuming that audience, or occasion for speaking, constrains a message and dictates form. The basic assumptions of generic criticism are that audience situations are repeatable and categorical, that it is such occasion rather than time and place which serves as the basis for categorization, and that through rhetorical practice evolve "rules" which guide future practice. Generic criticism expects to find that successful keynote addresses, for instance, emulate each other, that successful speeches of vindication are much alike, etc., or more loosely applied, that successful product advertisements subscribe to particular generic rules. Genres exhibit a degree of stability over time, but they also grow, change and decay in response to environmental change.

Historical Criticism is generally motivated by social rather than academic curiosity, focusing on rhetorical acts solely as causes or products of their time. According to Ernest Wrage, history is recorded in a vast "mosaic" of documents, including rhetorical artifacts which are conducive to the kinds of inquiry for which rhetorical scholars are uniquely trained. Such criticism attempts to view history through the perspective of the rhetorical critic. Rhetorical constructs are generally extrinsic to the criticism in that questions of form and eloquence are rarely addressed, and rhetorical strategies are assessed only as they relate to discourse-as-cause (situation-centered) or discourse-as-product (audience-centered criticism).

Narrative Criticism involves the popular application of Walter Fisher's work on the narrative paradigm. Fisher argues that narratives are ways of giving order to events and describing them to others in terms of characters, actions and settings. In other words, we process and discuss events in terms of *stories* — both in the traditional sense and in the sense of an intrinsic content to commentary. To Fisher, narratives provide rationale for decision and action, both constraining behavior and determining it. Since stories may be *mystifications* (masks for ulterior motives), they must be tested for *narrative probability* (coherence) and *narrative fidelity* (consistency with other stories known to be true).

Neo-Aristotelian Criticism involves the widest application of rhetorical principles to the narrowest range of rhetorical acts. Neo-Aristotelian criticism is limited largely to attempts to assess and nurture formal public address by assessing a speech or speeches, a speaker or speakers, according to classical principles of rhetoric, most notably those from Aristotle's *Rhetoric*. As such, neo-Aristotelian criticism is largely uncentered, attempting to examine the broad context of message, messenger, audience and situation in an effort to judge rhetorical effect. The two central questions guiding such criticism are "*Was* the speech effective?" and "*Why* was it or was it not effective?"

Situational Criticism, while potentially subsuming all situation-centered methods, is generally associated with Lloyd Bitzer's notion of the rhetorical situation. According to Bitzer, discourse obtains its character from the circumstances of the situation which generates it. A situation is *rhetorical* when it needs and invites discourse capable of altering its reality. Discourse is given rhetorical significance by the situation which invites it and controls it rather than by the rhetor or persuasive intent. The three constituents of such a situation are *exigence* (imperfection marked by urgency which invites discourse), *audience* (those to be constrained in decision and action), and *constraints* (persons, events, and institutions with the power to constrain audience decision and action necessary to relieve the exigence). Situational critics seek to assess discourse to determine whether it was a *fitting response* to a particular rhetorical situation.

What goes into a successful Communication Analysis speech?

A Communication Analysis speech is, first and foremost, a public speech. Irrespective of its substance, a successful speech must be clearly organized, must make its arguments clearly and cogently, and must be persuasively delivered (which is a matter of both verbal eloquence and oral style). What sets the Communication Analysis speech apart from other forensic speeches is its unique substance. Successful Communication Analysis speeches fulfill the four stages of good criticism.

Stage 1: Justify your selection of a particular communication event. Why did you select to analyze this particular communication event? What makes it worthy of such interest? Is the message of particular import? The messenger? The audience? The situation? What socially or academically significant concern do you hope to address? Answering such questions not only helps center your analysis, it relates your critique to your audience. Any successful speech must, explicitly or implicitly, create an exigence which motivates your audience to listen to your commentary. In the case of a Communication Analysis speech, exigence lies in the significance of your critical endeavor.

Stage 2: Select, justify and describe your critical method. What rhetorical perspective will you apply to the communication event? Why did you choose this particular perspective to guide your analysis? How will you apply this perspective to the event? Most Communication Analysis speeches draw from a popular school of criticism and attempt to apply standard methods. A successful speech clearly identifies what that method will be, explains why it is appropriate, and describes the procedures involved in applying the method to a particular artifact. When, for instance, undertaking a fantasy theme analysis of popular television programming, you should identify the fantasy theme perspective, justify the perspective as a tool for answering important questions about television programming, and explain how you will go about digging into the "reality" of television programming with the tools of fantasy theme analysis. A successful

Communication Analysis speech not only makes sure that the *audience* understands a method, it demonstrates that the *you* understand it.

Stage 3: Apply your critical method to the communication event. Critical methods generally involve two steps. First, you should *describe* the object of your criticism. When, where, why and by whom was it experienced? What did it look like, or sound like, or feel like? You are working with an artifact, and artifacts have substance. What is that substance? More importantly, an artifact is tangible evidence of a rhetorical act. What was the substance of that act? Critical methods provide ways of breaking down and reconstructing discourse. The first stages of any critical method involve seeing what is there, taking it apart, and putting it back together again into some newly recognizable form. Second, you should *interpret* the experience through the lens of a particular rhetorical perspective. What does the reconstructed discourse look like, sound like, etc.? How do realities which had existed only between the lines now standout in the reconstructed discourse? Rhetorical perspectives are ways of viewing discourse, and interpretation is a statement of what you see (or hear, etc.) when adopting that view.

Stage 4: Explain/evaluate the communication event. The critical act culminates in assessment. What has your analysis revealed? What do those revelations disclose? What questions have been answered and what questions remain unanswered? A fundamental feature of good criticism is that in answering such questions it makes an *argument.* It makes an assessment of a communication event and undertakes to support that assessment as reasoned and enlightened. You should be willing to risk confrontation. That is, to make judgments which are beyond the obvious and ordinary. Description, classification, appreciation, and obvious comments arguably explain or evaluate, but the assessments they make are insignificant and the criticism they produce is unimportant.

Closing Thoughts

Predicting the behavior of judges in any forensic event is next to impossible. Judges each take into an event personal expectations and preferences which make them unique evaluators of forensic performance. However, comments collected from Communication Analysis ballots instill an inkling of foresight. According to one such collection, the Top Ten ballot comments address: [5]

1. Delivery
2. Critical analysis (descriptions, proofs, illustrations, etc.)
3. Organization of the speech
4. Ability to explain and justify the critical methodology
5. Ability to justify focusing on a particular act or artifact

---

5 Dean and Benoit 101-106.

6. Effective documentation for claims and assertions
7. Ability to provide appropriate background about the act or artifact
8. Productive use of available time
9. Discussion of critical assessment
10. Discussion of critical implications

How particular judges will react to your Communication Analysis speech will always be open to conjecture. Descriptions which are clear to one judge may be unclear to another; arguments persuasive to one may be unpersuasive to another; analysis insightful to one may be mundane to another. However, time and effort invested in producing good criticism is always profitable. The two sure keys to success in the Communication Analysis event are to write the best criticism you can write, and to be willing to review, rethink and revise.

For Additional Reading

Articles Every Aspiring Communication Critic Should Read

Black, Edwin. "A Note on Theory and Practice in Rhetorical Criticism." *Western Journal of Speech Criticism* (Fall 1980): 331-336.

Brockriede, Wayne. "Rhetorical Criticism as Argument." *Quarterly Journal of Speech* (April 1974): 165-174.

Campbell, Karlyn Kohrs. "Criticism: Ephemeral and Enduring." *Communication Education* (January 1974): 9-14.

Rosenfield, Lawrence. "Anatomy of Critical Discourse." *Speech Monographs* (March 1968): 50-69.

Introductory Rhetorical Criticism Textbooks

Andrews, James R. *The Practice of Rhetorical Criticism.* Second edition. New York: Longman Publishing, 1990.

Arnold, Carroll C. *Criticism of Oral Rhetoric.* Columbus, Ohio: Merrill Publishing, 1974.

Brock, Bernard L., Robert L. Scott and James W. Chesebro, eds. *Methods of Rhetorical Criticism: A Twentieth-Century Perspective.* Third edition, revised. Detroit: Wayne State University Press, 1989.

Foss, Sonja K. *Rhetorical Criticism: Exploration and Practice.* Prospect Heights, Illinois: Waveland Press, 1989.

Rybacki, Karyn and Donald Rybacki. *Communication Criticism: Approaches and Genres.* Belmont, California: Wadsworth Publishing, 1991.

Articles About Critical Methodology

Baird, A. Craig and Lester Thonssen. "Methodology in the Criticism of Public Address." *Quarterly Journal of Speech* (April 1947): 134-138.

Bitzer, Lloyd. "The Rhetorical Situation." *Philosophy and Rhetoric* (January 1968): 1-14.

Black, Edwin. "Chapter VI: The Genre of Argumentation." *Rhetorical Criticism: A Study in Method.* Madison, Wisconsin: University of Wisconsin Press, 1978: 148-177.

Bormann, Ernest G. "Fantasy and Rhetorical Vision: The Rhetorical Criticism of Social Reality." *Quarterly Journal of Speech* (December 1972): 287-298.

Brock, Bernard L. "Rhetorical Criticism: A Burkeian Approach Revisited." Brock, Scott and Chesebro, eds. *Methods of Rhetorical Criticism: A Twentieth-Century Perspective.* Third edition, revised. Detroit: Wayne State University Press, 1989: 183-195.

Fisher, Walter R. "The Narrative Paradigm: An Elaboration." *Communication Monographs* (December 1985): 347-367.

Gronbeck, Bruce. "Rhetorical History and Rhetorical Criticism: A Distinction." *The Speech Teacher* (November 1975): 309-320.

Hendrix, Jerry A. "In Defense of Neo-Aristotelian Rhetorical Criticism." *Western Journal of Speech Communication* (Fall 1968): 246-252.

Jamieson, Kathleen Hall and Karlyn Kohrs Campbell. "Rhetorical Hybrids: Fusions of Generic Elements." *Quarterly Journal of Speech* (May 1982): 146-157.

Johannesen, Richard L. "Richard M. Weaver on Standards for Ethical Rhetoric." *Central States Speech Journal* (Summer 1978) 127-137.

Mohrmann, G. P. and Michael C. Leff. "Lincoln at Cooper Union: A Rationale for Neo-Classical Criticism." *Quarterly Journal of Speech* (December 1974): 459-467.

Do you like green eggs and ham?
I do not like them,
Sam-I-am.
I do not like green eggs and ham.
Would you like them here or there?
I would not like them here or there.
I would not like them anywhere!

Familiar words from your childhood? They were written by a three-time academy award winner, a man awarded an honorary Doctor of Letters by Dartmouth College, a man called a "genius" by his publisher. They were written by Theodore Seuss Geisel, better known to generations of children throughout the world as "Dr. Seuss." Born in 1904, Theodore Geisel graduated from Dartmouth College, and then moved on to Oxford with the hope of becoming a great English professor. His quest was sidelined by a temporary job animating advertisements for Standard Oil, which gave way to a career drawing cartoons for *Life, Vanity Fair,* the *Saturday Evening Post*, and inevitably his first children's book, *And to Think That I Saw it on Mulberry Street.* "Today," says the *Los Angeles Times,* "Dr. Seuss is the celebrated author of 47 books, having sold over 200 million copies and translated into 20 different languages."

He is loved not only for his animated creatures and popular verse representing a true, however altered, sense of reality, but as stated on his 1984 Pulitzer Prize, "for his contribution over nearly half-a-century to the education and enjoyment of America's children." In looking back at the life of Theodore Geisel, perhaps now is the best time to try to understand the guidance he provided his audience through his unique use of allegory. In order to analyze the allegories of Dr. Seuss, we turn to the concepts discussed by Kenneth Burke in his essay "Literature as Equipment for Living," first published in his 1941 text, *The Philosophy of Literary Form.*

Burke's essay, although ostensibly addressing literature, discusses much broader rhetorical principles which he claims are "based on the terms of a sociological perspective," and as such concern not so much aesthetic judgment as the *effect* literature has on its audience. He indicates, "the most highly alembicated and sophisticated work of art . . . could be considered as designed to organize and command the army of one's thoughts and images. . . . Art forms like

This speech was written by Jennifer Kanan Sawyer while she was an undergraduate student at California Polytechnic State University, San Luis Obispo.

'tragedy' and 'comedy' and 'satire' would be treated as equipments for living that size up situations in various ways, in keeping with correspondingly various attitudes." To Burke, allegories are "like philosophy, sufficiently 'generalized' to extend far beyond the particular combination of events named by them in any one instance." According to Burke, literature as equipment for living has three salient features: It *communicates a timeless, recurrent situation,* it is *used as a tool for organizing ideas* about that situation; and it *provides an accessible, strategic role* to be played in that situation.

Since it would be impossible within this time span to examine all of Dr. Seuss' works, I will concentrate on three representative selections: *Horton Hears a Who,* the 1954 story of an elephant who chooses to protect small creatures despite the scoffing of his larger friends, *The Lorax,* a 1971 tale about a protector of the trees who engages in a battle to save the "truffula forest" from the profit-minded "Once-ler," and the 1984 story *The Butter Battle Book,* which depicts the "Yooks" and the "Zooks," who take-up arms to defend their right to butter their bread on opposite sides.

To understand the way the stories of Dr. Seuss function as equipment for living, we must first look to his ability to communicate timeless and recurrent situations. In a sense, we must find allegories accessible to his adolescent audience. As such, we must ask ourselves whether *Horton Hears a Who* represents a relevant experience in the lives of children. The *New York Review of Books* commented in 1990 that "Horton [is] a charitable and self-sacrificing elephant [who] protects the rights of the unborn and small nations and obscure in spite of the ridicule and scorn of his friends." Or, as Dr. Seuss put it, "A person's a person no matter how small." For all those children who have felt too small and feeble to voice their ideas, Horton represents the brace of self-esteem. The references to "small nations" and "the unborn" in the quotation from the *New York Review of Books*, might somewhat exaggerate the allegory, or it might merely represent a deeper allegory accessible to Geisel's audiences as they mature. A 1989 story in *Time* magazine typified the timeless nature of *The Lorax.* Eight-year old Sammy Bailey of Laytonville, California, came home to his father, the owner of a logging company, and insisted, "If you cut down a tree then it's just like someone coming in and taking away your home." The comment eventually caused an uproar in the small logging community because the town's children interpreted the allegory as a plea for preserving the environment, an attitude at odds with that of the adult population. As the *Horn Book Magazine,* a review of educational materials indicates, "*The Lorax* is the first ever Seuss book to have induced a potential ban." *The Butter Battle Book* surprised even Gerald Harrison, president of the Random House Merchandise Division. "I had no idea it was about nuclear disarmament until [Geisel] brought it all finished to New York." Readers had no such difficulty understanding the story. "*The Butter Battle Book,*" says the *Christian Science Monitor,* "is the most thinly veiled allegory Geisel has written." The stories Dr. Seuss told children were framed in experiences with which they could identify, yet addressed issues children would continue to confront as adults.

Burke's second dimension of allegory as equipment for living deals with literature as a tool for organizing ideas. To understand this, we must step back from Geisel's messages and examine his medium. For children to understand such complex notions as environmentalism and the nuclear arms race, they must be packaged in a manner appropriate to adolescent experiences. "In the days before Seuss," writes Elizabeth Ritchley in the *Los Angeles Times,* "there are only books for adults and little adults." The Dr. Seuss books changed that. According to the *New York Times,* "His meter and language were irresistible, especially the Seuss-speak he created when English seemed too skimpy for so rich an imagination. . . . Think of the Once-ler . . . who stayed in his Lerkim on top of his store and made his own clothes out of miff-muffed moof." Author Anna Quinlen, in her tribute to Geisler's revision of children's literature, wrote, "Dr. Seuss was praised for many things, including the murder of Dick and Jane, which was a mercy killing of the highest order. [But] his stories taught morals." The Dick and Jane approach to children's literature was swept aside by the popularity of Dr. Seuss. Simply put, children comprehend and relate better to "Green eggs and ham" than to "See Spot run." As the *New Yorker* explained in 1984, "*The Butter Battle Book* is a satire designed to inform the young and remind [them] of the consequences of mindless hostility coupled with escalating invention." Says Judith Morgan, in the *Los Angeles Times,* "Three generations of readers responded to his books with personal allegiances and enduring affection. We all have known Grinches and Sneetches and Whos." The Who from Horton, the lovable Lorax, and Grandpa Yook are comprehendible to young readers and provide a way for them to organize Geisel's moral messages.

Finally, Burke indicates that allegory must provide an accessible, strategic role for the audience. He elaborates, "In so far as situations are typical and recurrent, people develop names for them and strategies for handling them. Another name for strategies might be attitudes." For Dr. Seuss, those strategies are defined in terms of attitudes which help form a child's perspective and ultimately affect behavior. Geisel tried to guide children toward "moral" behavior by affecting their attitudes. With Horton, writes the *New York Times,* we must understand that goodness and courage always triumph. Horton is every bit as uplifting as any engine that could." Says third-grader Samantha Calderon, "It's neat 'cause there's a happy ending no matter how big the mess." *The Lorax,* however, does not have a happy ending. Nonetheless, the attitude of the story is immediately evident. As Jenny Cothern, age 8, put it, "Don't chop down all the trees at one time 'cause the animals will have no place to live." The Dr. Seuss stories are not merely adolescent entertainment, they are fables which point to attitudes obvious to the children who read them and listen to them.

As might be expected given the worldly messages evident in the Dr. Seuss allegories, Geisel has borne a fair share of criticism during his fifty-year career. His critics think that children should be protected from images of avarice, selfishness, intolerance, and the other human foibles the Dr. Seuss characters confront. The *New York Review of Books* commented about *The Butter Battle Book* that "This story is far too close to international reality for comfort." Insisted

Geisel, "[Children] are living in an environment that we made. When enough people are worrying enough — about war, the environment, illiteracy — we'll begin to get these problems solved." In this sense, the stories embody the strategy Geisel intended. Dr. Seuss influences children and worries their parents, hopefully pressing toward change — if not from this generation then from the next.

Through the framework provided in Kenneth Burke's "Literature as Equipment for Living," it is possible to come to a greater understanding of the Dr. Seuss stories. Each tale represents experiences children have, and will continue to have, in language which is inventive, magnetic and effective. Through the trials of heroes like Horton and the Lorax, Dr. Seuss lays the foundation for attitudes which help equip children for living in a complex and confusing world. The allegories carry deep and important themes which children will carry with them into adult life.

Theodore Seuss Geisel died on September 24, 1991. But, the Cat-in-the-Hat, the Grinch Who Stole Christmas, Yertle the Turtle and friend Mack (who delivered the first ever burp on the pages of children's literature), will live on forever in the minds of children young and old. Only one year before he died, Geisel published his final Dr. Seuss story, *Oh, the Places You'll Go.* I can think of no better way to end this analysis than with the Theodore Geisel's last bit of advice to the children of the world:

Be your name Buxbaum or Bixby or Bray
Or Mordecai Ali Van Allen O'Shea
You're off to Great Places,
Today is your day!
Your mountain is waiting
So . . . get on your way!

Honor to bold Robin Hood
Sleeping in the underwood!
Honor to maid Marian
And to all the Sherwood clan!
Though their days have hurried by
Let us two a burden try.

In his romantic poem, John Keats laments the by-gone days of the legend of Robin Hood, and all the heroism and fantasy that went into his escapades of robbing the rich to give to the poor. However, I contend that those days are not dead; that there is a modern version of Robin Hood weaving its tale into the annals of American History, only this time, the actors have changed. The rich who are robbed of their wealth are portrayed by one person — the Ayatollah Kohmehni. Playing the down-trodden poor are the Nicaraguan Contra "Freedom fighters." And starring as Robin Hood, America's newest and brightest star to emerge in years — Lieutenant Colonel Oliver North. Yes, a man who was viewed favorably by only six percent of the nation last February was by July 11 considered a "real patriot" and/or "hero" by 64 percent, according to a July 11 *New York Times/CBS News Poll.* As stated by the *New York Times* on July 11, 1987, ". . . Colonel North has executed a remarkable public relations coup and was apparently successful in achieving one of his major goals: to turn around, what had been during his long period of silence, one of the more negative public images ever recorded in the recent history of polling." So today, by using a theoretical model, I would like to analyze how Oliver North overcame the defamation of the Iran Contra scandal by becoming a "clever hero," not unlike Jesse James, Huey Long, or Robin Hood.

When selecting a model to analyze North and his handling of the Iran-Contra affair, we should note that the model must explain how North achieved his popular status as a hero to the American people, as most of the major polls indicated like the previously cited *New York Times/CBS News Poll.* This being the case, I have selected an article entitled "The Clever Hero," appearing in the January 1954 edition of the *Journal of American Folklore.* In the article Klapp identifies four elements characteristic of the clever hero: the clever triumph, fraud and deception, the small hero as the underdog, and escapes.

This speech was written by Steve Schroeder while he was an undergraduate student at California State University, Chico.

There are two reasons why I have selected a model from a folklore journal. First, headlines in newspapers from the *New York Times* to the *Los Angeles Times* claimed North's status as a folk hero to the American public. Also, Klapp's Clever Hero analysis is no stranger to the field of communication, for it was used by Klapp himself to analyze the rhetoric of Will Rogers. It was also essential to the creation of the "Demagogue Analysis" by Dr. Paul Gaske of San Diego State University, where he analyzed the rhetoric of Huey Long.

So, let's begin with the first aspect Klapp identifies in the clever hero, the clever triumph. This element is described by Klapp as "...triumphant but sometimes shady transactions which, on the whole, amuse people more than they outrage them." In specific, the clever triumph is a single, minor victory that aids the clever hero in his/her overall objectives. Klapp isolates two elements that can lead to clever triumphs: humor and popularity.

As Klapp notes, humor is a value which will redeem many a personal defect. Oliver North used humor to his advantage, utilizing a folksy, down-home style of humor that appealed to the grass-roots American public. Probably the most famous, or if you will, infamous use of humor was when North was being hotly questioned by House of Representatives Counsel John Nields about the date of a specific transaction between North and the Iranians. On the fourth rewording of the question, North replied, "I'm sorry, counsel, I think my brain has been shredded (with the rest of the documents). Would you repeat the question?" Another example of this type of humor used by North was, "I would have offered the Iranians a free trip to Disneyland if we could have gotten Americans home for it." This style of humor made North look human in the eyes of the American public, Nields and the rest of the ill-humored committee looked inhuman, thus scoring a clever triumph.

The other element isolated by Klapp is popularity. Just as Robin Hood snubbed the likes of the Sheriff of Nottingham with the support of the peasants, so does Oliver North. He did this through one of the most powerful uses of non-verbal communication seen in recent years: the stacks of telegrams. As the days of the testimony went on, a stack of telegrams on a desk next to Oliver North grew and grew. This symbolized increased American support for the man and his cause. As he stated in his opening statement (which occurred four days into his testimony), "I would just simply like to thank the tens of thousands of Americans who have communicated their support, encouragement, and prayers for me and my family at this difficult time." Through this statement and through the telegrams, North shows the Iran-Contra Committee that the American public is on his side, not theirs, thus scoring another clever triumph.

Along with achieving clever triumphs, Klapp notes that a clever hero must be a master at fraud and deception. Here is how Klapp describes it: "The clever hero must tell his opponent a story, seem to be what he is not, or surprise him with an unexpected strategy that no signs in the previous behavior allow him to guess." Oliver North use the second tactic, seeming to be what he is not, and emphasizes deception to reach his goals. He justifies breaking the laws he allegedly broke, including the sale of arms to adversaries and the Bolan Amendment, with the ideals of the country that wrote those laws; more specifically, North cloaks his actions with the American flag. He does so by aligning with one of the largest symbols of democracy seen in a long time: President Ronald Reagan. North testified:

> I came to the National Security Council six years ago to work in the administration of a great president. I admired his ability to bring our country together. He tried, and in my opinion succeeded, in advancing the cause of world peace by strengthening our country, by acting to restore and sustain democracy throughout the world.

So, no matter how allegedly illegal North's actions were, they were all justified in the name of democracy. As Daniel Schur, noted American journalist and coverer of the Watergate scandal, stated in his introduction to the book *Taking the Stand*, "It was a triumph of projected personality over complicated issues, reminiscent of the simple evocation of patriotism that has made President Reagan so successful a political figure."

The use of democratic ideals and symbols carries over into Lapp's third aspect of the clever hero: the small hero as the underdog. As Lapp states, "The Clever Hero is at his best when pursued by an apparently larger superior who thinks he has him beaten, cornered, captured, or scared, and suddenly, it is the little fellow who is laughing." Oliver North uses his smallness (one man against the thirty or so on the Iran-Contra Committee) as well as the power of the committee against them with stabs like this:

> I believe that this is a strange process that you are putting me and others through. Apparently, you have been permitted to make the rules. You dissect the testimony to find inconsistencies and declare some to be truthful and others to be liars. You make the rulings as to what is proper and what is not proper. It is sort of like a baseball game in which you are both the player and the umpire. And in the end you determine the score and declare yourselves the winner.

With this stab and others like it, North sets up a "Mr. Smith Goes to Washington" scenario: little guy trying to find justice in big-time government. And indeed, even the members of the Iran-Contra Committee perceived North as the successful underdog. As stated by the *New York Times* on July 11, "The members said they felt helplessly behind the curve, unprepared for either the substance or winning style of their star witness."

The last aspect of the clever hero noted by Klapp is escapes. As he explains, "It must be recognized that continual escapes, especially those which are nimble and impudent; which leave the pursuer looking slow-footed and foolish, have the quality of the clever hero's victory. Obviously, Oliver North has escaped many a shady transaction with both the Iranians and the Nicaraguans, but his most significant escape was coming out of the hearing practically unblemished. As indicated by a *Wall Street Journal* poll taken after North's testimony, 69 percent of the American public did not want North prosecuted for his role in the Iran-Contra affair. Thus, no direct or indirect action was taken against North by the committee following his testimony, for fear of public backlash.

However, it is this aspect, escapes, that can also help explain the demise of popularity for North. He is facing a very trying time right now, with the publication of the Iran-Contra Committee's report and his indictment. He also cannot rely on "Ollie-mania" for as indicated by the August 31, 1987 *Polling Report*, North's popularity has declined to its pre-hearings position, only six weeks after his testimony. It is because North is no longer directly in the public eye, he has not maintained those "continual escapes" which Klapp notes as essential to maintaining a clever hero's popularity. So, if North can escape conviction in true clever hero fashion with clever triumphs, fraud and deception, and appearing as the small hero, his status as a popular figure should be restored. If not, his popularity is sure to decline even further, as well as support for the Nicaraguan Contras.

However, at least for last summer, America had a modern Robin Hood in the persona of Lieutenant Colonel Oliver North, at least in the terms that Orin Klapp laid down in his analysis of the clever hero. Specifically, North has been shown to win numerous clever triumphs, use fraud and especially deception to his advantage, appear as the small hero and underdog, and successfully achieve escapes. Who would have thought that the modern Sherwood Forest would have turned up on Capitol Hill, and revive the likes of the Sheriff of Nottingham and Maid Marian (who I incidentally did not cast in my introduction?) But Maid Marian is easy to cast — no, not Fawn Hall, but look at the polls; a lot of Americans seem to be having a love affair with Lieutenant Colonel Oliver North.

Impromptu and Extemporaneous Speaking
Allan McKissick, Sally Tannenbaum and David Hoffman

Nature of the Events

Impromptu and Extemporaneous Speaking fall into a category of forensic events generally known as "limited preparation" speaking. These events differ from standard platform speaking events in three important respects: First, you have a limited choice of topics. Unlike the other platform events, when you do Impromptu or Extemporaneous Speaking, you are presented with a short selection of topics (generally three), from which you must choose one. Second, you have a limited period of time in which to prepare your speech. In Extemporaneous Speaking, you are allowed thirty minutes in which to research and frame a speech. (You are given an additional seven minutes in which to present your speech.) In Impromptu Speaking, you are given seven minutes to *both prepare and present* a speech. Finally, once you have drawn your selection of topics, neither event allows you the luxury of seeking assistance from coaches, team mates, or friends. In Impromptu Speaking, there is no time to seek advice — you draw your topics, take a few moments to compose yourself and decide how to approach the topic you have selected, and begin speaking. In Extemporaneous Speaking, with its thirty minute preparation period, it is often tempting to seek advice on how to approach a topic, which arguments might be the more compelling, or what might make the best illustrations. However, the rules of the event expressly forbid outside assistance.

Impromptu and Extemporaneous Speaking test your ability to apply your rhetorical skills under the pressure of severe time constraints. A broad understanding of history, literature, philosophy, and current events, wit, ingenuity, the ability to think under pressure, an intuitive sense of organization, the ability to express yourself clearly and eloquently, and a dynamic delivery are the keys to success in these events.

Extemporaneous Speaking topics typically concern themselves with current events, and are usually expressed as a question you are expected to answer. Topics are generally chosen from stories given substantial attention over the past several months in major news magazines such as *Time, Newsweek,* and *U.S. News and World Report.* Impromptu Speaking topics vary from tournament to tournament. They may be provoking quotations, proverbial statements, slogans, cartoons, or abstract concepts such as "honesty," "integrity," etc. Some tournaments use "rhetor-

---

Professor McKissick is a former Director of Forensics at Modesto Junior College. Professor Tannenbaum is a former Director of Forensics at California State University, Fresno. Professor Hoffman, a former Director of Forensics at the University of Nevada, is currently an attorney in the law offices of David R. Sylva.

ical situations," in which the you role-play a speaker in a particular hypothetical situation, and present the speech you think that speaker should present.

In both events, you are allowed to use brief notes. Most experienced speakers carry small index cards, and use one side of one card for notes. Sometimes, your topic slip will be large enough for you to use the back side for notes. In either circumstance, you will want to jot down just enough to keep on track as you speak.

General Guidelines

Topic Management. Read each of the topic selections carefully. Take into consideration what you know about each topic (or, in Extemporaneous Speaking, what you know you can research in a few minutes), the potential thesis you could develop for each topic, the opportunities for vivid and pertinent illustrations, and the intrinsic interest each topic generates. Choose the topic about which you think you can give the best speech. Before you begin to prepare, make sure you understand what the topic is saying — nothing frustrates judges more than listening to a speech grounded in misreading or misinterpreting the topic.

In Extemporaneous Speaking, you are now ready to devote a few minutes to research. Extemporaneous speakers normally carry recent issues of major news magazines in a research file. Scan tables of contents for relevant articles. (Many experienced Extemporaneous speakers prepare a topic index before the tournament. While this is not necessary, topic indexes are simple to construct, and quicker to use than tables of contents.) Quickly read one or two of the articles, the more current the better. Remember, you have a limited amount of time for preparation, and very little of that can be devoted to on-the-spot research. In Impromptu Speaking, you have no time for research. You have to draw upon your own knowledge and experiences.

For both events, the next stage involves topic analysis. Decide upon a thesis. Be sure that it deals *directly* with the topic. You do not want to sound like you have prepared a generic speech which you have tried to connect to the specific topic. Settle on two or three main points you want to use to develop the thesis, and quickly think about the illustrations you might want to use.

Time Management. Impromptu Speaking involves the more limiting time constraints. While event rules do not specify how much time can be spent preparing and how much must be spent speaking, the standard practice is to use approximately two minutes thinking about the speech, and five minutes presenting it. Judges do expect that speakers who deviate from this practice do so with good reason. Beginning to speak almost immediately, and then presenting a very short speech or a rambling, redundant speech, is a sure sign that you should have spent more time thinking about what to say. Spending three minutes preparing means that the judge will expect a better organized, more concise, eloquently expressed speech. Before you draw your topic, ask the judge how he or she will give time signals. Some judges will give you a minute-by-minute countdown as you prepare, and then use hand signals to show your remaining time as you speak. Other judges will just tell you when you have prepared for two minutes, then use hand signals as you speak. On rare occasion, a judge will expect that you are watching the time for yourself. Obviously, you need to know whether the judge will let you know time passage during your preparation. It would be disgruntling to think you were using your time effectively and efficiently, begin speaking, and notice the judge signaling that you have only three minutes remaining! The easiest way to deal with this simply is to ask.

In Extemporaneous Speaking you have more time, but more to do. Unlike Impromptu Speaking, in this event you have time allotted specifically for preparation. Since judges have no idea how you have used your preparation time, there are no expectations to which you should conform. A good rule of thumb would be to divide your preparation time into thirds — ten minutes researching, ten minutes preparing, ten minutes practicing. One thing to keep in mind about Extemporaneous Speaking is that you normally will speak in a different room than the room where you drew your topic and prepared your speech. Since you are expected to begin speaking *exactly* thirty minutes after drawing your topic, the time it takes to get to your speaking room comes out of your preparation time. What most experienced Extemporaneous speakers do is practice on the way to the room. When you see students walking down a hallway, staring at index cards, and mumbling to themselves, you have probably happened upon Extemporaneous Speaking students on their way to speak.

In both events, it is important to pay attention to the time signals judges will give you as you speak. You will have two or three main points you want to discuss in developing your thesis, and your time should be divided fairly equally between them (setting aside a few moments for introduction and conclusion). You cannot afford to get so involved in one point that you have to rush through the rest of your speech. The most serious mistake you can make in time management is to begin adjusting too late. Have a general notion of how much time you want to spend on each section of your speech, and begin to adjust as you notice that you are falling behind. Hopefully, you will be back on track as you begin each new section. Above all, do not adjust your speech by eliminating your conclusion. If you are not able to bring your speech to closure, you cannot expect the judge to give you a high rating.

Content Management. As in all forensic events, arrangement is important to effective Impromptu and Extemporaneous speeches. The basic structure for speeches in these events conforms to the sage advice offered to all public speakers: "Tell them what you are going to tell them. Tell them. And, tell them what you told them."

Your introduction should prepare the audience for your speech. Your opening comment should grab the attention of the audience and direct them to your topic. You should identify the specific topic you have selected (stating it word-for-word), and explain to the audience why this topic is important to them. Finally, you should clearly identify the thesis of your speech and preview the main points you will address in developing your thesis.

The body of your speech should discuss in detail the two or three main ideas which support your thesis. There are numerous stock organizational patterns you can use: spatial sequence (east-to-west, top-to-bottom, etc.); time sequence (past, present, future); advantages and disadvantages; causes and effects; problems and solutions; goals-criteria-accomplishment; the political, social and economic aspects of a given topic; or even journalism's 5-W's: Who, What, When, Where, and Why. Whichever pattern you choose, make sure that your main points are parallel. For example, if you select a topic concerning foreign trade, you would be unwise to choose as your main points trade with Europe, trade with Asia, and your own personal experience with a can opener made in Taiwan. The last point, obviously, is on a different plane of abstraction than the first two, and thus is not parallel to them (although it may be an example you could use to illustrate your main point about trade with Asia). Also, your main points should be relatively balanced. Spending three or four minutes on one point, and less than a minute on another, makes the shorter point seem comparatively insignificant. Finally, as you work your way through your speech, make sure to use clear transitions. Sign-posting (i.e., "The first concern is. . . ," etc.) and posing rhetorical questions are effective ways of moving from point to point. Given the short nature of the speech, you probably will not have time to devote to internal summaries, so save your summarizing for your conclusion.

As with any good public speech, the conclusion of an Impromptu or Extemporaneous speech should draw your thesis out of the body the speech, and quickly summarize the main ideas which support it. Your goal is to bring the speech to obvious closure. One shortcut often used by forensics students is to relate the conclusion to the introduction. While not an original tactic, it brings the speech together nicely and is preferable to "Well, that's all I have to say. . . ."

Delivery. Unlike other forensic events, an Impromptu or Extemporaneous speech is delivered, to some extent, "off the cuff." As a result, you should speak naturally and your delivery should appear less rehearsed. This does not mean that delivery is unimportant. Even Impromptu and Extemporaneous speakers should remember Cicero's summation of the three most important elements of effective public speaking: "Delivery, delivery, delivery." What judges look for in these events is a fluent, *conversational* delivery style. The *ideas* you are discussing should dominate your delivery. In other words, you are expected to react naturally to what you are saying without overdramatizing. Humor, concern, anger, etc. can all be evident in your delivery without resorting to over interpretation. Remember, your voice is a tool. You can vary the volume, rate, quality and pitch of your voice to communicate interest in and involvement with what you are saying.

Vitality is another important ingredient. It is important that you sound energetic, interested, and concerned about the topic you have chosen to discuss. If you sound bored, your audience certainly will be bored.

In addition to vocal variety, use your body to reinforce what you are saying. Let your gestures happen naturally. Try not to restrict movement by holding your hands behind your back, or putting your hands in your pockets. Taking a step during transitions, or moving your hands and arms to emphasize an important point, is natural. Avoid rehearsed gestures. For instance, holding one arm straight down your side, bending the other across body at the waist, and emphasizing your points by repeatedly using one or two stock gestures makes you look as if you were announcing the local weather rather than discussing important ideas. You probably will have an index card with some notes on it. Let the card be an extension of your hand rather than an object to caressed, waved, folded, or rolled-up.

Good eye contact is essential. It is often awkward when you are alone in the room with a judge who is continuously writing, but make an effort to look into the judge's eyes. If you manage to engage the judge visually, he or she may become so involved in listening to your speech that they forget about taking notes. If other people are in the room, be sure to look at them, too. While the judge may be the only person evaluating your speech, he or she is paying attention to your general public speaking skills. One of those skills is your ability to use eye contact to engage the *entire* audience.

Miscellaneous Advice

Before the tournament. Limited preparation events, especially Impromptu Speaking, stress reflex skills. As with any skill, forethought, repetition and critical feedback are essential. It is easy to give thought to Extemporaneous Speaking. When you read interesting news articles, or listen to newscasts, think about how you would discuss those issues if someone would ask you to give a speech. Brainstorm about Impromptu topics with team mates. Many tournaments distribute in ballot packets the topics used during the competition. Save them and use them for practice. Sit around with team mates, and talk about how you would develop particular topics. Practice as much as possible. If necessary, you can always practice on your own, but it is particularly helpful to have your coach listen to you on a regular basis. As with any activity, you want to make sure you are practicing good habits rather than bad.

Collect a research file composed of several months worth of issues of major news magazines. Try to pick magazines which represent the breadth of the political spectrum. Read each issue as soon as it hits the newsstand. Construct an index. This may take some time at the beginning of the season, but an index is easy to maintain as the season progresses. After you read an issue, go back to the index and add notations. When you delete issues from your file, be sure to delete the references from your index.

After getting your topic. In Impromptu Speaking, do not just sit and wait for inspiration to strike. A useful three-step approach for beginners is to: *Quickly choose your topic.* Assuming you have a choice, you must make an almost instant decision. The event does not give you time to ponder your selection. Stick with the topic which first strikes your fancy. *Settle on your main points.* This will give you something to go on, and will prompt further invention, especially during the speech. *Think about introductory remarks and supporting materials.* Getting into the topic is often the hardest part of Impromptu speaking. Think of a quick introduction, and then think of a couple of experiences or illustrations you could use to develop your main points. Do not take time to arrange your speech beyond this. If you try to think about what you are saying while your are saying it, you will think of additional support and begin to fit it into the speech as you are speaking.

For Extemporaneous Speaking, do not spend so much time on research that you fail to save time for composition and practice. This event gives you sufficient time to mull over your speech, and successful Extemporaneous speakers take advantage of it. Make a brief outline of how you want the speech to progress, and do not be afraid to refer to your notes as you move from point to point. Finally, remember that Extemporaneous Speaking topics are usually in question form. Do not beat around the bush, answer the question!

Closing Comments

Limited preparation event speaking often seems less cohesive than the more practiced and polished platform speeches. There is a tremendous incentive to resort to stock tactics ("I will discuss the past, present and future dimensions of this issue," or "I will examine this issue from economic, political and social perspectives") whether or not they are particularly insightful. There is also a tendency to rely on shallow analysis, latching on the obvious rather than spending a few moments thinking about the topic. Finally, Impromptu and Extemporaneous speeches often seem short on purpose — if there ever was a central thesis, it seemed to get lost in the translation as the speaker rambled about.

Your immediate reaction might be to point out the obvious: "If I had a few days instead a few minutes to prepare, I would have given a better speech." The point is well taken, but remember, many Impromptu and Extemporaneous speakers thought the very idea of composing and delivering a speech on such short notice absurd until they tried it. On the one hand, Impromptu and Extemporaneous Speaking are contests in which skilled and experienced speakers compete for awards. On the other hand, the events are intended as laboratory activities where you can cultivate skill and experience. Do not be afraid to be a novice speaker. When you listen to award winning Impromptu and Extemporaneous speakers, remember that they, too, once were novice speakers. The key is not to feel disenheartened that your speeches are not as insightful, witty and eloquent, but to aspire to those heights. With time, patience, and practice, you can become an effective Impromptu or Extemporaneous speaker.

Sample Impromptu Speaking Topics

Abstractions

Amused . . . Angered . . . Confusion . . . Courageous . . . Creation
Depression . . . Determination . . . Entertaining . . . Fear . . . Fighting
Great . . . Gullible . . . Hope . . . Hypocrisy . . . Integral . . . Introspection
Metropolis . . . Nationalism . . . Nature . . . Peaceful . . . Prized . . . Remorse
Satisfaction . . . Scapegoat . . . Territorial . . . Unlikely . . . Utopian . . . Validation

Famous Quotations

"You can't hold a man down without staying down with him" — *Booker T. Washington*

"When a man knows he is to be hanged in a fortnight, it concentrates his mind wonderfully" —*Samuel Johnson*

"In a million people there are a thousand thinkers, and in a thousand thinkers there is one self-thinker" — *Ludwig Borne*

"There is no sin except stupidity" — *Oscar Wilde*

"I met what the psychiatrists call a "normal man" yesterday. I can't remember what he looked like or what he said" — *Anonymous*

"There is nothing harder than the softness of indifference" — *Anonymous*

"Nature, to be commanded, must be obeyed" — *Francis Bacon*

"All the evil in the world is caused by ignorance" — *Albert Camus*

"What is moral is what you feel good after" — *Ernest Hemingway*

"Show me a thoroughly satisfied man, and I will show you a failure" — *Thomas Edison*

"When you betray someone else, you also betray yourself" — *Isaac Bashevis Singer*

"The devil is a gentleman who never goes where he is not welcome" — *John A. Lincoln*

"Law never made a man a whit more just" — *Henry David Thoreau*

"When the people have no tyrant, their own public opinion becomes one" — *Edward George Lytton*

"I respect faith, but doubt is what gets you an education" — *Wilson Mizner*

"Diplomacy gets you out of what tact would have <u>kept</u> you out of" — *Brian Bowling*

"An error doesn't become a mistake until you refuse to correct it" — *O. A. Battista*

"Good advice usually works best when preceded by a bad scare" — *Al Batt*

"Habit, if not resisted, soon becomes necessity" — *St. Augustine*

"Whenever you find yourself on the side of the majority, it is time to pause and reflect" — *Mark Twain*

Rhetorical Situations

A fellow classmate approaches you on the eve of a big test in an introductory college course asking if you would like to purchase a copy of the test to be given the next day. Discuss with him/her why you feel his/her actions are inappropriate.

You have trouble starting your car and call a neighborhood mechanic to get the car running. Upon picking up the car the next day, you feel the mechanic's bill includes unauthorized work charges. Explain to him/her why you feel the bill is excessive and inappropriate.

A proposal by your college's student senate to abolish distinctions between student and faculty parking lots has created much controversy on campus. At a campus forum called by the student senate to address the issue, several faculty members open the meeting by arguing to keep the distinctions. You then address the group calling for elimination of separate parking.

You supervise a group of twenty hourly workers in a large computer parts factory. At your department's monthly meeting, several employees question a number of minor company policies regarding sick days, break times and the like. Explain to the employees why these policies exist.

Your city is planning to raze a city block near the downtown area to provide parking for businesses and shoppers. The area to be cleared contains several old historical buildings and homes. As a concerned citizen you attend a public hearing on the proposed action. A proponent of the leveling has just spoken to the issue. It is now your turn to argue against the proposal.

The state has just announced $300,000 of budget cuts to your college's educational fund. As a student member of the college's board of trustees, you have listened to board members argue for various criteria to be used in determining the specific cuts. You speak indicating the criteria you believe should be used.

Your city's park board has announced tentative plans to buy three acres of vacant property next to your house for a public park. Speaking at the meeting at which the decision will be made, take either side of the issue. A speech by your opponent will follow.

While picnicking at a state park with your family, you notice a group of youngsters defacing some park signs. Approach them with reasons why they should halt their actions.

Wait Until Your Father Gets Home

My mother and I have always fought like cats and dogs. We never seem to agree on anything. When I was younger and my mom and I were home alone arguing, and I came up with that one argument, that clincher in the last moments of my 1AR which she could not respond to, she would always stop, look at me and say, "Wait until your father comes home!" What a cop-out. The only reason she said that was because she couldn't think of anything else. That phrase has been said to children across the United States for many years . . . my mother probably heard it herself. But children are not hearing it as much any more. This is due to changes in the family unit and society, and we have to learn how to live with the changes in these fundamental aspects of our daily lives.

Everyone is a part of some type of family unit. Traditionally in America, this unit consisted of a father who worked a nine-to-five job, a mother with an apron and chocolate chip cookies in the oven, and a couple of swell kids. But as we look at the family today, we might well find ourselves asking, "Whatever happened to Donna Reed?" She certainly isn't living at my house! Things such as the increasing cost-of-living mean that more and more it takes two incomes just to survive. The role of provider is being shared, and this means other roles are shared as well. Household chores are no longer an exclusively feminine domain, and men do not have the monopoly on discipline. The increased divorce rates also mean in many cases that single parents have to take care of all roles. A mother can't say "Wait until your father gets home," if she's the only adult in the household. There is no denying a dramatic change is taking place in the American family today.

Because society is a collection of family units, society is changing as well. Women are entering the work force in ever greater numbers. This means issues such as child care at the workplace are receiving greater and greater concern. These concerns are changing the shape of businesses, which are becoming more and more attuned to family issues.

The loss of the highly structured family unit also means that society has to do more parenting. This is shown to bet true in our public school system. Teachers in public schools are increasingly caught in the dilemma of whether or not to teach morality in schools. With sex education, for example, many feel that the family is no longer teaching kinds what they need to know about sex. They feel that this issue must be addressed in school, to protect our children. Yet some parents believe educators are usurping their role. In addition, single parents also have

---

This recreates an Impromptu speech presented by Amy Kate O'Brien when she was an undergraduate student at Santa Rosa Junior College.

a hard time surviving. Many time they must turn to the government for financial help. Society is becoming more involved in all aspects of family units; things that used to be private matters now seen to be public domain. The changing family is changing the society we live in.

No one can deny the changes in the family of society. But how do these changes affect us? First of all, we must deal with the personal changes in our lives. Now we must cope with our parents and our brothers and sisters, (and our parents with us) in a completely new way. New roles will develop, putting more responsibility on children and more pressure on parents. We have to be adaptable and not bemoan lost days. We can't go back, so we each have to accept the present and try to make the future better. On a national level, we will have to adapt our way of thinking. Now more that ever, we must rely on each other for support — not necessarily financial, but emotional support. Many children are no longer growing up with Donna Reed, and we still have to look our for those who perhaps do not have anyone looking out for them. Currently, society has a great responsibility to take care of, at least watch over, its individual members.

When we look at the changes in the family unit and society today, it is no surprise that we do not hear "Wait until your father gets home" anymore. The structure, roles and attitudes of both are in constant flux. If we remain flexible and work to improve the structure of family and society, we can perhaps have something better. How we deal with the changes in family and society will determine our future. Hopefully, we will not have to use threats to deal with our children . . . we will find a better way. And hopefully, I won't fight as much with my daughter as my mother did with hers!

Sample Extemporaneous Speaking Topics

[Editor's Note: By the very nature of the event, interest in any particular Extemporaneous Speaking topic is of short duration. Although some of the following topics represent relatively timeless issues, for the most part they are outdated in the sense that they no longer qualify as "current" issues. You certainly would not want to use them as practice topics. However, they do illustrate the kinds of issues which work their way into forensics tournaments as Extemporaeous Speaking topics.]

Domestic Issues

College sports: Has the big business of intercollegiate athletics gotten out of hand?
How can America put a stop to teenage gang violence?
Minorities on TV: Do growing numbers mean real progress?
Designer diets: Is there any common thread of good health advice?
Can big city schools be saved?
Where does the responsibility for our health lie — in our habits or in our genes?
Do the gains from genetic engineering outweigh the cost?
Non-smokers: Are they denying the "rights" of a minority?
How has Affirmative Action helped the quest for gender, racial and ethnic equality?
Does the mass media play too great a role in Presidential campaigns?
Critically ill patients: Are we treating them like organ farms?
Alcoholism: If a gene's the problem, what's the solution?
Social Security: Can America afford to take care of the elderly?
Cocaine: Can America afford to "Just Say No?"
Is there any hope for the homeless?
Animal Rights: Is violence the answer?
Does America need another "New Deal?"
Private hospitals: Are they bankrupting the medical care system?
America's space program: Is it really worth it?
Will new technology help the oil industry find a gusher?
Do student achievement tests really test achievement?
"They're baaaaack:" What can California do to stop the medfly?
What effect has the NCAA's Proposition 42 had on intercollegiate athletic programs?
Will America's trash problem bury us all?
How will the graying of America affect our retirement system?

International Issues

How can America beat Japanese "judo" economics?

Can the Israelis and the Palestinians finally come to a settlement?

Does the break-up of the Soviet Union leave the U.S. unopposed as a world power?

Will the end of apartheid mean the beginning of peace in South Africa?

American manufacturing: Is it ready to reconquer the world market?

Is North Korea about to become the newest thorn in America's side?

Has communism gone the way of the buffalo (and the five-cent cigar)?

Will Japan make significant moves to reduce the trade problems with the U.S.?

Star Wars revisited: How likely is a major conflict in outer space?

Why the resurgence of nationalism around the world?

Should America use military force in the international war on drugs?

Can the America continue to allow terrorists to hold her hostage?

Techno-bandits: Are they selling our enemies the rope to hang us?

Cuba: Is it finally time to be neighborly?

Is America prepared to fight a conventional war?

What role did television play in the world-wide revolutions of the 1990s?

The lessons of Lockerbie: What needs to be done about airline security?

Will peace in Europe blow a hole in the U.S. economy?

Razing the rain forests: Just a Brazilian problem or everyone's concern?

Aid to Somolia: Was it a United Nations relief effort or American imperialism?

On February 25th of last year, a great step for worldwide democracy took place. Free elections were held in Nicaragua. After years of civil war, Daniel Ortega agreed to let votes take the place of fighting to determine the future make-up of the Nicaraguan government. Immediately, a contender, Violeta Chamorro, stepped forward with promises of hope should she become president. Those promises were evidently effective because Chamorro was elected as the new president of Nicaragua. Now, nine months after Chamorro's triumphant election there is again civil war in Nicaragua. Thus, the question arises: Has Chamorro broken her promises to the people of Nicaragua? Many people believe so. In order to understand why, we must first examine exactly what her campaign promises were. Next, we must look at the present government in Nicaragua to determine whether or not these promises have become reality. Finally, we must look at some of the drastic consequences which have resulted from this breech of faith.

Before being elected to office, Chamorro made many idealistic promises which were enticing to the people but almost impossible to attain. According to *The Economist,* November 24, 1990, her first and most important promise was to remove the revolutionary Sandinista movement which had seized power a decade before. Her key word was peace — a peace within the government and between the people. She contended that, should she become president, the Sandinista officials would have to turn their positions over to her Contra supporters. Once the government was secure and peace restored, Chamorro promised to improve the economy and to return stolen land to the people.

These promises sound like too much for one woman to accomplish. Unfortunately for the Nicaraguan citizens, this proved to be true. According to *Time,* July 23, 1990, Chamorro immediately began forming coalitions with Sandinista officials once her position as president was secured. She claimed these actions were to prevent strife within the government and military. In addition, she allowed many Sandinista officials to retain their positions. Perhaps most surprisingly, according to *The Economist,* May 5, 1990, she even allowed Daniel Ortega's brother, Humberto, to retain his spot as head of the army. Unfortunately, according to the November *Economist* article, these key Sandinista officials have been taking advantage of Chamorro's leniency. They are cheating the government, stealing thousands of dollars in goods and currency.

Yet, this is not the worst of the news for the Nicaraguan people. The land Chamorro promised them never appeared and the quality of life for the people began to decline. According to

---

This recreates an Extemporaneous speech presented by Amy Haddix when she was an undergraduate student at Santa Rosa Junior College.

the November *Economist* article, many citizens found themselves receiving worse wages than their Sandinista neighbors, a situation not uncommon during Ortega's rule. The economy as a whole is not at least as badly off as in the worst years of Sandinista rule.

So, what does this mean for the future of Nicaragua? The people who put Chamorro into power feel sold out and are beginning to complain that living under her is like living under Ortega. According to the November *Economist* article, the riots are beginning again, with twenty-four people killed and fifty wounded in early November. The people have not been fooled by false promises and empty speeches. Whether Chamorro is breaking her promises willingly or unintentionally makes no difference. The people, through their riots, roadblocks and slaughter of one another have made one thing clear — there is still discontent in Nicaragua.

The assumed victory for democracy seems to be an illusion in Nicaragua. Voting is easy. Yet making a democracy work is an entirely different matter. Unfortunately, Violeta Chamorro has shown that the future she promised the Nicaraguan citizens was not what she had in mind for the long run. We can clearly see by examining the current situation in Nicaragua that Chamorro's promises to remove the Sandinistas from power, restore peace and save the economy never made it off the campaign trail. Unfortunately, these broken promises have had dire consequences in that they have led to more dissent within the populace. The people of Nicaragua are sending a message to the world. They have seen that it is irrelevant who leads their country because a democracy founded on false promises will never satisfy the people.

Informative (Expository) Speaking

Diana Crossman

Informative speaking, sometimes called expository speaking, is defined in many basic public speaking textbooks as a speech designed to educate, one in which the speaker takes on the role of teacher. Although this definition works somewhat in a forensics setting, understanding the event requires going beyond informative speaking as you might have experienced it as a classroom assignment. My intent is to highlight for you the differences between classroom informative speaking and competitive informative speaking. I will concentrate on three important dimensions of the competitive speaking environment — topic selection, preparation, and presentation.

Choosing a Topic for Your Informative Speech

In forensics competition, choosing a topic for your informative speech is a primary concern. Your audience will expect several things from the topic you choose. First, they expect to learn something new. If you choose a topic your audience already knows a good deal about, they will expect you to add considerably to what they know. Some successful informative speakers might tell you that they try to find a topic their audience will know nothing about. This is a challenging task. Your primary audience in competitive speaking will be your judge, who is usually a college instructor, and is usually well-informed, widely read, and has been listening to informative speeches for a number of years. While your topic might be new to a few of your judges, it is not likely that it will be new to very many of them. While finding a unique topic would be nice, your time would be better spent searching for a topic which allows you to build upon what informed audiences already know. A new bent to an old subject might be just what you are looking for.

Second, your audience will expect your topic to be significant. Comments about your summer vacation to New Zealand might educate your audience, especially if they have never been there, but your experiences would most likely fail the test of significance. A bizarre birth defect that occurs in one of 100,000 infants might educate your audience, but because of its infrequency it would fail the significance test. Your audience might also learn something from your impressions about Madonna's latest world tour, or your personal predictions about future fashion, but these topics would also fail the test of significance. Information that does little more than entertain, amuse, or astound an audience makes for a meaningless educational experience. Generally speaking, the test of significance means your topic should be relevant to our lives, important to us as human beings, and subject to research, verification and validation.

Professor Crossman is currently Co-Director of Forensics at El Camino College.

I should also mention at this point that informative topics never should be overtly persuasive. Examine your reasons for choosing a topic, and be certain it is not to affect beliefs or attitudes about a controversial issue. Some coaches argue that all informative speeches are somewhat persuasive. To a degree, this is true — you choose a speech hoping to persuade a judge that your topic is more important that your competitors' topics. Just the fact that you have chosen a particular topic implies that you find it to be a significant issue, and that alone is a subtle form of persuasion. However, there is a substantial difference between persuading a judge your topic is significant, and examining a *persuasive topic*. Persuasive topics are inherently controversial, which is to say, merely addressing them before informed audiences invites controversy. *Informative topics* are not immediately controversial. That does not mean that you will not present your speech persuasively, merely that the topic you address should not raise immediate concerns about how people ought to feel or believe about the issues involved.

The final attribute a forensics audience expects of your topic is that it will fascinate them. The more fascinating the better. However, it is true that what amazes one person may leave another uninterested. You will have to make an educated guess as to what might fascinate a typical forensics audience. Your coach, and experienced team mates, can be of invaluable help here. However, it is best to remember that your judges are typically college forensics instructors, are often former forensics competitors, and are likely to be interested in a wide variety of subjects, particularly those which touch their own lives. As well-educated people, forensics audiences are particularly curious about the world around them. Innovations in science, medicine and technology, and new ways of looking at or understanding common experiences, often make good topics. With any topic, ask yourself what would make judges interested in it and how it would relate to their lives. The harder it is to answer these questions, the more you should shy away from the topic.

If you have taken a basic public speaking class, you may still be wondering how competitive informative speech topics differ from those you might have encountered in the classroom. Expectations about novelty, significance, and fascination are substantially greater in a competitive setting. In public speaking classes, simple, informative subjects such as the common cold, dreams, pyramids and carpel tunnel syndrome are very popular. At one time or another, each of these topics also have been used in competition. Only when they were novel, however, were they successful. Forensics judges simply are not impressed by speeches they might hear in the classroom, despite the fact that they are more proficiently researched, constructed, and presented.

Finally, topics which appear to be novel, significant, and fascinating might have occurred to someone else. Before you get too deeply involved with a topic, discuss it with your coach or experienced team mates. Ask if other students in your area have used the topic. While would be ideal to choose a topic that has never been done in competition, it is not necessary to be the first. It is advisable, however, to avoid jumping on a topical bandwagon — good topics may be reprised, but they die from over-exposure.

So, what are some examples of successful informative speaking topics? Some topics that stand out in my memory are: insects as a food source; magnetic resonance imagery; stealth bomber technology; spontaneous human combustion; homeopathy; designer foods; multiple chemical sensitivity syndrome; and synthetic blood. Many of these topics appear mundane today, but when they were novel ideas they fascinated forensics judges. To catch the next wave of good informative speaking topics, watch in-depth television news programs like *20-20, Dateline,* and *48 Hours,* science and technology programs like *The Next Step, Beyond 2000,* and *Nova,* and read popular magazines like *OMNI, Scientific American, Health* and *Psychology Today.*

Preparing Your Informative Speech

Research. After choosing a topic, your next step is to research it thoroughly. Focus your research on reputable sources. This means to resist the temptation to interview your next-door neighbor, even though she has done a tremendous amount of reading on the subject. Forensics speakers traditionally make use of information in the public domain (published, publicly-distributed materials). Public information is more easily validated and less prone to distortion by hearsay. In addition, forensic activities try to encourage library based research skills as a way of contributing to your critical thinking education. Judges will expect your speech to be documented from a variety of reputable sources. You can use transcripts from broadcast journalism. You can use books, newspapers, and current periodicals. You can use government documents and professional journals. Basically, you have available to you the wide range of resources commonly found in university libraries.

Construction. When you have completed your preliminary research, the next step is to organize your materials. Every basic public speaking textbook includes a chapter on speech organization, and many discuss arrangement tactics which relate specifically to informative speaking. It would be a good idea to check these textbooks before sitting down to outline your speech.

Begin your speech by trying to get the audience interested in your topic. There are a variety of strategies from which to choose — suspense, surprise, teasing, etc. Again, you will find your basic public speaking textbook very helpful. Next, you need a clear thesis statement explaining your purpose, followed by a preview sentence which indicates how you will go about developing your thesis.

The body of a competitive informative speech is typically composed of three primary ideas, although you may want to arrange your speech into two or four main points. (For a ten minute speech, one would be too few, and five would be too many.) The substance of your speech should be balanced and logically arranged. Balance means that you give relatively equal treatment to each of your main points. Logical arrangement means both that your ideas must be organized, and that there must be an intuitive sense to the way you have arranged them. Even the best researched speeches can be ruined by giving the impression that you are rambling, with no sense of where you are going or where you have been. Any number of stock organizing schemes are available. Choose one which is appropriate to your topic and stick with it.

Finally, your conclusion should bring the speech to closure. It should include a brief summary of the important points you have made (reiterate ideas, not evidence and examples), it should draw these points together in a way that makes the way they support your thesis clearly evident, and it should end with a powerful, motivating comment.

Visual Aids. Although visual aids are commonly used in informative speaking, they are not absolutely necessary. The main reason you might want to use visual aids is that they are capable of communicating complex information quickly. Your audience can glance for a moment at a chart, graph, or diagram and comprehend more than they would have understood from several minutes of explanation. Also, many people learn better visually. In fact, some research suggests that information processed visually and aurally is understood more clearly and retained longer than information presented without the aid of visual stimuli.

If you use visual aids, and I strongly advise that you do, there are several guidelines you should keep in mind. First, make sure that your visual aids are neat, clean and reasonably professional looking. While hand drawn charts and free-hand pictures might suffice for an assignment in your public speaking class, forensics judges expect that you will devote time and energy to constructing effective and impressive visual aids. Second, resist the temptation to talk to your visual aid — make sure you do not put your body between the visual aid and your audience, orient the visual aid so the audience can see it easily, and keep your eyes, head and body facing the audience. Third, do not pass objects to your audience. If you cannot find a facsimile large enough to show to the entire audience at once, you would probably be better off without the visual aid. You want to be in control of when your audience looks at your visual aid, and what they focus on when they look at it, and you lose that control the moment a visual aid leaves your hands. Fourth, leave a visual aid up for the audience only as long as you are discussing it. When you move to the next point, lay the visual aid down, turn it over, or somehow remove it from the audience's line of sight. Again, you want your audience paying to you rather than to the visual aid. Finally, use your visual aids when you practice your speech. Because experienced informative speakers make using visual aids look easy, you may be tempted not to practice with them before competition. That is always a mistake. The only way to avoid Murphy's Law is to practice, practice, practice.

Presenting Your Informative Speech

Successful informative speakers employ what is called "scripted" presentation. Rather than relying on their extemporaneous speaking skills to carry them through the presentation, they write a text of the speech in advance. The script is then memorized. Delivering a scripted speech without sounding as if you were reading from a teleprompter requires refined oratorical skills. Your goal is to make your delivery sound as fresh and energetic as if you were speaking extemporaneously, and as eloquent and fluent as if you were interpreting a speech text. The combination produces the kind of persuasive presentation judges expect of skilled public speakers.

Early in the season, you may feel that you need note cards as a crutch to help you through your presentation. Check with your coach about this. Even in the first tournament of the season, speakers who depend on note cards are likely to have their judges commenting on the fact that the notes were an intrusion. Also, speakers who use note cards generally are ranked lower than speakers who do not need notes. To give yourself a chance to do well, you should try to memorize your speech from the outset. If you must use notes, limit yourself to a single note card to remind you about the general order of your speech. Your goal is to present a polished performance, which requires hours of practice and a commitment to excellence. The sooner you begin the task of memorizing your speech, the sooner your work will begin to pay dividends.

Your voice should be energetic and lively, but not melodramatic. You convey your interest in your subject by how energetic you sound, and to some extent, this interest will be contagious. Speakers who sound disinterested generally are perceived to be boring speakers. Show your interest in your speech by getting excited by the prospect of presenting it to the audience. One of the things you most want to work on when you practice your speech is maintaining an appropriate energy level.

It might be helpful to record or video-tape yourself when you practice. Check yourself for a monotone delivery. Work on eliminating as many "ums," "aahs," and "OK's" as possible. In the beginning, it will be difficult to eliminate all of these vocal distractions, but as you begin to get comfortable with the idea of speaking from memory, you will be able to start polishing your delivery.

When you speak before an audience, it is essential to make eye contact with the people who are listening to you. Although there may be anywhere from one to a dozen or more people in your audience, your goal is to be able to comfortably and naturally make eye contact with everyone. Look into the eyes of audience members. When you see them seeing you see them, you have made eye contact. Let your eyes rove around the room, but avoid falling fall into a left-center-right-center-left pattern. You are supposed to be watching your audience for feedback, not merely looking around the room. Use your posture, arms and hands to create a positive visual effect. You do not want to choreograph your gestures, but you do want to gesture for emphasis. Avoid rocking and pacing, but do not stand stiff and still — it is perfectly acceptable for you to move a little as you speak. Your hands and arms should gesture freely and naturally, and your body should be relaxed, and any movement should be slow, graceful, and with purpose.

In Summary

The first key to preparing a successful informative speech is to choose a good topic. Look for subject matter which is novel, significant and fascinating. That does not mean that you must be the first forensics speaker to deal with the subject, but avoid over exposed topics, and try to find an angle which will make your speech more interesting than the way other speakers have approached the topic.

The second key to preparing a successful informative speech is to pay attention to effective techniques of speech construction. Your speech ought be well researched, your ideas effectively organized, and should you choose to use visual aids, they ought to be neatly constructed and competently managed.

The final key to success in informative speaking is develop proficient presentation skills. Take advantage of the opportunity to script your speech, but learn to present it energetically, fluently, and eloquently. Look your audience in the eyes, and keep your body relaxed and your gestures and body movement natural and graceful.

No amount of instruction can substitute for practical experience in public speaking. Do not expect to be a proficient informative speaker when you begin competing. Give yourself time to learn from your coaches and your experiences, practice diligently, and success will follow in due time.

Nobody wanted to talk about it. It wasn't exactly polite dinner conversation, yet Ruth Johnson was having a problem with incontinence. Not even June Allison and her "Depends" commercial could provide comfort for her. After consulting several different physicians and after rejecting surgery, the August 1990 edition of the *HMS Health Newsletter* reports that Ruth had exactly what she needed to cure her embarrassing problem. By exercising her options and learning to depend on her own muscle structure Ruth completely alleviated her bladder problem. Also to her surprise, Ruth discovered a pleasant side-effect — she experienced orgasm during intercourse more easily than ever before.

The muscle that accrued such health benefits for Ruth Johnson is one that you probably never studied in school. There is no machine in any gym that can work this muscle out for you. It is not a muscle that is attractive to human sight like bulging biceps or well-defined calves. The technical name for this is the Pubococcygeus muscle, but for practical pronunciation purposes, we will refer to it as the "PC muscle."

Some people may feel uncomfortable talking about this while others might not even know that they have one. I'll break the suspense.... You all do, and you learned to use it when you were very little and you needed to "hold it!" I am certain that any uncomfortableness will soon go away when you see how this muscle can actually affect you life.

If the PC muscle is exercised properly it can decrease the risk of cancer, cure bladder and urinary infections, alleviate menstrual cramping, improve a women's experience in child birth, and for both men and women it can cure urinary stress incontinence, and heighten sexual pleasure. To fully comprehend how these benefits are attributed to this obscured part of our anatomy, we will embark upon an anatomy lesson. This course will center on the research that has elevated the significance of this muscle, the health benefits, and the techniques suggested for developing a healthy PC muscle.

Let's begin by focusing on the research that brought the PC muscle out of anatomical obscurity. According to the July 1993 issue of American Family Physician in the early 1950's pioneering gynecologist Arnold Kegel, forged ahead of his colleagues by giving the PC muscle the attention it deserved. Instead of operating on women with urinary stress incontinence he taught women how to strengthen their PC muscle through exercise. In doing so, he spared most of his patients from surgery. To assist with the evaluation of the PC muscle, Kegel invented a

This speech was written by Sara Wright while she was an undergraduate student at El Camino College.

device called the Perineometer. With the use of this device, which was probably the world's first biofeedback gauge, patients could observe the strength of their contraction and with practice improve them. The practice of prescribing PC muscle exercising became so effective that Kegel began prescribing them not only after surgery but as an alternative to it.

This initial discovery by Kegel first highlighted the significance of the PC muscle. Prior to this, physicians usually bypassed the PC muscle because it is located in the most private region of the human body.

To demonstrate, the PC muscle runs from the pubic bone in front, to the coccyx in the back. According to Alice Kahn-Ladas landmark book *G-Spot*, the muscle supports the anus and adjacent internal organs and helps to keep them from sagging. The PC muscle connects the lower spinal cord to the bladder and uterus in females and in males to the bladder and prostrate gland.

Dr. Stephen Kiesling, writing in the April, 1993 *Journal of American Health*, refers to the PC muscle as the master muscle of the pelvis, and compares it to a hammock. When healthy it holds a taut straight line. When it's weak, the muscle and the pelvic organs it supports tend to sag. This can lead to urinary incontinence, childbirth trauma, lower back pain and decreased sensation during intercourse. With Kegel's research other physicians began to explore the potential of the PC muscle as a remedy for at least 18 gynecological and obstetrical conditions.

Now that we have a clearer understanding of the PC muscle itself we will turn the focus of our anatomy lesson on these numerous health benefits. The best way to examine the plethora of health benefits derived from the PC muscle would be to consider 3 areas; Preventative, therapeutic and sexual benefits.

From a preventative standpoint, exercising the PC muscle can decrease the risk of cancer. According to medical writer Edward Breecher, many post-menopausal women subject themselves to a ninefold risk of vaginal cancer by using estrogen cream to keep their vaginas moist. PC muscle exercises may accomplish the same goal with out the risk of cancer.

Also, Kegel and others observed that weak muscles were more often the cause of problems with childbirth, and today many experts are prescribing prenatal exercises to strengthen the PC muscle. According to Sheila Kitzinger's 1983 book *A Women's Experience* most women experience much greater ease during childbirth when the PC muscle is in good shape, and they have a prompt return of the muscle to its original condition after the birth of a child.

The PC muscle produces even more benefits when prescribed as therapy. If you are bothered by lower back pain urinary infections or incontinence, or if you suffer from severe menstrual cramps, PC muscle exercises can improve these conditions. Alice Kahn Ladas, previously cited states, "some clinicians believe that often what is described as "lower-back pain" is really PC muscle tension. We have treated a number of patients who initially complained of lower-back pain and found relief by learning to relax their PC muscles."

After hysterectomy, some women feel their vagina is atrophied. Toning the PC muscle not only restores a healthy vagina but increases a women's sense of femininity.

PC exercise is also prescribed in cases of incontinence which effects about 10 million Americans. Incontinence is one of the major reasons elderly people are admitted into nursing homes. This is due to the fact that family members can much more easily tolerate mild forgetfulness than they can the smell of urine. Dr. Neil M. Resnick, who is a gerontologist at Harvard Medical School, states in the February 1993 *Gerontology Newsletter* that physicians can now eliminate incontinence in a third of those who have it, and can make leakage much less frequent in another third by prescribing PC exercises.

Both men and women benefit greatly from a strong PC muscle in order to control urine and bowel movements, especially in later years. But in addition both can also improve their sexual performance. As Dr. Lucy Waletzky, writes in *American Health*, August 1993, "orgasm is an important part of optimal physical and emotional health for everyone. This is due to the fact that a flabby, unexercised muscle is not very responsive; a healthy muscle is more sensitive to physical stimulation.

People who regularly exercise their PC muscle develop a greater capacity for experiencing orgasms. Kegel reported in a clinical study that 78% of 123 women who completed the exercise program had orgasms during intercourse for the first time.

Dr. William E. Hartman and Marilyn Fithian, sex researchers and co-directors of the Center for Marital and Sexual studies in Long Beach, CA report that PC exercises alone can make erections possible or even more frequent and increase sexual endurance by 50%. Hartman states that, "the control of the PC muscle is probably the most simple and the most direct answer to a man becoming multiply orgasmic. You see ejaculation and orgasm are not the same thing. At the moment of orgasm the male is able to hold back the fluid and refrain from ejaculating while still having an orgasm

The final aspect of our PC lesson involves the actual techniques used to strengthen the muscle. According to Dr. Mona Coates, professor of Human Sexuality, at Orange Coast College, warms both men and women should identify their PC muscle before attempting exercise. With a full bladder start and stop the flow of urine, so only a little bit is let out at a time. The PC muscle is the only muscle that can accomplish this task.

Once a person has learned control of the muscle, they can squeeze it periodically throughout the day in order to strengthen it. With about ten minutes a day of exercising, stress incontinence is often dramatically lessened in a month or two.

For women preparing for childbirth, a more strenuous technique is required. This exercise is refereed to as "Bear Downs," and involves bearing down as though trying to have a bowel movement or helping to push out a baby during child birth. Each contraction should last at least 3 seconds. Kegel often said that 300 contractions per day were necessary for noticeable improvement. As with any exercise, start out slow, you wouldn't want to have a sore PC muscle.

The good about these exercises is nobody has to know you are working out. Some of you could be doing it right now!These exercises can be done in a variety of ways. One traveling saleswomen has gotten into the habit of contracting her PC muscle every time she stops at a traffic light. A stockbroker does several quick contractions when the telephone rings. One musically inclined women used to put on her favorite music and practice moving her PC muscle to the beat.

Many cultures incorporate dances such as the hula or Middle Eastern belly dancing or Oriental dancing into everyday activities in order to exercise the PC muscle. Even disco dancing has been known to improve the strength of the PC muscle.

In retrospect, we have considered 3 aspects of the PC muscle, the significant research, the numerous health benefits, and a few of the exercise techniques for developing a healthy PC muscle.

From an educational point of view, certainly we have learned a relevant aspect for improving our health and well-being.

From a practical point of view, the role of the PC muscle takes on even greater importance, because through a few simple exercises all of us can do something about our own muscle tone, and have a positive influence on our health, our expressions of love, and ultimately, on our quality of life.

In 1956, a Hungarian ferry captain was accused of stabbing a mailman to death. The mailman's body was discovered near the ferry docks a few hours after the captain had reported for work. The autopsy report revealed the presence of newly-hatched larvae on the corpse, but the entomological evidence was ignored by the court. The ferry captain, all the while protesting his innocence, was condemned to life in prison. Six years later, the case was reopened. The best witnesses for the defense turned out to be the maggots that have been found on the corpse. Ferenc Mihalyi, of Budapest's Natural History Museum, testified that the bugs found on the mailman's body proved that the captain could not possibly have murdered him. Why? Because the captain had reported for work at 6 p.m., and in order for the eggs to have hatched by the time of the autopsy they would have had to have been laid before 6 p.m. (which means the mailman was dead before the captain had arrived for work). This testimony persuaded the court to overturn its previous verdict, and the skipper was released.

You may have thought that the only connection between bugs and crime was in the motion-picture, "Silence of the Lambs," however the use of bugs in solving crime has become a sought after practice.

When death transforms a body into a corpse, hundreds of species of insects descend upon the scene. Attracted by what scientists think may be a "universal death scent," ground beetles, green flies and other insects migrate to a corpse to lay eggs on the body or to find nourishment. To the squeamish, these bugs are the stuff of nightmares. To homicide squads, they have long been considered a nuisance. But entomologists have come to realize that the creatures they study are witnesses, and that the stories these bugs have to tell can solve mysterious crimes. Bugs are proving they're an asset to justice. So today, we'll unearth the facts as we investigate exactly what forensic entomologists are, we'll look at how these bugs are really "bugging" criminals, and also how this forensic science will metamorphize the future.

Bugs have roamed the earth for 280 million years, but the study of insects associated with death is just now coming to life. According to International Wildlife, the field known as "forensic entomology" was virtually unknown in the United States 20 years ago and today fewer than 30 scientists practice this speciality. But these pioneers are increasingly being called upon to comb crime scenes for bugs, using the evidence they find to help solve cases of rape, child abuse, neglect and even murder.

This speech was written by Brandi Wallace while she was an undergraduate student at Modesto Junior College.

The earliest case history involving a crude form of forensic entomology dates back to 13th century China, when a farmer was murdered with a threshing sickle. The mystery was solved when all of the farmers were forced to lay their sickles on the ground. When flies were drawn to the blade containing minute traces of blood the guilty farmer confessed his crime.

So now that we know that insects are the basis of a growing but grisly branch of sleuthing called forensic entomology, exactly how does this science aid in the conviction of criminals?

According to U.S. News and World Report, Oct. 14, 1991, "the death of a human triggers very predictable patterns of insect activity that entomologist can trace through time." Although this isn't the most pleasant of topics, the details are important in order to understand how these bugs are an asset to justice. For example, Audubon magazine, Sept./Oct. 1991 reports that in open air, various blowflies, and flesh flies lay thousands of eggs in a body's mouth, nose, and ears within 10 minutes of death. The eggs then hatch about twelve hours later and the bugs feed on the tissues. When they're finished, the bugs move away from the body and cocoon in nearby soil. A second wave of insects, which are usually beetles, come to live on the now drying skin. Later, still more insects, such as spiders, mites, and millipedes, arrive to prey on bugs already at the site or to work on the remains. The San Francisco Chronicle, Jan. 26, 1992 claims that "the life cycles of these creatures are so fixed and precise that they act as a natural clock. This natural clock gives entomologists a highly accurate estimate at the victim's time of death." The Chronicle recounts that in a Chicago murder case, a coroner estimated that the victim had been dead for 6 weeks, but the insect evidence pointed to a more accurate time of 6 days.

Kenneth G. V. Smith, in his book, "A Manuel of Forensics Entomology" points out that "the key to this track of succession or the life stages of these natural undertakers, as they feed and develop in a cadaver." The ability to recognize the species as they develop, combined with a knowledge of their rates of development, can give the scientist an indication of the age of the corpse.

The longest interval between the death and the discovery of victims was a 1987 case in which two elderly women were found dead in their home. On the basis of insect remains, the women were determined to have been dead for 10 years - during which time a relative had been cashing their $140,000 pension checks.

Not only is insect evidence useful in dating the time of death but also the place of death. Different insect species have unique and predictable behaviors that can help scientists recreate the scene of a crime. According to E. Paul Catts, a forensic entomologist at Washington State University, "bug behavior can indicate whether the deceased was killed indoors or out, during daylight or night, in warm or cool weather, or in the shade or in the sun." For example, certain species of insects will lay eggs only indoors, at high noon, and in warm weather, while others insects prefer cool climates, shade and moisture.

Science writer, Joannie M. Schrof, claims that in other cases, it is the absence of bugs that gives suspicion of foul play. For example, a man came home and claimed he found the windows open and his girlfriend dead. He was convicted of her murder when none of the usual creatures had made their way indoors to the body which had been dead for four hours. A close look at insect clues made it obvious that the man had thrown open the windows moments before the police had arrived. "This World," January, 1991 tells us that "because bugs tend not to stray far from where they live, their presence around a corpse can tell investigators whether the deceased was killed at the scene or transported from somewhere else. If certain urban-dwelling insects show up on a corpse in a cornfield, for example, entomologists can often specify not only the city but the neighborhood where the crime had taken place.

Criminals are even arrested and convicted with the help of insect association. As in the case of a Florida murderer who dropped his victim in a swamp region during the few days of the year when mayflies were active. He was later convicted of murder when the same breed of mayflies were found smashed to his car radiator. In a rape case, the assailant had worn a ski mask. When a ski mask was collected from a closet of a likely suspect, entomologist Bernard Greenburg found larvae from caterpillars that emerge only in late summer and were known to dwell in the woods around the scene of the rape.

Obviously, criminals are being brought to justice by this new branch of science - and yet it's still in the larval stage. Although forensic entomologists have aided in hundreds of investigations and insect sleuthing is quickly becoming a sought-after and respected source of evidence in the courtroom, bug scientists say they now understand only about half the insects that frequent corpses. The future implications of forensic entomology will be even a greater asset to justice. As they build up their base knowledge, entomologists are using computer simulations to make investigations quicker and more sophisticated. Ted Suman, a forensic entomologist in Maryland says, "One day, we'll be advanced enough to glean clues from mere splotches of bugs on car windshields." Entomologists are also working on techniques to detect the presence of drugs like cocaine and heroin, which may have vanished from a body but leave traces in bug carcasses.

Also, planning is underway to begin teaching the police and coroners the value of insect activity on a corpse and training them to collect specimens. Clemson University entomologist, T. R. Adkins says that investigators sometimes overlook or even destroy the bug evidence needed to solve a crime. Along with other entomologists, Adkins is developing a procedural manual for police departments. The science of forensic entomology will definitely metamorphize the future.

Today we've learned that forensic entomologists are not a new breed of speech coaches but a quickly advancing science using bugs to solve crime, we've also looked at how these bugs are really "pestering" criminals and also, exactly what the future holds for this grueling yet very helpful branch of forensics. If knowledge involving forensic entomology had been available in 1956, Mr. Milhalyi would not have spent six unnecessary years in prison. So as we've seen today, insects promise to become one of sleuthing's most tools as they prove they really are an asset to justice.

Persuasive Speaking

Joe Corcoran

Of all of the forensics events, persuasive speaking is perhaps the most challenging. Although it is possible to inform or entertain an audience in ten minutes, it seems as if little can be done to affect attitudes or beliefs in a single speech. Effective persuasion usually requires an extended effort (such as during a political campaign), where repeated exposure to a messages makes opinion change more plausible. However, much can be accomplished in a single exposure. In order to be a successful persuasive speaker, you need to understand the tools you have at your disposal. Specifically, you need to understand how topic selection and research, arrangement tactics, language style and delivery can affect your success.

Topic Selection and Research

Probably the most important aspect of topic selection is choosing a topic about which people are not likely to be strongly predisposed. That may sound cynical, but you simply do not have time to loosen tenaciously held beliefs and attitudes, especially as they relate to emotionally charged topics such as abortion. However, you may well be able to affect the way people feel about less loaded topics such as indoor air pollution, health care and foreign policy. Some coaches may disagree with this, but years of observing successful persuasive speakers suggests that less emotionally charged topics fair much better than their counterparts. (This suggestion is not meant to dissuade you from choosing topics you genuinely feel need to be addressed. There is much more to forensics than winning trophies.)

You should also try to choose a topic that you feel strongly about. Picking a topic that you dislike makes it difficult to engage in exhaustive research or speak with energy and conviction. The best place to start looking, therefore, is among those issues which you personally consider important. Start by brainstorming. List as many topics as you can think of without evaluating them. Then, go back through your list and pick out the two or three that seem most interesting. Go to the library and do some preliminary research. See what you can find our about the topics.

If fails to produce a topic you are interested in pursuing, try going through the current periodicals section of your library. Peruse the contents pages of current issues of major publications. One thing to keep in mind is that you are seeking a "fresh" topic, one that has seldom been used in competition. This is not as important on the novice level, but it will be important as you move up to junior and open division competition. Check with your coach, or experienced team mates, for advice about questionable topics. Other sources of fresh topics are television programs such as *20/20, Sixty Minutes,* or PBS' *MacNeil/Lehrer News Hour,* the daily debates on

---

Professor Corcoran is currently Director of Forensics at California State University, Chico.

the editorial page of *USA Today,* or offbeat magazines such as *Mother Jones* and *Rolling Stone.* If you are still stumped, ask your coach for assistance. He or she is an old (or not so old) hand at topic selection.

Sometimes, taking a new angle on an old topic can make a refreshing and successful speech. I remember a student who placed third the AFA-NIET with just such a presentation. He spoke about how to save the family farm. His speech was insightful, well documented, and slightly different from speeches or debates heard previously on the subject. In this age of the knowledge explosion, often new studies and research can change our perspective on entire bodies of thought. Just look at the evolution of our understanding of issues like AIDS, computer technology, or the Strategic Defense Initiative ("Star Wars"). So, if you run across a study or article with a fresh perspective on an old topic, it may serve as the source for a successful speech.

Once you have a topic, you need to find out as much about it as possible. There are many ways to discover information, but probably one of the best ways is to talk to the experts. Your school serves as a great source for these experts. Ask your coaches or teachers if they know people on campus who might make good sources, or phone academic departments which might have faculty with an interest in your topic. Make an appointment and interview your expert. You will find that most faculty will be more than happy to speak with you. While you may not want to use the interview as a source for your speech (personal interviews are not in the public domain), it can be a great lead for special insights and excellent writing on the subject. If your school lacks experts in your field of interest, letter writing or research trips can often be fruitful ventures.

The next stop on the research journey is the library. Here, you will need to do a substantial amount of resource gathering. You see, persuasive speeches need to be well documented. One of the theoretical traditions handed down to us by classical rhetorical scholars an understanding that persuasive speakers must be perceived as highly credible individuals. In order for you, a non-expert, to enhance your credibility, you must quote and paraphrase experts often. Even tournament event descriptions make reference to citing and using "multiple sources." You can use the *Reader's Guide to Periodic Literature,* the card catalog, newspaper indexes, journal indexes, the *Congressional Information Service*, on-line computer indexes, or even full-text computer data banks. If you do not know how to use some of these resources, your librarians or coaches are usually more than willing to guide you. Start with the most recent resources. Not only do you need a fresh topic, but you also need fresh information. The more recent the better. Try to gather a substantive number of articles, documents, and books on the subject.

Once you have collected relevant materials, you are ready to read through the it. As you do, look for three types of support: testimony, statistics, and examples.

Testimony refers to what journalists or experts have to say about the subject. In your speech, this information can be either quoted or paraphrased. As you find information of this type, copy individual quotations and citations onto separate note cards. Incorporate these references into your speech. Ideally, each time you introduce a new source you ought to cite the author, qualifications, title, and date of that source. However, that is rarely practiced, and few critics seem to demand full citations. (However, there are areas of the country, such as in the Northwest, where critics are more likely to do so.) Kim Horan, a CSU-Chico student who place third in persuasion at the 1987 AFA-NIET, introduced testimony this way in her speech on chlamydia:

> We must realize that the infertility cases caused by chlamydia are more than mere numbers on a page. There is a huge emotional toll involved for women as well as men. As Eugene Washington, Assistant to the Director of the CDC's Sexually Transmitted Disease Unit states, "People can't see into the hospital when a woman is told she is infertile, or follow a couple into therapy or divorce because they cannot conceive.

Note that the quotation is introduced in Kim's own words. Be sure to do the same. Novice competitors often commit the error of stringing together quotation after quotation without giving any of their own analysis. The speech should be in your own words, using testimony as support, not as text.

As you read through your resource materials, also look for statistics. Statistics are important because they quantify the extent of a problem, and many critics demand quantification. When establishing that a problem exists, for instance, use statistics to show the extent of the harm. In a speech on cancer, you might point out that 56 million Americans are likely to contract some form of the disease in their lifetime. Also, make the statistics real to the audience. To do that, compare the statistics to something to which the audience can relate. For instance, the number of Americans who are likely to contract cancer could be compared to the population of the U.S. by saying, "that's one in four Americans." Kim Horan uses statistics effectively in her chlamydia presentation. She writes:

> [Chlamydia] is the Number One sexually transmitted disease in the USA today, infecting, according the Center for Disease Control anywhere from 3-10 million Americans a year. That makes this virus-like bacterium 3 times more common than gonorrhea and 10 times more common than herpes, according to the May issue of Science '86. Medical studies reported in the April 21, 1986 issue of Newsweek indicate that 10% of all college students are infected with the disease whether they know it or not.

Notice how Kim establishes the prevalence of the disease, and then relates that directly to her college audience. Also, pay attention to the way the sources for the statistics are woven into the text of the speech.

Finally, you need examples. The example is a form of proof which is imperative for persuasive presentations. Examples bring quotations and statistics to life, which provokes emotional responses from your audience. Many scholars feel that these emotional arguments may even be more persuasive than logical appeals.

Kim Horan does a good job using examples. In supporting testimony and statistics that doctors cannot properly diagnose chlamydia, Kim gives an example of incorrect diagnosis.

> The ineptness of doctors' abilities to diagnose chlamydia correctly manifests itself painfully in the case of Maureen . . . who suffered with chlamydia for 12 years before she was properly diagnosed: "I went to many doctors, but they all told me the same thing — that I had non-specific cervicitis and that my cervix was so eroded it looked like hamburger meat. I must have tried every treatment known — including having my cervix frozen, having it painted with iodine, vaginal ointments, suppositories — but none of these worked. One doctor even suggested that I see a sex therapist!" Maureen's is not a unique case.

There are three things to pay particular attention to in this example. First, be as detailed as time allows. Vivid detail provokes a deeper emotional response. If Kim would have said simply, "one chlamydia victim tried for a long time to get help but could not," it would not have been nearly as effective. We empathize more with illustrations when speakers *personalize* them — give people names, describe settings, or include incidental details (like having her cervix frozen and spending 12 years searching for a cure.) Second, avoid using extreme or atypical examples. Maureen's case may seem extreme, but Kim's point is that many doctors are inept in diagnosis, not that the average chlamydia sufferer goes through 12 years of hell. In that respect, the illustration is not atypical. You can avoid the perception of over-generalizing by combining examples with statistics, testimony, and complimentary examples. In her speech, Kim continues with a second example to help reinforce the credibility of Maureen's story. Finally, vivid metaphors and graphic details sometimes have a lasting impact on the audience. Kim mentions a cervix looking like "hamburger meat." While that is certainly not a pleasant comparison, the audience will remember that image. In a close competitive round, such details may make the difference between first and second, or even last place. A note of caution — do not overuse graphic details. One or two appropriately worded and placed details will suffice. And, not every topic lends itself to that kind of development.

Organization

Just as source citations affect your credibility, so does speech organization. A disorganized presentation will adversely affect your credibility. There are many ways to organize persuasive speeches. For our purposes, I will discuss problem-solution formats, the Motivated Sequence, comparative advantages, and criteria assessment formats. The first three organizational patterns are used when discussing matters of policy, the last is normally associated with matters of value.

Problem/Solution Format. A policy issue asks the question: What action, if any, should be taken? Consequently, a problem-solution format may be appropriate. The problem section discusses two distinct aspects of the present situation: What are the harms of present policy, and what are the causes of those harms? Obviously, if you can prove that harms exist, you will have accomplished the first step toward proving the need for policy change. A former NFA national championship speech on rat infestation, did a good job of demonstrating the harms of a seemingly obscure problem. The speaker reported that in New York City, there were approximately two rats for every human. The speech pointed out that rats have been known to chew the fingers off babies, they eat food stores, and generally spread disease. Obviously, urban rats are a serious problem. In this speech, significant harms were established both quantitatively and qualitatively. The quantitative dimension of the problem was illustrated through the use of statistics (two rats for every human). The qualitative dimension of the problem was demonstrated by the pathos inherent in the illustration (rats chewing the fingers off babies). To be successful with a policy topic, it is essential that you establish significant harms.

You should also try to pinpoint the causes of a problem. Unless you can identify a cause, there is little chance you will be able to convince an audience that you have found a solution. Perhaps rats are infesting New York because people leave pet food out, or are not picking up garbage, or the sewer systems are inadequate. Identifying the cause of a problem is a necessary step to finding a solution.

After isolating problems and causes, you must focus on solutions. A good place to start may be to eliminate the obvious causes. Stop-gap measures may offer temporary respite, but they are unlikely to provide long-term results. For instance, much of the debate over the U.S. welfare system has centered around whether to focus on mitigating the effects of poverty, or to work on eradicating its fundamental causes. However, do not assume that eliminating root causes will necessarily eliminate your problem. Once a problem gets out of control, simple solutions may no longer work. It may be too late for garbage collection and improved sewers alone to solve the problems of urban rat infestation. While those programs might keep the problem from getting worse, they would do little about the millions of rats which already infest metropolitan areas. The more complex a problem becomes, the more complex the solution it is likely to require.

Make sure you document the effectiveness of potential solutions. One way to do this is by analogy. Find where similar solutions have been tried for similar problems, and offer that experience as proof. Kim Horan suggests that mass screening be adopted as a solution to stop the spread of chlamydia. She then illustrates how this method has been effective on a limited basis:

> The Seattle-King County Department of Public Health, where the first chlamydia control program has been in operation for four years, reports that the prevalence of chlamydia in the Seattle Metropolitan Area has dropped each year.

Quantification also helps document your solution. For example, if you were trying to alleviate family violence through intervention counseling, you might provide evidence that pilot counseling programs have an 80 to 90 percent success rate. Believable quantification is usually quite persuasive.

While documenting institutional solutions is important, many critics prefer that you also try to engage your audience in personal action. Writing letters to congressional representatives is an overused personal action step. Focus on realistic and effective personal action. Kim Horan tried to involve the women in her audiences by pleading with them to have a chlamydia test, be choosy about sex partners, and use barrier methods of contraception.

The Motivated Sequence. An alternative way to arrange a policy speech is around the Motivated Sequence, a five-step approach to persuasive speaking.

- *Attention step.* Many studies demonstrate that unless you get your audience's attention immediately, they will begin thinking about other things, such as their own problems. Engage them immediately.
- *Need step.* This is similar to the problem step of the problem-solution format. Show your audience that there are problems which need to be addressed.
- *Solution step.* This is the first of three steps which focus on solving the problem. This step has you describe the institutional solutions you are advocating.
- *Visualization step.* The next solvency step has you describing for your audience what the world would be like were your solutions adopted. This is where you would begin to document your solution.
- *Action step.* The final solvency step has you trying to get the audience to become personally involved. What can they do to begin solving the problem, or to help bring your solution to fruition? Give the audience something to do: become educated, tell others, boycott a product or company, vote a certain way, etc.

The problem-solution and Motivated Sequence formats are largely similar. The primary differences are that the problem-solution format does not include an overt attention step, and the Motivated Sequence does not expressly investigate causes. Functionally, however, they are merely alternative ways of addressing the same basic issues.

Comparative Advantage Format. The final format for policy speeches is substantially different. Rather than focusing on problems which need to be solved, this format focuses on ways to improve fundamentally tolerable conditions. For instance, the trusty IBM-XT or Mac I you have been using as a word processor is still a reliable computer. However, a new computer, built around a faster processor, more memory, and a color monitor, might make writing easier and more enjoyable. People constantly yearn for things which are comparatively advantageous. Individuals buy new cars even though their old cars run reliably, they buy bigger television sets even though nothing is wrong with their old sets, and they buy gadgets for tasks which are easily done manually. Institutional decisions are often made on the same basis. Old programs are cast aside for new programs which are more economical, more efficient, or more effective. The comparative advantages format differs from the problem-solution and Motivated Sequence formats in that it focuses on what is *not* rather than what *is.* The trick is to make the audience want what they do not have.

Criteria Assessment. Sometimes, persuasive speeches defend value judgments, subjective opinions grounded in abstract philosophical notions such as good and evil, right and wrong, or justice and injustice. The primary difficulty you will encounter in defending value judgments is that they are by their very nature *personal.* People simply have different ideas about goodness, rightness and justice. The challenge is to find a way to reduce subjective valuing to an objective decision. Generally, you do this by creating philosophical common ground (criteria) which can be used as a basis for common evaluation (assessment). When people agree on what it means to be good, right or just, their value judgments are more likely to coincide.

When addressing a hostile audience, many theorists advise that you seek agreement about abstract values before indicating your views about more concrete concerns. For instance, if you were giving a speech on school prayer, you might try to get the audience to agree philosophically with the values inherent in separation of church and state and freedom of religion. Then tell them that you favor school prayer, and argue that it enhances freedom of religion without violating the constitutional separation of church and state. Having committed themselves to the importance of separating church and state and promoting freedom of religion, your audience is less likely to reject school prayer. Your speech might be arranged something likc this:

I. Separation of church and state and freedom of religion are important because...
(supported by explanation and documented by testimony, statistics and examples)

II. I advocate that students be allowed to pray in schools because ...

III. School prayer enhances freedom of religion in that ...
(supported by explanation and documented by testimony, statistics and examples)

IV. School prayer respects the separation of church and state in that ...
(supported by explanation and documented by testimony, statistics and examples)

Whether your involves policy decisions are value judgments, you still have to consider the order in which you will address your proofs. Some researchers suggest that you place your strongest arguments first, to take advantage of the *primacy* effect; others suggest that you place your strongest arguments last, to take advantage of the *recency* effect.[1] I advise that you place your strongest argument first, your second strongest argument last, and your weakest argument in the middle. That way, you benefit somewhat from both primacy and recency. In some circumstances (e.g., speaking before a hostile audience), you may want to opt for an *anti-climatic* arrangement, where you begin with your strongest argument and work toward your weakest. With hostile audiences, primacy is your most important concern since you must overcome hostility at the outset of your speech. In other circumstances (e.g., speaking before a highly sympathetic audience), you may want to use a *climatic* arrangement, where you work toward a logical/emotional climax. With sympathetic audiences, the recency effect is more likely to dominate audience reactions.

---

1 Mary John Smith, *Persuasion and Human Action: A Review of the Social Influence Theories* (Belmont: Wadsworth, 1982).

Language Style

Your eloquence, a rhetorical byproduct of word choice and modes of expression, will have a tremendous effect on reactions to your speech. Eloquent speakers are more impressive and better remembered than speakers who just plod through their ideas. A few simple suggestions can help you succeed at this important aspect of persuasive speaking.

When appropriate, employ humor. While there remains professional skepticism about the persuasive effect of humor, there is little question that it makes your speech more memorable. Kim Horan did a good job of incorporating humor into her speech on chlamydia. When urging women to take steps to reduce the risk of chlamydia, she says:

> If you do choose to be sexually active, at least be like those mothers who buy Jiff Peanut Butter for their children, and be a little choosy about your partner.

This statement helped to relieve tension during the discussion of a touchy subject, and Kim rarely failed to get a laugh. Some topics do not lend themselves to touches of levity, and misplaced humor can easily destroy your credibility and diminish your chance for success. However, appropriate humor will make you a more interesting persuasive speaker.

Other ways to help make your speech memorable include using antithesis, alliteration, repetition, metaphors and other stylistic devices called *tropes.* Antithesis juxtaposes opposing ideas to give emphasis. President Kennedy was fond of using this trope. The phrase most people remember from his Inaugural Address is "Ask not what your country can do for you, ask what you can do for your country." Had JFK said simply "Come on guys, let's all do something for our country," few people would have remembered his plea. As it is, the phase is part of the Kennedy legacy.

Alliteration involves repeating certain sounds in a sentence. Winston Churchill delighted in using this stylistic device. He once said, "The task is heavy, the toil is long, and the trials will be severe." Here, the "t" sound is repeated in the words, "task," "toil" and "trials." This device is probably the easiest to use, but also the easiest to abuse. Make sure that your alliteration is subtle. Read the first sentence in this paragraph aloud. Note the repetition of the "sss" sound in the "certain," "sounds" and "sentence." When you first read the sentence, you probably did not notice the alliteration, but it sounded pleasant. That is how subtle alliteration should be.

Key words and phrases also can be repeated for effect. Dr. Martin Luther King was particularly adept at using repetition. In his address to the crowds gathered for the March on Washington, he repeatedly used the phrase "I have a dream . . ." to introduce his visions of the future.

The metaphor is probably the most common trope. Metaphors involve subtle comparisons in which one thing is represented as another. Referring to the federal government as "the ship of state" is a metaphor — governments are not ocean going vessels. President Nixon was addicted to sports metaphors, often speaking about hitting home runs, calling his own plays, and scoring points. Other types of comparisons include using similes ("float like a butterfly, sting like a bee"), and literal analogies (extended metaphors and similes).

A complete discussion of tropes could fill volumes. Consult your coach or a fundamental public speaking text for further guidance. When you begin working on the precise wording of your presentation, try to incorporate some of these linguistic techniques. The more memorable your speech, the more likely you are to be successful. In fact, one study indicates that the less linguistically diverse your speech, the less credible you will appear to your audience.[2]

Delivery

Winston Churchill is generally regarded as one of the most effective speakers of the Twentieth Century. He was not a master technician, in fact he spoke with a gruff lisp, often talked with a cigar in his mouth, and he looked like an aggressive bulldog. He was, however, obviously sincere. When as, British Prime Minister, he spoke out against the evils of Hitler and fascism, his voice reinforced his conviction. The best delivery does not draw attention to itself. Truly persuasive delivery is derived from sincerity, not from an overly dramatic presentation.

When it comes to delivering your persuasive speech, there are basically two approaches you can use. You can give present speech extemporaneously, or you can script your speech and deliver it from memory. I suggest that you give your speech extemporaneously at first, and later work on memorizing it. That way you will be able to concentrate on the ideas that you want to get across, without getting bogged down with trying to remember exact words and phrases. If you can, try not to use notes. Have a general outline of the speech in your mind, and go from there. If you do not feel comfortable speaking without notes, use a brief outline, preferably on a single note card. The best delivery is not noticed, and your audience will surely notice if you begin to shuffle through a bunch of papers or begin to read your speech. You may want to include quotations and transitions on your note card.

A credible presentation must be free of "ums," stumbles, and other vocal distractions. Studies indicate that audiences perceive speakers as less credible when they stumble through a speech.[3] The best prevention against disfluencies is practice, and the best cure is concentration.

Eventually, you will want to prepare a final script so you can take advantage of the linguistic tactics discussed in the previous section. Memorizing a ten minute text is difficult, but not as

---

2 James J. Bradoc, Catherine W. Konsky and Robert A. Davies, "Two Studies of the Effects of Linguistic Diversity Upon Judgments of Communication Attributes and Message Effectiveness," *Communication Monographs* 43 (1976): 70-79.

3 John Waite Bowers, "The Influence of Delivery on Attitudes Toward Concepts and Speakers," *Speech Monographs* 32 (1965): 154-158. See also, Kenneth K. Sereno and Gary J. Hawkins, "The Effects of Variations in Speaker's Nonfluence Upon Audience Ratings of Attitude Toward the Speech Topic and Speaker's Credibility," *Speech Monographs* 34 (1967): 58-64.

difficult as presenting a speech which does not *sound* memorized. Try to sound conversational. Your expressions should seem spontaneous, as though you were saying them for the first time. When competitors deliver memorized speeches, usually the first thing that suffers is vocal variety, especially pitch variation. Studies indicate that a monotone delivery severely hinders speaker credibility.[4] Vocal variety comes naturally when you speak with conviction. However, it is sometimes hard to maintain a sense of conviction when you present the same speech over and over. If you are having difficulty with vocal variety, you will have to work on your delivery skills. Tape record yourself and, with your coach, analyze your specific problems. Learn to alter your pitch and rate, and vary the number and length of your pauses. Above all, try to achieve an easy, conversational style.

Eye contact is particularly important in persuasive speaking. As with any public speech, you want to use eye contact to help involve the audience in your speech. Beyond that, effective eye contact is an important tool for selling speech. Looking people in the eyes often is interpreted as a sign that you are sincere and trustworthy, which is why the expression "shifty-eyed" has such a negative connotation. People like to be noticed, so notice them and talk to them. No one wants to listen to a talking essay, but when you avoid eye contact, that is what your speech becomes.

Conclusion

Persuasive speaking cuts to the heart of forensics competition. Steeped in the finest traditions of Western democracy, it is free speech in practice. In forensics competition, you learn about being an ethical communicator — persuading people through the worth of your ideas and the sincerity of your convictions. In persuasive speaking, you learn not only the value of free speech, but develop the skills to frame your opinions for public consumption.

---

4 David W. Addington, "The Effect of Vocal Variations on Ratings of Source Credibility," *Speech Monographs* 38 (1971): 242-247.

Jennifer and Tom met in college, fell in love, graduated, got married and eventually decided to start a family. It is here, however, that their happy story begins to fall apart. After a year of unsuccessfully trying to conceive a child, Jennifer and Tom decided to seek fertility counseling. Testing revealed that Jennifer was suffering from a sexually transmitted disease known as chlamydia which had silently festered inside her for years. The disease had left her sterile, unable to have the children she and Tom had wanted so badly.

Unfortunately, Jennifer and Tom are not a "1 in a million case." Despite the fact that most people have never even heard of chlamydia, it is the #1 sexually transmitted disease in the United States today, infecting, according to the Center for Disease Control, anywhere from 3-10 million Americans a year.

That makes this virus-like bacterium 3 times more common than gonorrhea and 10 times more common than herpes, according to the May issue of *Science '86*. Medical studies reported in the April 21, 1986 issue of *Newsweek* indicate that 10% of all college students are infected with the disease whether they know it or not.

As Dr. Thomas Quinn of the National Institute of Allergy and Infectious Diseases states, "We are in the midst of a chlamydia epidemic." Obviously, it is time that we begin to understand chlamydia and take immediate steps to alleviate the problem.

In order to facilitate this, I will do several things. First, I will look at some of the serious dangers associated with chlamydia. Second, I will examine why this disease is so prevalent. And last, I will suggest specific steps to be taken to stop the spread of this epidemic.

There are several serious dangers which often accompany chlamydia. One of these dangers is that, if left untreated, chlamydia can lead to sterility in both men and women. For example, The Center for Disease Control, or CDC, estimates that chlamydia is responsible for 1/2 of the 1 million cases of pelvic inflammatory disease which develop yearly. Chlamydial PID is extremely dangerous. Dr. King Holmes, Chief of Medicine at Seattle's Harborview Medical Center suggests 150,000 women become infertile yearly due to this condition.

We must realize that the infertility cases caused by chlamydia are more than mere numbers on a page. There is a huge emotional toll involved for women as well as men. As Dr. Eugene Washington, Assistant to the Director of the CDC's Sexually Transmitted Disease Unit states, "People can't see into the hospital when a woman is told she is infertile, or follow a couple into

This speech was written by Kimberly Horan while she was an undergraduate student at California State University, Chico.

therapy or divorce because they cannot conceive." Even if a couple is able to conceive, there's a second major danger the two of them must often face. According to Dr. Holmes, pregnant women with chlamydia increase their chances tenfold of having a tubal pregnancy. Tubal pregnancies, where the egg begins to develop in the fallopian tube and ruptures there, are not only painful for women, but they can be fatal as well.

Sadly, tubal pregnancies are on the rise. They quadrupled between 1972 and 1981 to more than 68,000 per year. According to the *American Journal of Public Health*, 1982, they are increasing at a rate of 8.6% per year in California alone. And Dr. Holmes and other researchers agree that chlamydia is largely to blame for this increase.

So suppose a couple can conceive and they are fortunate enough to escape the danger of a tubal pregnancy, there is yet a third hazard they must often confront — that their newborn child will contract the disease. According to the May 1986 issue of *Essence* magazine, there's a 66% probability that infected women will pass the disease on to their baby during childbirth. This translates into 182,000 innocent infants being born yearly with pneumonia or eye infections as a result of this sexually transmitted disease. These are serious conditions for newborn babies.

Additionally, pregnant women with chlamydia are 3 times more likely to give birth prematurely than women without the disease. And considering that a study conducted by the University of Washington concluded premature birth is the #1 cause of death in newborns, we can recognize the very serious and devastating nature of chlamydia.

So, why is it that a disease, which if diagnosed early enough can be easily cured with just 7 days of tetracycline, continues to spread at such epidemic proportions? The answer to this question lies primarily in the diagnosis of the disease. Diagnosis is complicated by the fact that, according to the April 21, 1986 issue of *Newsweek*, in 70% of all cases, there are no symptoms at all until the disease has already done its damage. Thus, the term "silent epidemic" is often associated with chlamydia. And according to Dr. Holmes, 50% of chlamydia's destructive consequences occur because of the 'silent nature' of the infection. What about the other 50% of the damage? To further complicate matters and make them a whole lot worse, we find that when symptoms do occur, doctors are diagnose often incredibly inept at diagnosing the disease correctly.

Perhaps one reason doctors have a difficult time identifying chlamydia, is that medical students, on average, are only required to have 3 hours of training, 180 minutes, on diagnosing and treating *all* sexually transmitted diseases. And until recently, according to *Public Health Review*, May 1984, this training had nothing to do with chlamydia. Obviously, this is a problem. I mean what if you happen to miss class that day?

The ineptness of doctors' abilities to diagnose chlamydia correctly manifests itself painfully in the case of Maureen, a 35-year-old registered nurse who suffered with chlamydia for 12 years before she was properly diagnosed: "I went to many doctors, but they all told me the same thing — that I had nonspecific cervicitis and that my cervix was so eroded that it looked like 'hamburger meat.' I must have tried every treatment known — including having my cervix frozen, having it painted with iodine, vaginal ointments, suppositories — but none of these worked. One doctor even suggested that I see a sex therapist!"

Maureen's is not a unique case. Debbie Milligan, a 1977 graduate of the University of Massachusetts, was tested for a urinary tract infection. Three months later when the symptoms returned, it took her 4 years, 30 doctors, and $15,000 before her problem was finally diagnosed correctly. Along the way she was told she had low-grade appendicitis, premenstrual syndrome and psychological problems of all things! The real culprit of course, chlamydia.

The fact is, according to *Newsweek*, that when doctors and victims are faced with symptoms such as painful urination, unusual discharge and abdominal pain, they simply don't consider the possibility of chlamydia. But chlamydia isn't a mere possibility, it is often a very harsh reality. Confronted with this reality, steps must be taken to stop the spread of this epidemic.

The first step in solving this problem is mass screening of all high risk groups. Doctors should convince sexually active men and women between 15 and 24 years of age, those with a history of sexually transmitted diseases and all pregnant women who may have contracted the disease, that testing for chlamydia is in their best interest.

It has been proven that mass screening is, indeed, effective. The Seattle-King County Department of Public Health, where the first chlamydia control program has been in operation for four years, reports that the prevalence of chlamydia in the Seattle Metropolitan Area has dropped each year.

It is miraculous that chlamydia cases are going down in Seattle, because they are going up in most other places. And to prevent the cases of this epidemic from education continuing to climb, health education about this disease should be improved. According to Dr. Holmes, "Public education regarding chlamydia ranges from grossly inadequate to nonexistent." This pitiful amount of knowledge about this pervasive disease is not sufficient. The public must learn about this disease in their schools, in the media and in their doctor's office. They should know that barrier methods of contraception such as the condom, the diaphragm and the sponge, are fairly effective ways of preventing the spread of infection. In addition to increasing the public's education about chlamydia, the required hours of study for doctors should also be increased beyond the ridiculous 180 minutes that it is now.

The more we learn about this disease, the easier it will be for doctors to diagnose. Therefore, increased research funds is the third step toward a solution to this STD. According to Dr. Washington, "Chlamydia is a major, major problem which requires more research funds." We currently spend approximately 4 million dollars a year on chlamydia research, which may sound like a lot at first. But considering that, according to the CDC, this country spends 1.3 billion dollars every year on health care costs related to chlamydia, 4 million dollars is merely a drop in the bucket.

The answers to this increasingly important problem are fairly simple. Equally as simple as the steps which you, personally, can take to prevent the spread of chlamydia. For starters, become educated about this disease. Secondly, if you do chose to be sexually active, at least be like those mothers who buy Jiff Peanut Butter for their children and be a little choosy about your partner. Third, use barrier methods of contraception just to be on the safe side. And finally, don't be embarrassed to ask your doctor for the simple $7.00-$30.00 test. It isn't worth the risk.

The bottom line is that chalmydia is the #1 sexually transmitted disease in the United States today, but most people don't hear about it until it is too late. However, if we implement the steps I have outlined, and if individuals, such as yourselves, are willing to take responsibility for their own actions, then unfortunate cases such as Jennifer and Tom, who want to have children of their own so badly, but can't, will at least be minimized, if not one day, completely eliminated.

"What is so terrible as war?" I will tell you what is ten times, and ten thousand times more terrible than war: outraged nature. I see that three persons out of every four are utterly unaware of the general causes of their own ill-health, and that it is due to stupid neglect, or what is just bad, stupid ignorance."

In 1859 Rev. Charles Kingsley used these powerful words to address the cholera epidemic, which created a 40% infant mortality rate in England, simply because of a lack of sanitation.

Today we face a similar situation. There is a problem that most are unaware of, which is causing influenza, smallpox, pneumonia, tuberculosis, meningitis, air-born lead poisoning, and most fatally, legionnaires disease. This problem is . . . Sick Building Syndrome. Sick Building Syndrome describes any building with actual or potential health hazards due to contaminated air.

The incidence of SBS is rising, partially because buildings have been planned with maximum energy savings in mind since the energy crisis of the 1970's.

Dr. Tony Pickering, who is currently studying SBS, states in the May, 1987 issue of *World Press Review* that, "SBS affects 90% of super sealed buildings, and in some cases sickens up to 70% of the building's occupants." Super sealed buildings describe any building which uses mechanical ventilation. In basic terms, a building whose windows cannot open or close.

SBS is a serious problem that we need to become aware of, because if we don't do something to cure this disease today, then, like England in the 1860's, thousands of Americans will die in the 1990's.

So today we will investigate SBS, by first, examining the general causes of the problem, then looking at the symptoms of SBS, and finally, we will find ways to end the outraged nature of SBS.

There are three major causes of SBS. The first, is that buildings are using ineffective heating, ventilation, and air conditioning systems, also known as HVAC systems. Architect William Heineman describes these systems in the December, 1985 issue of National Safety and Health News, "Once we enter these air-tight buildings, we are completely dependent upon its support systems for survival. The quality and quantity of air we breathe are totally contained within the system."

This speech was written by William Fort while he was an undergraduate student at California State University, Chico.

Not only do these systems pick up fungus and bacteria, and recirculate it throughout a system, but also airborne viruses, germs from co-workers, and cigarette smoke. "Microbiological health hazards are the most wide spread of the many hazards in mechanically ventilated buildings," declares environmentalist Sandy Moertz in the February, 1988 issue of Occupational Hazards magazine. Ms. Moertz goes on to state, "The vast majority of this microbial growth is caused by stagnant water, and dirt build-up in air filters, and condensation drainage trays, that are not regularly cleaned." Or, in Kingsley's words, "Stupid neglect and stupid ignorance."

The third major cause of SBS is the lack of governmental support. The Environmental Protection Agency's Eileen Claussen states in the June 6, 1988 issue of *Time* magazine that, "Some Americans spend an estimated 90% of their time indoors, however no specific federal regulations have been adopted for control of air in offices, even though the air in some buildings is 100 times as polluted as the air outside the buildings."

Ineffective HVAC systems, lack of maintenance on existing systems, and no governmental support, all perpetuate the problems associated with Sick Building Syndrome. And those problems are significant.

The symptoms of SBS don't start out with your building throwing up or your elevator doors getting a fever, rather as minor annoyances such as dry throat, headaches, or drowsiness. In fact, the May, 1987 issue of *Occupation Health and Safety* printed a survey of over 10 thousand office workers, half of whom worked in naturally ventilated buildings and half in mechanically ventilated buildings. The results showed that while only 15.7% of those in naturally ventilated buildings had frequent headaches, 37.4% of those in mechanically ventilated buildings did. When it came to drowsiness, 13.8% in naturally ventilated buildings, 51.4%, four times as many in mechanically ventilated buildings were frequently drowsy on the job.

These lopsided figures translate into a monetary loss by building owners. James Rapace, the indoor air specialist with the EPA, states in the January, 1989 issue of *Discover* magazine, "The millions of workdays lost each year (due to SBS) translate into billions of dollars in medical expenses, diminished productivity, and compensation claims."

In May, 1988, 70 workers boycotted their office building, claiming that the air inside the building was so contaminated that it caused frequent headaches, dizziness, eye irritation, chest pains, and breathing difficulties. The Washington DC building is the National Headquarters of the Environmental Protection Agency.

Although usually the symptoms of SBS are the ones I've previously mentioned, sometimes just one visit to any super sealed building can be fatal. In May, 1985, 37 men, women, and children who stayed on the fourth floor of Stafford General Hospital, mysteriously died. Later the cause was found to be Legionnaires Disease, a harmful bacterium which originated in the air conditioning system, which blew the deadly disease through the air ducts, right into the unsuspecting patients rooms. The HVAC system hadn't been cleaned in over a year.

This incident outlined in the June 3, 1985 Air Conditioning, Heating, and Refrigeration News, is not an isolated one. In fact, the September 2, 1985 issue of *US News and World Report* says, "Legionnaires disease strikes 25-50 thousand Americans a year, and about 15% of the victims die." Translating these figures, we can see that the outraged nature of SBS causes around 5,000 deaths annually.

Hospitals, hotels, the Environmental Protection Agency, and school buildings are places where we should be able to go and feel safe and secure. However until we, as individuals, and as a nation do something to stop the outraged nature of Sick Building Syndrome, then each and every trip into a super sealed building will be potentially life threatening.

On an individual level, the one sure fire way to prevent becoming a victim of SBS is to wear a gas mask at all times. But since gas masks are uncomfortable, hard to find — and lets face it — unattractive, I'll recommend other means of survival. First, we need to become aware of general causes of our own ill health in these buildings. Realize that if you have frequent headaches, dry throat, drowsiness, eye irritation, chest pains, or breathing difficulties inside a building, that it is probably a sick building.

Once this awareness is achieved, please act. Pick up the phone and call your local building inspector and ask him or her to examine your sick building, and let you and the building owner know what actual or potential health hazards are there due to contaminated air. Another practical step we can all take is to tell others about the problem so they can also help find these sick buildings and pressure building owners to start a preventative program against SBS.

On a larger level, we can see the need to attack the number one cause of SBS, which is microbial growth in HVAC systems. Davis Custer, the Vice President of Environmental Management Systems, says in the February, 1987 issue of *Buildings*, "Microbiological health hazards are the most preventable of the many hazards in super sealed buildings. They can be virtually eliminated through simple maintenance."

The types of simple maintenance which Mr. Custer speaks of include replacing all dirty air filters, emptying all condensation drainage trays, and treating the entire system with an inexpensive anti microbial solution. By spending a few dollars today, they can save millions tomorrow, and end their stupid neglect. This is a simple and logical solution which will be easy and inexpensive to implement.

Finally, Federal legislation which, A) requires building owners to use certain types of tested, effective HVAC systems, and B) requires them to clean and maintain their existing systems, would be a great help in calming the outraged nature of SBS.

In 1859, one of England's major problems was a cholera epidemic which created a 40% infant mortality rate. This could have been solved by taking simple preventative measures and being more sanitary. Unfortunately, most ignored Rev. Kingsley, and because of it hundreds of thousands needlessly died.

Research scientist Michael McCawley said in the June 6, 1988 issue of *Time* that, "Unless we realize the severity of the problem today, Sick Building Syndrome will be one of the major problems of 1990's."

If we follow the simple steps which I've outlined, we can learn from the English mistakes of the 1860's, and end the stupid neglect, stupid ignorance, and outraged nature associated with SBS, and in the process we can all play doctor, and save the thousands of lives lost each year to SBS.

Speaking to Entertain

Jack Perella and Steven R. Brydon

Entertainment speaking is a forensic activity in which original speeches are constructed and presented in such a manner that they serve the ends of both public address and public entertainment. Known both as "After Dinner Speaking" and "Speech to Entertain," the common descriptions of the event focus on three salient concepts — public entertainment, public speaking and personal originality. The fusion of these concepts give it a character which makes it both like and unlike the other platform speaking events.

Public Entertainment

Public entertainment is the most obvious defining feature of this event. This focus does not imply that an informative or persuasive speech *cannot* entertain. The difference is one of emphasis. Professors Swanson and Zeuschner noted the reason for this emphasis in their discussion of the origins of entertainment speaking.

> After-dinner speaking has always been a genre of American public address. Anthologies of American public addresses frequently have examples of these speeches. Organizations having dinner meetings would hire a well-known speaker to give a short talk after the meal. This wasn't as easy as it sounds. The speaker had to address a group of people that he wasn't a member of; had to compete with the liquor and heavy food that was served at dinner; had to be witty and yet eloquent. It is no wonder that the great after-dinner speakers were highly prized during their day![1]

The relationship between persuasive and informative speaking on the one hand, and entertainment speaking on the other, was originally not one of goals (since both might examine serious issues), but one of techniques. The after-dinner speech made exceptionally heavy use of interest devices and operated on the assumption that the audience would rather go home or go to sleep. Thus "entertainment," primarily in the form of humor, was used to finesse a possibly trite or controversial idea past an uncooperative audience.

Since humor is the essential technique of entertainment speaking, you need to develop an understanding of what people find funny. Many people seem to have an instinct for humor; they seem "naturally funny." But, humor can also be seriously studied. While elaborating a "theory of

---

Professor Perella is a former Director of Forensics at Santa Rosa Junior College. Professor Brydon is a former Director of Forensics at California State University, Chico.

1 Don R. Swanson and Raymond F. Zeuschner, *Participating in Intercollegiate Forensics* (Dubuque: Gorsuch Scarisbrick, 1983) 43.

humor" is beyond the scope of this chapter, we can offer you some insight into what people generally find humorous.

Distortion. Humor often distorts reality, treating the unreal as if it *were* real, while communicating an attitude that "this is all in fun." A similar distortion, presented "straight-faced" as an informative or persuasive speech, might be likely to irritate an audience. But, a distortion treated facetiously is likely to evoke laughter.

Exaggeration. How funny is an annoying baby in a restaurant? Usually not very. But exaggerate the annoyance, make it seem outrageous, and it is funny.

Incongruity. Something that does not seem to fit can be funny. Woody Allen's famous story about having a brother who thought he was a chicken shows how the incongruous can be humorous. When asked if the family sought help for his brother, Allen replied "We couldn't afford to. We needed the eggs."

Sarcasm. Saying one thing in a biting manner which suggests that you mean quite the opposite, is a potent but dangerous source of humor. Sarcasm often comes off bitter rather than satiric, and can actually create sympathy for your victim.

Irony. This is an extremely powerful source of humor, and one which is well suited to making a serious point in an entertaining fashion. The fact that President Reagan spent a few hundred thousand tax dollars flying to his ranch in California so he could chop wood to save money on the White House heating bill, was both funny and serious.

Puns. Known both as "the lowest form of humor" and "intelligent humor," puns can be extremely effective when employed creatively and infrequently. Because they are grounded in abstract dimensions of language, subtle puns are rarely effective. Oddly enough, obvious "groaners" work better in entertainment speeches.

Attacking authority figures. How many forensics entertainment speeches pick on coaches? Attacking authority figures has been a staple of humor as long as anyone can remember. Will Rogers made a career of attacking Congress. Johnny Carson continually took shots at Day Quayle. Joan Rivers made fun of everybody.

The rule of three. Comedian Milton Berle once claimed that he could make an audience laugh at anything, if he preceded it with two funny jokes. Reflecting the old adage that "the third time's the charm," American humor is traditionally packaged in threes — it always seems to be the third doctor, the third salesman or the third victim who generates a punch line. Position your punch line three levels deep to increase its humor quotient.

Perhaps the best advice on discovering the truly humorous comes from the British philosopher Thomas Hobbes:

> The passion of laughter is nothing else but SUDDEN GLORY arising from a sudden conception of some EMINENCY IN OURSELVES by comparison with the infirmity of others,

or with our own formerly: for men laugh at the FOLLIES of themselves past, when they come suddenly to remembrance, except they bring with them any present dishonour.[2]

Public Speaking

The fact that event descriptions mention "speeches" rather than "presentations" or "routines" should remind you that all public speaking events benefit from purpose and structure. An entertainment speech should follow the same principles of good public speaking which would guide you in other speaking events.

An entertainment speech should resemble any other good speech in organization — you need an effective introduction, including a clear statement of purpose and general preview of the content, a body which develops a thesis, and an appropriate conclusion. The presence of structure is one of the ways in which entertainment *speaking* is distinguished from an entertaining *monologue.* (A comedic monologue is also organized in the sense that it is arranged to facilitate its purpose. Such routines, however, subscribe to poetic rather than rhetorical patterns.)

The Introduction. It is very important to capture the audience's attention almost immediately. This is not the time for a belabored story leading to a punch line. So, try to get a laugh in the first sentence or two. Sometimes, merely an outrageous statement will suffice. Once you have the attention of your audience, give them at least a general notion of where you are headed. Another difference between speaking to entertain and performing comedy is a sense of exigence. Entertainment speeches use humor as a device rather than as an end in itself. It is generally expected that you aspire to express a *significant idea*, and that you use humor to amplify that idea and to impress it upon the audience. The various event descriptions commonly note that an entertainment speech "should not resemble a night club act, an impersonation or comic dialogue" and that it "is not merely a series of jokes or a 'stand-up' routine." To be sure, your idea may have an absurd sense, such as "organized crime is a growth industry which can provide job opportunities for the unemployed," and your intent to poke fun. Nonetheless, there is a central purpose to your speech. When you wait until the conclusion of your speech to reveal an underlying thesis, you risk making your speech seem relatively insignificant, somewhat along the lines of a poor comic's "but seriously folks. . . ."

The Body. This is where your idea is humorously developed. Depending on the nature of your topic, there are several ways to arrange your material. A narrative or simple chronology works well, especially when describing experiences or events. A topical arrangement may be appropriate in other situations, e.g., "Man Watching: Where to Look, How to Look, What to Do After You've Looked." Sometimes a mock problem-solution approach is the answer, as in

---

2 Thomas Hobbs, *Treatise on Human Nature*, cited in Charles R. Gruner, *Understanding Laughter: The Workings of Wit and Humor* (Chicago: Nelson-Hall, 1978) 29-30.

the speech which addressed a strategy for protecting an endangered species — the rat! Many entertainment speeches are parodies of what would, on another subject, be an informative or persuasive speech. Such speeches often borrow the topical pattern or motivated sequence arrangement expected from the "serious" speech.

The Conclusion. Unlike a traditional speech, a review of the "points" you have made is generally not appropriate — no one wants to listen to a summary of your punch lines. Focus on what you have accomplished rather than on how you accomplished it, but you do want to make sure that the point of your speech is clearly evident. The best advice for your conclusion is the old adage: "Leave 'em laughing!"

Delivery. While the entertainment speech is rhetorical rather than poetic, the demands on delivery exceed those for informative or persuasive speaking. The timing, facial expression and vocal variety needed for comedy require a high level of fluency, energy and practice. Manuscripts are intrusive. In humorous interpretation, a manuscript is present to stress that you are interpreting someone else's work. Since an entertainment speech is your own work, and since putting the audience at ease is necessary for comedy, avoid speaking from a manuscript.

Personal Originality

A creative wit has long been an appreciated part of the speaker's art. In fact, an underlying premise of the British style of public address is that by demonstrating wit, you are also demonstrating intellect. The wit you display when speaking to entertain should be your own. The clear intent of this dimension of the event is to prohibit the wholesale plagiarism of professional comedy routines. There have been a disturbing number of instances in which contestants have been disqualified because their speeches were virtually indistinguishable from routines performed by a popular stand-up comic. This does not mean that an entertainment speech is composed in a vacuum, anymore than are informative or persuasive speeches. But, you should quote or paraphrase infrequently, and you should be sure to give credit where credit is due. When you get to the point where attribution seems awkward or burdensome, you have encountered a sure sign that you are slipping away from the "original" dimension of the event. By convention, the event allows for some degree of unattributed "communal composition," in which you prepare a draft of a speech, and then seek suggestions from friends, teammates and coaches.

Some Tips for Beginners

How do you find a topic for your entertainment speech? The best place to begin is with yourself. Have you had experiences which, at least in retrospect, seem hilarious? A good topic needs to have the potential for ten minutes of development, not just one or two good punch lines. A good topic should be something your audience can relate to — which is what Hobbes' meant by comparisons with our own infirmities. Many of the funniest speeches are about the frustrations of everyday life. Avoid the temptation to tie-in to the latest *Saturday Night Live* schtick, or building on a routine from *Commedy at the Improv.* Work from your own experiences and from experiences all of us tend to share.

How do you develop the content of your entertainment speech? Brainstorming is a useful technique. In brainstorming, a group of people get together and rapidly fire-off ideas. Someone keeps a list. No criticism or evaluation of ideas is permitted (that comes later). The key to brainstorming is to piggy-back one idea on another. The wilder and crazier the ideas, the more they are likely to stimulate creative thinking.

Once you have a substantial list of ideas for jokes, select those which fit best with your purpose. Write each one on a card or slip of paper. Sort them out, arrange them in a manner which helps them emphasize your thesis, and work on transitions which mold them into a cohesive whole rather than a series of punch lines.

Some tips for presenting your entertainment speech. Humor depends on direct audience contact, and reading a joke destroys the spontaneity of the experience. Even if the speech is fully memorized, it should sound fresh and spontaneous. All good speakers make genuinc contact with their audiences, but for entertainment speakers it is particularly important that you remember that you are speaking to an audience rather than a room. An entertainment speech should be delivered in a lively and animated fashion, and should be as interesting to watch as it is to listen to. Make the audience feel that *you* are having fun, and they are more likely to have fun, also.

What special problems might you encounter presenting your entertainment speech in a tournament setting? The biggest problem is what to do when there is no audience. Sometimes your "audience" will be a single judge, other times just the judge and a few competitors. Be sure that your speech can be adapted to that situation. Also, try to prevent the problem. Encourage friends and teammates to attend rounds — and to stay for all the speeches. (It is rude, not to mention depressing, when the audience gets up and leaves just before somebody speaks.) Also, remind them not to force their laughter. When you've written a good speech, a sympathetic audience will laugh when it is appropriate. When friends try to "pump-up" your performance by laughing outrageously at mild witticisms, it is likely to detract from the real quality of your speech.

Feel free to enjoy the round yourself. Laughing at the other speeches doesn't lower your score, but it might help everyone to enjoy the round more. Courtesy and common sense should always prevail.

Finally, remember to be guided at all times by good taste. Stay away from the possibly obscene or potentially offensive. Locker room humor is rarely funny in public places, and some issues just hit too close to home to be approached in an entertaining fashion. Humor always has a victim, and you should be sure that your speech is one in which your "victims" would also see the humor.

[Start theme to Prince's "Let's Go Crazy" on keyboard] Dearly beloved, we are gathered here today to get this thing called death. That's right, I said death. Because you're going to die and you're going to have a funeral. And when you have a funeral it's going to cost somebody some money. Maybe not if your services are run-of-the-mill, humdrum or just plain. **[Play ending notes to "Taps"]** But consider financing if you play to have services like those of Oakland's dearly departed (drug lord) Felix Mitchell. The man had a procession three miles long **[Play Addinsell's "Warsaw Concerto"]** complete with horse-drawn hearse, three Rolls Royces, five limousines, motorcycle escorts and professional mourners. But, unless you can pick six and be right, you're not going to have that kind of money.

In a recent study, the Federal Trade Commission found funeral services are the third largest expense to the American family budget, third only to insurance and housing. Aren't we all surprised! With this information in mind, it seems appropriate to reassess the industry that so efficiently markets death, with the resulting coalition of grief, greed and guilt.

I will advise you on what to expect in today's services. First, we will plot our way through the marketing of death, then under take the requirements of services, and, finally, come to rest on our attitudes toward funeral homes. Now that we have those markets "plotted" — let's begin.

Let's face it, death is a very profitable business. Paul Fuller, an authentic mover-and-shaker in the marketing of death, operates a chain of funeral homes in California, with innovations such as rental caskets and drive-through viewing. It is suggested that he wants to be to funerals what McDonalds is to hamburgers. Although in his case, the Grimace takes on an entirely different meaning.

When you enter the doors of a funeral home, you're not there just to browse — you're sold. The only question is how much. Be prepared to encounter sales pitches such as, "He lived a BMW life — would you bury him in the Pinto of caskets?" Understand that entering a mortuary is like entering a Galleria of amenities. And it you're looking for services, it's not a buyer's market. It is not like a short, annoying guy is screaming at you, "Dying costs too much and that's why I opened Crown Homes." The attitude of the home is more like . . . . **[Play musical theme]** The mark-up on the never-ending list of amenities is higher than that at Abdul's AM-PM Mini-Market. Most of the parlors I interviewed were in Oakland. Jackie Taylor, Dean of Students at San Francisco School of Mortuary Service, says, "There are no guarantees on the integrity of a

This speech was written by John Favors while he was an undergraduate student at Chabot College.

mortician." If there are no guarantees, what are the requirements of services? Bob Yount, from the San Francisco School, the only man I know with the distinguished title "Professor of Embalming Science," says "Most people have only twisted ideas about our profession." No doubt, Bob. That's why I brought this short and concise list of affectionately titled **[Roll our visual aid — a six-foot long scroll]** "41 things to do on the most difficult day of your life," graciously provided to me by Hudson's Funeral Home in Oakland. It shows us people and places we must notify, things we must select, items such as providing vital statistics about the deceased down to cleaning and renovating the some, and some things you may have to — not, count on paying for all the items on this list.

Okay, pop quiz! Is embalming required by law? **[Very long pause]** I can see we have a lot of impromptu speakers here. I'll give you some time to think about that. **[Play theme to "Jeopardy"]** Okay, time's up; pencils down. The answer is . . . only if you play to transport the body by scheduled courier. For those of you who answered correctly, here's Bob to tell you what you won. **[Play game show "prize" music]** You've won a shake-and-bake. **[Hold up visual aid — a piece of cardboard with matches and lighter-fluid mounted]** That's right, an immediate home cremation kit. It features Ronson lighter fluid and a box of blue tip safety matches **[Fold down hinged piece of cardboard that says, "Burn Rites Inc." on it]** provided by Burn Rites, Inc. Their slogan: We're hot for your body."

The California State Trade Commission Funeral Home Act requires that homes provide a price list of services they typically perform. In 1963, Jessica Midford published her book *The American Way of Death*. When she did, we became a nation of frugal funeral consumers. However, between now that then, something happened. David Klugman, president of the Bay Area Funeral Society, attributes this to our attitudes. Mr. Klugman says, "America is a death-defying society, and we have a tendency to turn our backs on this most tragic day." Imagine with me that America were not a death defying society, and funeral homes could advertise more aggressively. They would not give us five minutes of dead air, they would give us something like . . . . **[Play "Addam's Family" theme]**

We have a cemetery, so you can come and bury,
Your mom or Uncle Larry, at our cemetery.
We're neat, our prices are discreet.

Or, they might give us . . . . **[Play Beatles' "With A Little Help From My Friends"]**

What would you do if the crematory you selected forgot the urn?
Or how would you feel if the Pinto Wagon you saw out back was their hearse?
OOH, you can't die without help from our firm.

NOO, you can't die without help from our firm.
If you're in bereavement and you've got a body to burn,
You can't die without help from our f—i—r—m.

Or, get us with . . . . **[Play Cal Worthington Chevrolet theme]**

If you need a casket real bad go see Cal.
If you need a casket real bad go see Cal.
If your credit's in the red and your loved one is not dead,
Go see Cal, go see Cal, go see Cal.
Hi! I'm Cal Worthington and this is my dog's plot.
Y'tambien en Cal Worthington nosotros hablamos espanol.
Sì tu puede un casketto muy malo va a ir Cal.
Sì tu puede un casketto muy malo va a ir Cal.
Sì to credito es en el rojo y to homara esta morta.
Va a ir Cal, va a ir Cal, va a ir Cal.

You have seen the marketing of death, the requirements of services, and your attitudes have been affected slightly; but what do you care? You pick six numbers every week, and not once has your number come up. **[Play Chopin's "Prelude in C Minor]** Unfortunately, many of us wait until the time of bereavement to make plans concerning our loved one's services. There we were faced with a frenzy of emotional and economic decisions which could have been made sooner. Making these plans sooner would make life more palatable both emotionally and economically. Remember, today it is not a question of when, only a question of how much! **[Play wind sound effect on keyboard]**

I know what you're thinking. You're thinking of one word . . . one word that would really capture this picture. MACHO. It has fallen onto me, appropriately enough, to discuss this topic of overwhelming cultural import. Where has macho been and where is it going? In order to answer that question we must look at the history of Macho in America.

First, there was the Golden Age of Macho, which actually began with the Vikings. But I would like to look specifically at post-World War II to the mid-1960s. Then came the Dark Ages, the mid-1960s to the late 1970s, when it was unpopular to be Macho in America. And finally, I'll look at the new campaign of macho, the late-1970s to today, which I think will be logged in history books as the Renaissance, the re-birth of Macho in America. In order to show the full scope of Macho in America, I will consider movies, violence, sex and, of course, crying for men.

First off, there was the Golden Age of Macho. This was a time when men were men and women were frigid. This was the age of the real man, and Hollywood was producing and projecting twenty-foot macho heroes across screens all over America — men like Gary Cooper, John Wayne and Humphrey Bogart. This was the age of the strong, silent type and violence was the primary method of conflict resolution.

The American man was at is best in war movies and cowboy movies. And we all know how macho you have to be to kill off a troop of Stupid Germans retreating into a mine field.

But, even in defeat America rose to new levels of macho. Even at Pearl Harbor, where we got creamed, we kept our composure and said rude things about the enemy (those lousy, dirty, stinkin' creeps who didn't fight fair). The enemy was sneaky, immoral and cowardly; the only way they ever killed any of us was by accident, by surprise attack or by overwhelming numbers. Even in the face of death, we had men like John Wayne saying stuff like, "Well men, there's 8,000 Germans out there and only five of us, but nobody said it was going to be easy."

All of this violence on the screen was reflected in the everyday guy who wasn't afraid to step outside to settle an argument. During this time, any real man would step outside . . . and often did. Men like truck drivers, lawyers, dentists, ministers and forensics coaches (especially forensics coaches). But did you ever notice that in those old movies they would never show the two guys fighting outside? The camera would always stay on the girl they were fighting over, and

This speech was written by John Corgiat while he was an undergraduate student at Modesto Junior College.

she would always look all panic stricken (probably because she knew she would have to kiss the bloody mess that came back in to fetch the prize).

But nevertheless, women encouraged fighting with likes such as, "If you were a real man you wouldn't let him get away with that." Men would never say, "If you were a real woman with clear vision you would see that he is twenty times bigger than I am!"

This was a time of dominance for men. This was the age when the man was the boss around the home (that average Leave-it-to-Beaver home with a two-car garage and 3.6 kids — 2.5 of them Republicans — and a wife bringing her husband the nightly newspaper in her mouth). But oddly enough, during a very macho time in America, sex was sort of kept under the covers. I believe it was the most sexually frustrated time in America; it was like ten years of foreplay. You knew it was going on, but you didn't talk about it. And when a baby did show up, the cause was usually blamed on immaculate conception or the stork.

Yes, the American man was truly the king of his castle . . . except for the bedroom. There the woman was queen and t he man was court jester. Women were not allowed to like sex in the Golden Age, and they didn't. This is why they encouraged fighting, to get their men out of bed and into the boxing ring. The most commonly used phrase by married women during this time was, "Not tonight dear, I have a headache." And instead of saying something like, "I'm not asking you to think," men would just give in, get up and go pick a fight with another sexually frustrated male. In the bedroom, these men were helpless. They had to keep their pride and not beg like you or I would today:

HE: "Please, I'll be done in a second"
SHE: "Huh-Uh!"

So picture this poor guy. He's sexually frustrated, he's just been beat up, and he's not even allowed to cry. Because in the Golden Age, real men didn't cry. Unless, of course, it was in time of war and you were having a temporary mental breakdown — in which case your best friend was required to slap some sense into you:

MAN: "I can't take it anymore!"
FRIEND: "Charlie, what's the hell's the matter with you? Pull yourself together [slap]!"
MAN: "Thanks, I needed that."

Then came the Dark Ages of Macho. Things changed dramatically. It was no longer popular to be macho. In fact, it was mandatory for men to cry almost as much as women. And the women loved it. It made a woman's day if she could call her best friend and say, "Susan, I just saw Serge cry. It was so for-real! Oh yes, he's so sensitive." It was important to be sensitive, caring, passive, gentle . . . wimpy! the movies had changed. The most macho heroes on the screen at this time were Jane Fonda and Barbra Streisand. Pseudo-intellectual wimps like Woody Allen, Alan Alda and Kermit the Frog were the leading men. Fist fighting between men had been reduced to verbal abuse (which usually wasn't even exciting to listen to). "Listen, Apollo, like I really don't dig where you're coming from. Put yourself in my frame of reference. I don't think you even know what kind of negative karma you're giving out."

Demonstrations were about as violent as men got during the Dark Ages. Men would arm themselves with daisies and shout abuse like "Fascist pigs!" at the police. This was not particularly smart because the police were holdovers from the Golden Age of Macho, armed with nightsticks and guns, and loved to beat the bejesus out of men holding daisies.

Women were against fighting during the Dark Ages — because they wanted to save their man's energy for the bedroom. It was the complete opposite of the Golden Age. Sex was much more free, much more open and much . . . more! In fact, I think the only thing American men didn't pull out during this time was Vietnam. Women, after being sexually repressed for so long, now had been unleashed. During the Golden Age, men were frustrated in the bedroom; during the Dark Ages, they were terrified.

Once, women suffered in silence. Now, all of a sudden, men had a critical audience demanding multiple orgasms. For example, if love-making was brief **[point to an audience member]** (*you* should know what I mean), women would say something especially sensitive like, "Can I get you anything else?" or "You selfish pig-face! Now I'll never be satisfied!"

But then, in the late-1970s a movie came out that changed the face of Macho in America. Let's hear it for *Saturday Night Fever.* The macho man was back. He was new. He was improved. He was even better dressed. **[Assume John Travolta disco-pose]** the campaign for the renaissance of macho was led by ultra-violent guys like Arnold Schwarzenegger, Chuck Norris and Sylvester Stallone.

The new Macho Man is somewhat different than his Golden Age counterpart. First, he's less articulate. Even John Wayne made little speeches. But the new macho man has to know only a half-dozen or so English words. I was *Rambo II* on video tape, and I was prepared. I had my Rambo Thesaurus nearby, I had earphones penetrated deep into my ears only to hear lines like "Comarrdee!" What is this man saying? I'm just waiting for the sequel to this one, *Rambo: First Noun.* The non-articulate macho continues:

Mr. T:	"Yo' foo', I bust yo' head!"
Clint Eastwood:	"Make my day, punk."
Rocky I:	"Yo, Adrienne, should I fight or wha'?"
Rocky II-III-IV:	"Yo Adrienne, should I fight or wha'?"

Another difference between the new and old macho — macho violence is more sophisticated. Fist fighting is out, unless you're a boxer or a Karate expert. After all, it messes up your clothes. And in the war movies, the Stupid Germans have been replaced by Stupid Asians who the lone macho hero mows down with sophisticated weapons. High tech is very important — Clint Eastwood with his .44 magnum, Rambo with his M-60 machine gun, and Ronald Reagan with his Star Wars. (I'm a little worried about Ron, buddy. Not only does he want the Star Wars weapons, he wants the action-figures that go with them.)

About crying. Crying is optional for the Neo-macho. You may shed a few manly tears, but then you must immediately: (a) beat-up a Russian boxer; (b) rescue 15 or more POWs; or, (c) invade Grenada.

The Dark Ages did leave us with one nice thing — sexual equality between men and women (which is to say now days women *want* sex as much as men do). The Neo-macho is not expected to be super-human in bed, partly because a woman wouldn't take him seriously. Also, the male population is now divided into *three* groups. For the first group, having sex is the most important thing in their lives. The second group would rather make money than make love. The last group is having a gay old time. The idea of two guys stepping outside to settle an argument has more or less died out. In fact, now days when two guys step outside, they may still exchange blows, but nobody gets hurt. (My coach said I was allowed one crude joke.)

In closing, I would like to pose a question. Will the new heroes of macho lead American men to a new Golden Age? Or is this Renaissance the last gasp of Macho in America before a final Dark Age? Ultimately, for each American male, it comes down to three things: *One — Who are You? Two — It's really up to you. Three — That's the way it should be!*

Oral Interpretation Events in Forensics Competition

Susan Stathas Houlihan

The Art of Oral Interpretation

To begin this discussion of Oral Interpretation Events in Forensics Competition by describing the various forensics interpretation events would be doing a great disservice to any reader new to the art of oral interpretation. You might develop the misconception that the art originated for the sole purpose of forensics competition. Since nothing could be farther from the truth, it is important to examine the nature of the art of oral interpretation, thereby putting events for forensics in some sort of perspective. According to Charlotte Lee and Timothy Gura:

> Interpretation is the art of communicating to an audience a work of literary art in its intellectual, emotional, and aesthetic entirety. . . . The writer of a literary selection is a creative artist who orders ideas, words, sounds, and rhythms into a particular form, putting them into written symbols. The interpreter, in turn, takes these symbols printed on a page and brings personal experience and insight to bear on the clues the author has given. . . . The introduction, transitions, and program arrangement become part of a *new* artistic product . . . a creative act of the interpreter. The interpreter is "director, arranger, and performer, all in one.[1]

While dramatic art and acting are vehicles for performing dramatic literature, oral interpretation is a vehicle for performing all genres of literature — poetry, prose, and drama. The difference between oral interpretation and acting is not the presence of manuscripts nor absence of blocking movement, but the fact that oral interpretation focuses on the *text*. Whereas drama has been written to be performed by actors, most other literature is written in the expectation that the work will be read silently (exceptions are some poems and children's stories which have been explicitly written to be read aloud). The mission of the oral interpreter is to make the text of *all* genres of literature "come alive" for the audience.

Even though oral interpretation in forensics competition requires that you use a manuscript, the physical presence of the manuscript does not define the art. The art of oral interpretation can be very skillfully and enjoyably performed without a manuscript at all — interpreters simply memorize the literature, performing it "off book." This approach has some advantages, such as allowing both hands to be free for gesturing and eliminating the barrier or distraction of the infamous "black binder." However, most of the rule-makers in the world of forensics compe-

---

Professor Houlihan is a former Director of Forensics at Santa Rosa Junior College.

1 Charlotte I. Lee and Timothy Gura, *Oral Interpretation*, 7th edition (Boston: Houghton-Mifflin, 1987): 3.

tition have taken a conservative approach and required the presence of a manuscript during performance, perhaps with the idea that the manuscript distinguishes oral interpretation from acting. If this is the reason, unfortunately, it is not the right one. As a forensics coach who must live within the rules, yet respects the freedom of the art of oral interpretation, I like to justify the use of manuscripts by reminding myself that the manuscript *represents* the text, which keeps our focus on the literature, and that a manuscript *can* be creatively integrated into a performance. If you come to forensics with a background in theatre and find the manuscript requirement restrictive, try seeing oral interpretation as a separate and unique art with special challenges, and you will grow from the experience.

Having taught and coached oral interpretation for more that a decade, I am often asked to distinguish between acting and oral interpretation. I usually start by saying that there is a "fine line" between the two, and there are some similarities and some differences, but that the distinction really comes down to this: While the purpose of each is to "make the literature come alive," the primary technique employed by actors is *reenactment* and the primary technique employed by oral interpreters is *suggestion.* Oral interpretation invites members of the audience to participate by using their imaginations.

The Oral Interpretation Events

The following events are standard fare in intercollegiate forensics competition. You will notice that the events are generally divided by genre. I have attempted to define the different events as I would for novice or beginning students during the first week of class. Each of the events requires that you use a manuscript. Except for Readers Theatre, your presentation is limited to ten minutes, including introduction and any transitions.

Dramatic Interpretation. Typically, this event involves a single individual's portrayal of one or more characters from a play. Material may be drawn from stage plays, screenplays, teleplays or radio plays. You may present a monologue, a dialogue, a scene involving three or more characters, or any combination of the above. Regional preference, individual taste, and the material itself will often dictate your decision as to which will be more effective or successful, a single-piece program or a multi-piece program. When more than one selection is used, they ought to be tied together thematically.

Prose Interpretation. The purpose of this event is to interpret for the audience literature from a novel, short story or essay — generally, any work written in paragraph form, except for "prosaic poetry." Plays are prohibited. The work (or works) interpreted may be from any number of points of view — first person characterization or narration, third person narration or second person characterization. Any of these styles may include characters or dialogue *within* the narration. Again, regional preferences, individual taste or the material itself may determine your decision to choose to perform a single-piece or a multi-piece program. When more than one selection is used, they ought to be linked thematically.

Poetry Interpretation. This event involves interpreting literature which is poetic in form or style. It may be *lyric poetry* (poems describing or expressing feelings or emotions from the perspective of the poet), *dramatic poetry* (poems portraying characters created by the poet) or *narrative poetry* (poems which tell a story). Once again, regional preferences, individual taste or the material itself may determine your decision to perform one long poem or two or more shorter poems linked thematically.

Oral Interpretation of Literature. You are probably asking, "Don't all of these events involve oral interpretation of literature?" The general category is called oral interpretation. However, this is a distinct interpretation event which crosses genre lines, and is called simply Oral Interpretation of Literature (or sometimes Program Oral Interpretation). Programs used in this event must include selections from at least two *genres* of literature (i.e., drama and prose, drama and poetry, prose, poetry and drama, etc.). The program must link the selections thematically.

Duo Interpretation. This event involves a cutting or cutting presented by *two* interpreters. Some organizations limit the event to material drawn from plays (e.g., AFA), while others allow material to be drawn from any genre of literature (e.g., Phi Rho Pi). Most rules agree with the notion that the portrayal of two or more characters must be the central focus of the presentation. The broader definitions allow the script to include narration, usually performed by the characters themselves. Acting is discouraged; presentation should use the technique of "suggestion" rather than "representation." Traditionally, focus is "offstage," not to each other. Costumes are not allowed.

Readers Theatre. Three to fourteen students (typically three to six students) from one school form a cast who compete against casts from other schools in group performance of literature. This event combines oral interpretation and conventional theatre. Scripts are usually developed by the coach/director; in some instances students create the script. Material used may be published or original, fiction or non-fiction, from any genre of literature. Scripts may be single-piece programs or thematic compilations. Oral interpretation techniques, blocking, set pieces and ensemble dress are all used to communicate the literature to the audience. A manuscript, which represents the text, must be used in the performance; however, readers often go "off-book" at times during the performance. Focus is primarily "offstage," but "on-stage" focus is sometimes used during a performance. The time limit is twenty-five minutes, not including set-up. (Phi Rho Pi allows two minutes for set-up and take-down.) Although hours of scripting and tedious rehearsals make this the most time consuming interpretation event, it is also considered by many to be the most creative, exciting and moving event in forensics competition.

Some Important Variables in Event Descriptions

Event descriptions often vary from tournament to tournament. A situation in which two tournaments offer events entitled "Oral Interpretation" with radically different rules is not uncommon. For instance, at one tournament the rules may call for a mixed genre approach, while another may allow any genre of literature, either singularly or paired with another. You should read event descriptions for each tournament carefully.

The second thing to consider is that most tournaments, particularly the national championship tournaments sponsored by AFA, NFA and Phi Rhó Pi, stress interpretation over acting. The distinction is not always clear, and, in fact, actions which would be regarded as acting in one region may be quite acceptable in another region. Carefully reading tournament announcements and consultation with your coaches help to minimize problems in this area.

A third problem is that the definitional lines which separate genres of literature are quite vague. The distinction between prose and poetry is particularly troublesome. In fact, when pressed for a criterion upon which to base the distinction, one critic has maintained, "If it looks funny on the page, its poetry." For some, the definitional lines probably will never become clear. I have, however, seen the works of some "poets" that have taken the form of something resembling a short paragraph. That poet and her critics may maintain that it is not the *form* it takes that defines the genre, but the *style* in which it is written. Some define poetry as literature which is clearly rhythmical and, perhaps, rhymed or metered. Others claim that the use of metaphor and vivid images appealing to sound and sense define the genre.

While the distinction between prose and poetry can sometimes be difficult, the distinction between drama and poetry can also be a puzzle. Into which category does a cutting from a play which has been written in poetic form belong? Much of Shakespeare's drama is written in rhythm, meter and rhyme, so where do we put it? My personal inclination is to categorize it as drama since the cutting is from a play. Others may disagree, or merely play it safe and include the piece in a multi-selection "oral interpretation" program with a prose piece.

The distinction between prose and drama could cause some confusion when the piece is a narrative monologue from a play. Usually, when we hear a narrative with characters voices within the "story" we think of it as prose. One of my former students competed with a selection from the one-man play "Redthroats," by David Cale. The cutting he chose was a narrative monologue from a section of the play called "The Weirds." If you just heard the selection performed without the introduction, you might think it was a prose story. But since the piece was taken from a play (albeit delivered in the style of a performance artist much like Lily Tomlin or Laurie Anderson), my student entered "Dramatic Interpretation," had no problem (other than a few stray comments that the piece sounded "prosey"), and actually was quite successful competing with the program. Nonetheless, you should be aware of the problem of clear definition and seek your coaches' guidance on questionable matters.

The final problem to consider is the confusion regarding the acceptability of reading original material (drama, poetry or prose you have authored). Phi Rho Pi tournament rules explicitly require that programs be drawn from "published material available to everyone through normal research methods." The American Forensic Association skirts the issue by requiring literature "of literary merit," which many coaches interpret to mean, at a minimum, published literature. National Forensic Association tournament rules avoid the issue altogether. A few years ago, a Poetry Interpretation national champion "confessed" to me that she had written two of the pieces in her program, but used a pen name when crediting the poets during the transitions. I had always loved her program, and thought the pieces were wonderful. Would I have thought differently had I known she had written them? I doubt it. I know good literature when I hear it. Others may have been affected. In any case, if you want to include your own work, ask your coach's opinion on the literary merit criterion and, if you get the go ahead, my advice is to be discreet.

Preparing Your Program

Getting started. There is not just one way to "start" an oral interpretation program. Some begin by deciding which event they would like to compete in, and focus all of their research on reading only that genre of literature; others try to begin with a theme and then use indexes to research selections on that particular theme; some start by reading *widely*, finding several selections that they believe are especially good, then trying to build a program using one or more of those selections as a foundation. Most literary selections contain more than one theme, and can be taken in several different directions.

Although each of these methods is appropriate in its own way, my experience coaching students tells me that, for several reasons, the latter approach typically yields the most satisfying results. First, by drawing a theme from general reading, you are assured that the selections in the program are those that you will enjoy reading. Remember, you have selected a piece because there is something about it that you really like — perhaps you can identify with a character, perhaps you find the message particularly meaningful, perhaps you find the images vivid and compelling, perhaps you like the sound of the language, perhaps you are emotionally moved by it, perhaps it makes you laugh. The second reason I prefer to recommend this method is that starting with a theme in mind and then looking for material to support it is often like "looking for a needle in a haystack." Even if you are lucky enough to find material that supports the theme, chances are that you won't really connect with the selection(s). The third reason for my preference is that focussing on one genre (like focussing on one theme) is limiting. For instance, if you have your heart set on finding a dramatic piece, you may be missing a great poem that could be just perfect for you. The fourth reason that I prefer the "find a selection, then figure out a theme approach" is that it challenges you to be more open-minded in interpreting the literature. If you already have a theme in mind, you are less likely to be open to the other messages it may be conveying. A side benefit to this approach is that for multiple piece programs you are more likely to pull together diverse and unique pieces, rather then presenting three selections saying the same thing with essentially the same tone. Finally, this method asks you to draw upon your existing literary knowledge — novels, stories, poems, and plays you've read before — or, if you have not read much, it forces you to start reading, familiarizing yourself with literature.

If you are lucky, your coach may suggest a specific selection or selections to you. If you are *really lucky* your coach will hand you a photocopy of the poem, dramatic scene, or short story. And if you are *truly blessed*, the program will be already edited down to the time limit! I have a few things to say about this. First, don't *expect* pennies from Heaven; your coach has several students to work with and many other duties. If you do have access to an edited program, be grateful. Second, as a coach, I have been known to pass material on to a student, but only if I've known and worked with the student long enough (at least several months) to get a feeling for his or her personality, abilities, and level of commitment (I want to be sure that if I give a student a "gem" that it will be polished to perfection). Finally, if you do the lion's share of the work — researching the program, selecting the material, editing it, and polishing the performance — you will have the satisfaction of knowing that it came from *you*, and this should give you a great sense of pride and accomplishment. Also, your heart will truly be "in it." Realize, however, that a coach's guidance is very valuable, and you should seek assistance from your coach at *every step* of the process of formulating a program. Before you begin polishing a program, make certain that your coach approves of the choice of material, theme and format. Your coach probably has years of experience in forensics, so pay careful attention to that valuable feedback.

Researching and choosing your material. Each student interested in competing in the oral interpretation events has a very different base of literature from which to draw. You may be quite well read — perhaps you are a re-entry student, perhaps you had some particularly demanding high school English instructors, perhaps your family background is one which encouraged reading, so you now have a love and interest in the activity. In any case, because of your experience with literature you are at an advantage. You may have a great interest, but not much experience with literature thus far in your life. Do not despair! It is never too late to begin your quest for literary savvy. There are plenty of research aides to help you, some of which will be discussed in this chapter. In the meantime, you can start by going to the library and finding the works of authors you may have read in the past. If you have a big chunk of time, sometimes spending an afternoon or evening in the library — or even in a good bookstore — just browsing through the stacks and thumbing through anthologies that look interesting, may uncover a poem, story or play that you really like. If this sounds too unstructured for you, narrow your focus by examining who you are or what you are interests are and proceed accordingly. If you would like to explore your ethnic heritage, you may choose to research poets who share your heritage. There may be certain issues which interest you that you can use as a general focus — poverty, the environment, mass media, women's concerns, homosexuality, etc. You may choose to develop an "author program" on a particularly interesting author, poet or playwright. A student of mine once competed with a marvelous interpretation program of Noel Coward's works using selections from all three genres. If you would like even more focus, consider asking your coach (or other instructors on campus, particularly those in English or Theatre) to suggest authors or works that you might research. Take the lead you have been given and start digging. You may not care for what you originally set out to find, but the process of digging just may unearth another little treasure! Also, book reviews in magazines and best seller lists may be of use.

Your college library should have a variety of indexes which will help you. The indexes contain lists of stories, plays or poem titles, and are usually listed by author and subject. Ask your reference librarian to instruct you in the use of these indexes. He or she will be happy to assist you, and once you get the hang of it, you will be glad you learned. These books are great for getting the title of a poem or the synopsis of a story or play. The librarian will show you how the index leads you to an anthology from which you can get a copy of the selection. Three of the most popular indexes are: *The Columbia Index to Poetry,* a reference work indexing anthologies published through June, 1989; *Short Story Index, 1989,* an index to stories in collections and periodicals, listed by author, title and subject, and *Play Index, 1983-1987,* a reference work indexing almost 4,000 plays by title, playwright, and description. In addition, two important periodical publications, the weekly *New York Times Book Review* and the biweekly *New York Review of Books*, are very helpful. Copies of plays can be purchased from play services. Catalogs with brief descriptions of each play are available from the following companies:

Samuel French, Inc.
7623 Sunset Blvd
Hollywood, CA 90046
(213) 876-0570

Dramatists Play Service, Inc.
440 Park Avenue South
New York, NY 10016
(212) 683-8960

Clear your selections with your coach. Once you have found a piece you think you'd like to perform, before launching headlong into analysis, editing, and memorization, you may want to consult with your coach. I imagine every coach has a different policy about this. Your coach may not want to even discuss a program until you think it is ready for tournament competition. Personally, I strongly urge my students to "report" to me before proceeding past the research stage, so I usually ask for the title and author. If I am unfamiliar with the piece, I'll ask for a casual, cold reading by the student. The issue here is not censorship, I am merely trying to save them some time that might unnecessarily be spent working with a program that has inherent problems resulting from the choice of material. Just because you starred in your high school drama production of "Arsenic and Old Lace," or your favorite book in sophomore English class was "1984," does not necessarily mean that these are good selections for forensics competition. My assumption as a coach is that, as my student, you want a program that will increase your chances of doing well in competition. So *trust* your coach when you are cautioned about your choice of material for any of the following reasons:

- The piece does not really fit your natural "persona" (e.g., you are 18 years-old trying to portray a 70 year-old) and without make-up and costumes, and with your current interpretation ability, it's a bit of a stretch.
- The piece demands an accent or dialect that may be too challenging for you at this time.
- The selection is overexposed. Unfortunately, the piece is so good it has been very popular and "done to death." Judges may be tired of it. Find something fresh instead.
- The selection was superbly performed very recently by a student in your region, making such an impression on so many judges that to undertake it now would be seen as either stealing a good idea or competing against a legend.
- The selection is actually from the screenplay of a very popular movie, or "box-office hit." In this case, your audience is probably so familiar with the characters and the actors that play them that you will have a hard time measuring up to, say, Robin Williams in "Dead Poets Society" or Dustin Hoffman in "Rainman." In addition, it may be difficult to maintain an audience's attention when they already know the plot so well. Try to find material from a play that has yet to be made into a movie; or if you love screenplays, at least find a relatively obscure one. But remember, screenplays have been written for a visual medium and sometimes do not translate well into the oral interpretation format.
- Larson and O'Rourke suggest that you should consider the quality of the literature: "S. I. Hayakawa, in *Language in Thought and Action,* argues that high quality literature allows the audience to draw its own conclusion, to become active participants in the literary process, while low quality literature spells out the conclusions. Others have argued that high quality literature is timeless in its appeal on truthfulness, still others have based the judgment on the reputation of the author."[2]

As a beginning student of oral interpretation, you may feel that you are still shaping your values and tastes with regards to literature. This is normal. On the one hand, you want to trust *yourself*—you know what you like. On the other hand, your tastes are often guided by exposure to great works and the opinions of others, so listen to the advice of your coaches, teachers and other students and then decide. Realize, however, that there are judges out there that absolutely retch when a competitor announces he or she will be reading a selection written by Rod McKuen, Erma Bombeck, or Neil Simon. I, myself, don't want to hear an entire program of Judith Viorst or Shel Silverstein poetry either, but one, good, well-placed piece may be just the balance and levity the program needs. Since it's impossible to make black and white judgments about literary merit, you may want to seek advice, weigh it, then trust yourself.

---

2 Suzanne Larson and Sean Patrick O'Rourke, "Some Thoughts on Oral Interpetation," Paper presented to the Northwest Forensics Association, Eugene Oregon, October 1982, revised 1983: 3.

Analyzing your selection. Careful analysis of each selection you will perform is important for an intelligent reading. If you have taken an English literature class, you should use the same techniques that you learned in that class to understand the literature. If you haven't taken a literature class, you should pay particular attention to this section on analysis. You should also consult the other chapters in this publication on specific genres.

If your selection is drama or prose, you should read the entire play or novel in order to understand the entire plot and each character's motivation. It is tempting to find a one- or two-minute cutting in an anthology of monologues or scenes and rely only on the editor's brief comments about each to guide your interpretation, but you will be more knowledgeable if you analyze the play or novel yourself. The relative length of poems and short stories make them a less time-consuming analytical undertaking, yet these works also need careful study. A particularly complex poem may need to be read several times before all of the metaphors, images, and symbols are understood. As an interpreter, you must understand the feeling or attitude behind each line or idea before you can perform it believably. The following items need special attention in your analysis of each of the genres:

Drama. Playwright, setting, time, social climate, tone, mood, characters (background, purpose, motivation, personality/psychology, mannerisms, dialect, appearance), plot, dramatic shape (introduction, inciting action, rising action, climax, falling action, denouement, conclusion), language, themes or message.

Prose. Author, narrative style and point of view (first person? third person?), suitability of material for the reader (gender-specific or not?), setting, characters within the narration (number, personalities, attitudes, dialects), plot/action climax, tone, changes in mood, themes or messages.

Poetry. Poet, genre (lyric, narrative, dramatic), "the speaker" (poet or character), point of view (first person or third person?), suitability of the material, prosody (rhythm, meter, rhyme, sound effects), figures (metaphor, simile), images, tone (ironic? argumentative? comic?, etc.), character analysis (if applicable), climax (if narrative), setting (if applicable), changes in mood, themes, or messages.

Cutting your selection. Since forensics competition imposes strict time limits on all events, most literature you select your program (with the exeception of short poems) will need to be edited. When cutting literature, Larson and O'Rourke advise:

> Two major considerations are involved. First, you must attempt to keep intact the author's intent. That is, be true to the literature. Second, you must cut with an eye for the purpose of your selection: the theme it supports, the humor it portrays, and the characters it reveals.
>
> Recently, forensic educators have become increasingly concerned with the ethical ramifications involved in cutting an author's work. Some argue that any cutting represents a mutation of the author's end product, the author's art. Others argue that interpreters have

a right to "poetic license," for interpreters are artists too. The question is a subjective one and must be answered by each competitor in his or her own way.[3]

As you begin to edit your material for competition, there are a number of things you should keep in mind. Here are a few practical tips:

- Never mark in the book you are using. Make a photocopy to work on.
- Use a pencil, not a pen, so you can change your mind.
- Put parentheses around the words or lines you want to cut. You can completely strike these parts out later, when you are certain.
- When cutting prose, once you have established the characters through name and voice identification, cut tag lines ("he said," "she said," etc.), unless it is clear that the writer is using them for effect.
- Cut whatever is not necessary. This may include repetitive statements, description, ideas that have already been made clear. Be careful, however, not to cut the style which the author intended. For example, sometimes description is necessary to set the scene or create the mood.
- When cutting drama, omit all stage directions and unnecessary or repetitive dialogue, unless, of course, it's there for effect.
- Cut characters or plot lines that are not central to your purpose.
- When cutting poetry, *never* cut single words, as this will destroy the rhythm or rhyme involved; cutting single lines will also cause damage. If you must cut rhymed poetry, cut whole stanzas. When cutting free verse, these concerns still apply, but are less crucial.

Arranging your program. If your program will include more than one selection, you will need to make some decisions about how to order the pieces, or "program" the material. Which piece should open the program? End the program? Traditionally, the trend is to begin with a humorous piece and progress to the more serious. This is known as the "make 'em laugh, make 'em cry" philosophy. One of the advantages to this approach is that the program will have "range" or diversity, thereby keeping the audience entertained while exhibiting the scope of your talent. As far as I'm concerned, the most important thing to remember is to "take the audience somewhere." The selections in the program should follow in some logical pattern that leaves your audience with the idea or feeling that you established as the theme in your introduction. This may even involve ending on a rousing, upbeat, humorous note.

Choosing a theme. After you have analyzed your material, you should be able to choose a theme, or decide upon the message. Sometimes the work will "say" many things, so you will need to focus on one main idea. The biggest pitfall for beginners is the inclination to think a topic (such as "mothers" or "lying" or "anger") is a theme. Such topics are too broad, vague and shal-

---

3 Larson and O'Rourke 4.

low. What *about* mothers? If you go with the adage "The hand that rocks the cradle rules the world," then you have a theme, a thesis, a central *idea.* Another pitfall is choosing topics that are overused. If you are avoiding general topics such as "war" and "love" and are choosing thematic *ideas*, your choices are endless, naturally eliminating the trite topic problem.

Introductions and transitions. The purpose of an introduction is to prepare the audience for the literature that is to follow. Whether your program is a single selection or multiple selections, you will need an introduction. The items you will want to include are the title of the selection, the author's name, and any orientation information the audience may need to understand the piece (setting, character relationships, etc.). You will also want to state the theme of the piece, or the universal idea it addresses (for instance, Sophocles' "Antigone" deals with the conflict between obedience to authority and following one's own conscience). Usually, an introduction will begin with a catchy attention getter, such as a quotation that expresses the theme or a personal statement that establishes rapport with the audience, moves on to clearly state the theme, then proceeds to the title and author of the selection with some background information for the audience to set-up the cutting. Sometimes, the introduction is preceded by a short "teaser." This is a brief excerpt from the single selection to be read after the introduction, or a brief piece from an entirely separate selection. (My general rule of thumb for a teaser is one minute maximum for a ten minute program.) A teaser often serves to get the audience's attention with literature, rather than with your own words. Introductions should be delivered extemporaneously, naturally, and conversationally. You should not assume a persona other than your own. The length of the introduction is entirely up to you, but most competitive introductions are proportional to the ten minute time limit, usually ranging from 45-90 seconds. To write an introduction, make a short list of all of the ideas you want to get across, arrange them in the order that you think will help the audience understand them, and write a sentence for each idea, making sure the sentences flow together clearly.

Multiple selection programs usually use transitions to link the pieces thematically. Recently, however, especially with poetry programs, there seems to be a trend toward the "collage" approach wherein all the titles and authors are stated in the introduction, and the interpreter proceeds to read the works one after another, or creatively spliced together, without transitions. I have seen this done very effectively, especially when the pieces are short or happen to lend themselves to creative arrangement. It is certainly an approach to consider when developing your program. Traditionally, however, you should close your binder and expresses to the audience, in two or three sentences, how the following piece is linked thematically to the preceding one. The transition might point out that the next piece is similar, another angle, a contrast, more serious, a resolution, etc.

Preparing your script. Make your manuscript work for you by carefully preparing it. The first inclination, especially if rushed, is to simply read from photocopied pages. There's no doubt that this method has, and does, work in a pinch. I suggest, however, that you type the material yourself (on a word processor if available) — first, because the activity of typing is helpful in the process of memorization, and second, because it is easier to read, especially if you can adjust the font to your liking.

The size of paper you use will depend on the binder size you choose. Experiment with different sizes and choose the one with which you feel most comfortable. Recently, the trend is toward the smaller-sized binder, probably because it is less obtrusive, easier to hold, and more mobile. Most students use black binders because black is neutral, but there is no rule about this. In fact, I once judged a speaker with a poetry program about "food" (I forget the precise theme) who used a red and white checked binder reminiscent of a Betty Crocker cookbook. It worked quite well.

You may want to mark your script by underlining words you plan to emphasize, or highlighting certain lines. For instance, if you are reading two characters, you may want to highlight character "A" in yellow and character "B" in green. When you glance down at the line, the color will trigger the voice, facial expression, and focus you plan to use for that character.

Often students place the pages of their script into plastic sheet protectors. These not only preserve the paper, they help avoid page turning sounds and make it easier to turn each page.

Oral Interpretation Techniques

Once you have chosen, cut, and prepared your manuscript, you are ready to begin rehearsing. Practically speaking, you may have informally begun reading the script aloud before this point to get the feel of the material, to time the selection, and to experiment with different voices and other techniques. Now, the intensive rehearsals begin.

If you are sure you are within the time limit, you should begin by reading the material over and over, becoming thoroughly familiar with it, eventually to the point of solid memorization. Depending upon how much time you have with it before the tournament, you will reach some level of familiarity. My experience is "the more, the better." I believe that other coaches and veteran competitors will tell you that memorization is generally the key to a polished performance. Memorization allows you to have a sense of control with the material so that you can anticipate ideas, and thus plan and execute your nonverbal communication accordingly. This control will make your performance more believable. An acting instructor once told me (and I believe this advice applies to oral interpretation as well): "Let us see you *think the thought*, then move in *action*, and finally, hear you say the *words*." As you can imagine, you must have the material memorized in order to apply this technique. If you are engaged in reading the words, you are unable to anticipate the idea that you wish to communicate.

The nonverbal channels of your performance, or "delivery," include everything except the words of your material. Sure, you could take your carefully prepared script to the tournament and read to your audience, your eyes glued to the pages, with little vocal inflection or physical responsiveness (not unlike some poets at coffeehouse readings), and you wouldn't be disqualified from the event. Your performance would not, however, be critically acclaimed, successful or even mildly interesting. Judges at forensics tournaments are analyzing your ability to share the experience through a disciplined use of voice and body. There are many specific elements involved in this aspect of the art, and they fall into two general categories: vocal characteristics and physical responsiveness. Pages could be written about each of their elements, but, for purposes of brevity, this section will list and briefly define them.

Vocal Characteristics. Another name for this dimension of nonverbal communication is "para-language." Employing this dimension in oral interpretation involves having *your* meaning of the author's words, or "language," in mind, and then using the various elements of your voice to convey that meaning to the audience. In other words, para-language is not *what* you say (content/language), but *how* you say it (vocal variation). For instance, the three simple words "I love you" can be said in a soft, slow, sweet and sensitive way to mean one thing, but can also be shouted from a distance in a loud, terrified and breathless way to mean something else entirely! Varying the characteristics of the voice is one of the two primary ways oral interpreters convey meaning, making the literature "come alive" for the audience. Important variables of the voice include:

Volume. The loudness or softness of your voice. You should try to vary volume for meaning and emphasis. Also, project your voice to be heard.

Rate. The speed with which the words are delivered. Again, variety is important, as is attention to the rate(s) demanded by the text. You should not be afraid to pause for dramatic effect, or to interrupt one character's lines for another's. Try to create realistic timing.

Breathing. The natural and relaxed process of inhalation and exhalation. Controlling your breathing is central to good vocal tone.

Pitch and Quality (Tone). The rate and complexity of the vibration of the vocal bands. You can use inflection (from high to low tones) to suggest meanings. Variation of pitch is important in order to avoid the "worst sin" of public speaking — the monotone (no changes in pitch).

Pronunciation and Enunciation. Pronunciation is the "correctness" of sounds and accents in spoken words. Enunciation refers to the "clarity" with which the words are spoken. Correct pronunciation is a factor in your credibility as an interpreter. Consult dictionaries when you encounter unfamiliar words or proper names. Clear enunciation (or diction) will insure your intelligibility. Say each syllable separately and distinctly. Fast talkers tend to "telescope" multi-syllable words, or smash them together. For example, "politics" becomes "poltics." However, in your concern for clarity, be careful not to *over* enunciate. For instance, "often" should not be pronounced "of*ten*." In some cases, interpreters with individual speech patterns (regional or ethnic) may need to develop Standard American Speech. Then again, the selection may call for a dialect or accent. If so, it should be performed as authentically and believably as possible, or not at all. No accent is better than a bad one.

Physical Responsiveness. Another name for this category is "kinesic behavior," or body language. It has long been recognized that we all communicate with our bodies, sending and receiving messages without ever uttering a word. We have all had experiences in which we have picked up a sense of how people feel by noticing their facial expression or how they are moving at a particular moment. Body language is a very central, natural and "telling" way of communicating, so it cannot be ignored by the oral interpreter. Effectively employing your body in oral interpretation involves deciding what you think the literature means, and giving the audience clues about that meaning by physically responding to the ideas. Remember the order that the acting instructor suggested: "Thought, Action, Word." A person would not say "I'm so mad at you!" and *then* wag his finger at you, would he? He would *think* about how mad he is, then start the *action* (i.e., wagging his finger at you), and finally he would say the *words*, "I'm so mad at you!" Keep this in mind as you physically respond to the ideas you are expressing. Physical responsiveness includes:

Posture. Stance. Good posture requires standing straight so that the various parts of the skeletal structure fall naturally into place. You may want to assume the posture of the character(s) being read.

Gestures. Any movement that helps to express or emphasize an idea or emotion. Gestures should be motivated by the material and the interpreter's natural physical response. During rehearsal, you may want to try using large, exaggerated actions in response to the emphatic cues and muscle imagery in the literature. This is the basis of "muscle memory" in which your muscles "remember" practiced movement. Muscle memory reflects the remembering, even after a specific gesture has been modified or discarded. Typically, gestures in forensics should "suggest" rather than "act-out." Mime is often effective.

Facial Expression. Meaning projected by the face. The key to effective facial expression is congruity with the verbal and vocal message. Make sure your face reflects the idea or feeling you intend to convey. A well-timed facial expression can often precede a group of words, setting the tone before the words are uttered.

Eye Placement. Where you fix your gaze will affect the audience's perception of what the literature is expressing, "who" is speaking and what is going on. The term we use to discuss eye placement is "focus." Interpreters, as public speakers, use "offstage" focus: the focus is "offstage" in the imagination of the audience. Facing the audience in full view facilitates the audience's participation in this presentational style of performing literature. Actors turn profile and look "onstage," which is only effective in representational performance of drama. There are four types of offstage focus:

When using an *open focus,* you look at the audience, making varied and direct eye contact with everyone. Use open focus when you are reading narration, when your character is addressing a large group, when your character is expressing a less private soliloquy or when stating an "aside."

When using a *closed focus,* your eyes are placed "on the back wall" or just above the heads of audience members giving the illusion of speaking to a character. This technique is useful when reading dialogue, or when reading a monologue that is clearly directed to one individual. If portraying more than one character, place the most central in the center and others angled to the right and left. Angles should be very slight, no more than 45°. Avoid angling wide into a profile as the audience will miss your facial expression and your head movement will become too severe and distracting. Consider the relative weight of each of your characters and look up or down a bit, accordingly.

When using an *inner-closed focus,* your eyes are placed in order to affect looking inward. This technique is useful when communicating your character's private, personal thoughts and feelings. To achieve this, you may want to glance upward, as if thinking or remembering, to the side and around in a non-directed way, or angled down at a non-specific place, as if in fixed, deep and pensive thought.

When using a *semi-closed focus,* your eyes are placed in order to affect addressing something or someone other than a present person. This technique is used when your character is communicating to a god, a spirit, an absent person, or an inanimate object. To focus on a god, you may want to angle your eyes up and out toward the back wall. To focus on an inanimate object, "place" the object somewhere, perhaps on the back wall if the object is supposed to be at a distance, or directly in front of you, about waist high, if it is supposed to be close. You may even want to mime picking up the object, as if you are "seeing" it in your hand.

Focus is also integral to communicating shifts in times and place. "Changing the direction in which you look when speaking the line that contains a shift in time or place is a way to suggest change."[4]

Visualization of Images. A final aspect of physical responsiveness, one closely associated with focus, is the visualization of the images in the literature. In response to an image in the literature (i.e., an airplane on the horizon), you should place the image "out there" using offstage focus, visualizing it in the place you have put it. Magically, as you "place" an image and speak about it, the audience will "see" the image as well.

Conclusion

Oral interpretation is one of the most fascinating and entertaining aspects of forensics competition. You are exposed to various genres and styles of literature, learn something about

---

[4] Judy E. Yordon, *Roles in Interpretation* 2nd Edition (Dubuque: William C. Brown, 1989) 119.

literary criticism, hear diverse interpretations of classical and contemporary literary themes, observe both traditional and novel techniques of presentation, and often find yourself laughing hysterically or being moved emotionally, all in the span of 60-75 minutes. You now have a basis for beginning your work in oral interpretation events, and are about to embark on a journey that is never ending, and through which you will never be the same.

For Additional Reading

John Greenfieldt and Juliette Yaakov, eds. *Short Story Index, 1989.* New York: H. W. Wilson, 1990.

Edith P. Hazen and Deborah J. Fryer, eds. *The Columbia Index to Poetry.* New York: Columbia University Press, 1989.

Charlotte I. Lee and Timothy Gura. *Oral Interpretation* 8th Edition. Boston: Houghton-Mifflin, 1992.

Kristin B. Valentine and Eugene Valentine. *Interlocking Pieces: Twenty Questions for Understanding Literature.* Dubuque: Kendall/Hunt, 1991.

Beverly Whitaker Long and Mary Frances Hopkins. *Performing Literature: An Introduction to Oral Interpretation.* Englewood Cliffs: Prentice-Hall, 1982.

Juliette Yaakov and John Greenfieldt, eds. *Play Index, 1983-1987.* New York: H. W. Wilson, 1988.

Judy E. Yordon. *Roles in Interpretation* 2nd Edition. Dubuque: William C. Brown, 1989.

Dramatic Interpretation

Kathrine Lemke Waste

"All the World's a Stage, and All the Men and Women Merely Players"

What makes dramatic interpretation work in competition? How does a beginning performer pull together a program? How can experienced competitors revitalize their approach to the event and realize new goals within the framework of competitive performance? I will answer these questions by discussing how dramatic literature works in the context of oral interpretation.Second, I will construct a sample program complete with selections, theme and performance notes. Finally, I will provide a list of useful reference material that no forensics library should be without.

In forensics competition, dramatic interpretation is an event that is usually defined as an eight-to-ten minute cutting from a stage, screen, radio or television play . More than one selection may be used if the selections are tied together by theme. A manuscript must be present. An appropriate introduction — usually preceded by a short "teaser" is the standard bill of fare. However, all too often, performers hastily pull together a program from monologue collections or cutting files without fully understanding the text from which the piece is drawn. Nothing is more frustrating to a judge than to listen to a performer who does not understand the material, or who has taken it out of context. Nothing is more frustrating to a competitor than to work on a program that falls flat in performance. The key to avoiding these situations is to begin by learning how dramatic literature works.

"An Honest Tale Speeds Best Being Plainly Told"

When we go to a movie or to live theater, we experience a visual, kinesthetic story that unfolds before our eyes through a series of actions in a setting. For example, in Jane Campion's 1993 film, *The Piano,* we are plunged into the lush rain forests of 19th century New Zealand as we listen to a mute woman play a haunting refrain on her beached piano. In Shakespeare's *Macbeth,* the action of the play begins with thunder and lightening, while three witches cast their spells. As a forensics performer, you lack such theatrical or cinematic accouterments as sound effects, costumes or exotic locales. You must rely on the basics — rigorous textual analysis, character development, language and the imagination of your audience.

Plays develop character through action, rarely through narrative. An excellent guide to understanding the relationship between action, dialogue and character is the book *Backwards*

Professor Waste is currently Assistant Director of Forensics at California State University, Chico.

and Forwards by David Ball.[1] Ball provides a step-by-step analysis of Shakespeare's *Hamlet,* and through his textual analysis of the play, provides a clear blueprint for understanding the construction of any play. Knowing how a play works is the first step in understanding what the play means.

Playwrights develop a dramatic arc constructed through performance over the course of two to four hours. A dramatic arc is a series of actions. *Plays are action.* Plays are not about action, nor do they describe it. An action contains two events. When one event causes or allows another event to happen, the two events together create an action, as we can see in *Macbeth.*

Upwardly mobile Macbeth discovers his hopes are dashed when King Duncan announces (the event) that someone else will inherit the throne upon his death. Macbeth conveys (the connected event) his dismay in a letter to his wife. Lady Macbeth, knowing her husband to be a weak and indecisive man, plots (the action) to do away with her soon to be arriving house guest — who just happens to be King Duncan himself. And so it goes. Connected events set into motion a chain reaction of actions and before we know it, Duncan is murdered, Macbeth is hallucinating, ghosts and witches dabble in the affairs of men, while bloody hell is loosed upon the land. Shakespeare's dramatic arc takes shape, determined by the action or the unfolding of the plot.

Plays begin with a *stasis* — or unchanging state in which all forces are in balance. The action of the play is initiated when the stasis is interrupted with an *intrusion.* The intrusion sets in motion the conflicting forces that battle throughout the play in order to reestablish stasis once again. Dramatic conflict rises and crests into a *climax* — that moment when all the major forces of conflict "have at each other."[2] The climax is followed by *denouement* — falling action — and return to stasis. Dramatic conflict is the lifeblood of a script. Dramatic conflict occurs when a character wants something; this is referred to as an objective or motivation. Macbeth wants to be king. So does Lady Macbeth. Events occur which cause obstacles to be placed in the path of the Macbeths, making it difficult for them to get what they want. Conflict happens between the wanting and the obstacle. Words are spoken and actions are taken in order to overcome the obstacle.

Character analysis involves the careful examination of dialogue and actions in order to determine a character's objectives, and in so doing, discover the inner nature of the character. Lady Macbeth goads her wavering husband into committing murder, and then takes action by drugging the King's guards so Macbeth can carry out the evil deed. Clues can be found in the

---

1 David Ball, *Backwards and Forwards: A Technical Manual for Reading Plays* (Carbondale: Southern Illinois University Press, 1983).

2 Ball 92.

text that give the performer a sense of the character's psychological makeup. Character choices are made through careful analysis of dialogue. The personality and inner landscape of a character are shaped by dialogue. For example, Lady Macbeth, upon learning that her husband will not inherit the throne, cries out, "Come, you spirits that tend on mortal thoughts, unsex me here, and fill me from the crown to the toe top-full of direst cruelty! Make thick my blood; stop up the access and passage to remorse, that no compunctious visitings of nature shake my fell purpose." This is a woman with a mission, a corporate raider on the prowl. Duncan will die and so will a host of others. In the end, vaulting ambition overreaches itself and we are left with an enduring psychological portrait of evil.

"Play Out the Play"

When a producer selects a title for performance — besides budget — a number of considerations must be made. How big is the performance space? How many characters are in the script? What are set and costume requirements? How do the demands of the script balance against the producer's available resources? In other words, *proportion* comes into play. As a solo performer, you are your own producer, and you must be concerned with many of the same issues. Because the format of interpretation places physical limitations on performance, the relationship between character and action must be carefully weighed. How many characters and how much action can one successfully cram into eight to ten minutes? Finding the right script is always a challenge, especially when your resources are limited to your body, your voice and a manuscript.

Finding the perfect cutting for DI (forensics lingo for dramatic interpretation), typically involves a frantic search through your library's monologue collection. A last minute reprieve is issued when some sympathetic soul produces the perfect, already edited, selection. Novice competitors sometimes turn to beginning acting teachers, who suggest titles like *Agnes of God* or *Shadowbox,* not realizing that such overexposed selections frequently work to the disadvantage of competitive dramatic interpreters. It is best to begin your search at the beginning, and that means looking inside yourself.

Write down what you want to accomplish with your entry into competitive dramatic interpretation. This seems simple and obvious, but frequently students pull together programs that are at odds with their personal goals for the activity. Like a character in a play, the performer needs an objective. Your list might look something like this:

- I want to qualify for nationals . . .
- I want to perform more than one character . . .
- I want to challenge myself with a "classical" piece . . .
- I want to focus on women's issues . . .

Armed with an articulated list of goals, you can now track down appropriate selections. The first thing to do is find out what made it to final rounds at national tournaments the previous year, since, strategically, it is a good idea to avoid repeat performances. Talk to people who read scripts. English or drama professors, local community theater directors, dramaturges, or reviewers are people to contact for ideas. In your college library, you can read through national theater reviews such as *New York Times Theater Reviews* or *New York Theater Critics' Reviews.* College Drama departments usually have their own script libraries; however, access usually requires permission. Script libraries subscribe to the latest catalogues from suppliers of plays and musicals. The Samuel French and Dramatists' Play Service catalogues contain thousands of titles — each with a short synopsis. Titles are arranged in different categories by ethnicity, gender, age, number of characters, etc. Scripts can be ordered over the phone and are delivered within a few days. Your forensics program should consider keeping copies of these catalogues on hand for easy reference.

For the purposes of illustration, let us now build a sample program using cuttings from *A Doll's House* by Henrik Ibsen and *The Taming of the Shrew* by William Shakespeare. Both plays can be considered "classic" examinations of the societal repression of women. Ibsen's Nora Helmer transforms from dutiful housewife into emancipated woman, rebelling against her status as housewife and property. Shakespeare — a firm believer in the conventions of his day — guides his exuberant Katharina through Nora's journey in reverse. The two women, created some three hundred years apart, provide a wonderful mirror image of each other and of ourselves. And both selections allow us to fulfill three of the four goals stated above.

Because a ten minute program cannot possibly allow you to convey effectively all the twists and turns of plot, proportion dictates an economy of scale. This is where the rhetorical nature of the event will help you decide what to cut and what to perform. Let theme guide your editing decisions. Our goal is to allow Katharina and Nora to exist side by side, each speaking for herself as she voices the changes that have occurred through the action of dramatic conflict. Katharina embraces the role of traditional wife, while Nora rejects it. Given our theme — or rhetorical position — the actual events that worked as catalysts for their newly-honed positions are less important than the positions themselves. The purpose of *this* program is not the journey, but the destination.

Let's look at the defining moment in *A Doll's House,* as Nora explains her decision to leave her marriage to her befuddled husband in the play's dramatic climax.

Nora: I shall not sleep tonight.

Helmer: But, my dear Nora —

Nora *(looks at her watch):* It isn't that late. Sit down here, Torvald. You and I have a lot to talk about.

(She sits down on one side of the table.)

Helmer: Nora, what does this mean? You look quite drawn —

Nora: Sit down. It's going to take a long time. I've got a lot to say to you.

Helmer *(sits down on the other side of the table):* You alarm me, Nora. I don't understand you.

Nora: No, that's just it. You don't understand me. And I've never understood you — until this evening. No, don't interrupt me. Just listen to what I have to say. You and I have got to face facts, Torvald.

Helmer: What do you mean by that?

Nora *(after a short silence):* Doesn't anything strike you about the way we're sitting here?

Helmer: What?

Nora: We've been married for eight years. Does it occur to you that this is the first time that we two, you and I, man and wife, have ever had a serious talk together?

With that question, Nora tells Torvald in no uncertain terms that great changes are to follow. This short passage is a good way to introduce the theme of the program and can be used as a *teaser* or opening introduction. As a performer, you can elect to present both characters or you can "cut to the chase" and present only Nora. Let's see how the previous passage can be edited down to one character while leaving the author's intent intact.

Nora: Sit down here, Torvald, You and I have a lot to talk about. *(pause)* Sit down. It's going to take a long time. I've got a lot to say to you. *(pause)* No, that's just it. You don't understand me. And I've never understood you — until this evening. No, don't interrupt me. Just listen to what I have to say. You and I have got to face facts, Torvald. *(pause)* Doesn't anything strike you about the way we're sitting here? We've been married for eight years. Does it occur to you that this is the first time that we two, you and I, man and wife, have ever had a serious talk together?

Editing for performance means maintaining the integrity of the script. While lines can be removed, they cannot be rewritten. You also need to consider the content, rhythm and pacing established through dialogue. Editing a dialogue into a monologue may not always work. Here, the edited passage works as an opening teaser because it hints at great conflict to come, establishes the use of language to define that conflict — "I have a lot to talk about" — and reveals the relationships to be examined — "You and I, man and wife." You can use the pauses to "listen" to Torvald and establish his presence with off-stage focus.

After the opening teaser comes the introduction. The introduction must identify the selections, provide necessary exposition and your clarify theme. Many judges consider interpretive events to be rhetorical in nature, and just as in platform speaking, expect you to establish the significance of your material. The sample introduction which follows identifies the selections, establishes the theme, and links the relevance of two "old" plays to a modern audience.

In 1879, Norwegian playwright Henrick Ibsen shocked conservative audiences when he created Nora — a character who leaves behind her husband, her children, and the conventional mores of the day with a "door slam heard 'round the world." In contrast, in *The Taming of the Shrew,* William Shakespeare's irrepressible Katharina makes the opposite choice as she knuckles under to the demands of her husband Petruchio, proclaiming, "Thy husband is thy lord, thy life, thy keeper, thy head, thy sovereign . . ." Well, you get the picture!

As war rages between men and women — he won't clean the house, she won't mow the lawn, he won't do windows, she won't take out the garbage — gender diplomacy begins with understanding how we reached this impasse. And as with most things in life, we can turn to literature to better know ourselves. *The Taming of the Shrew,* by William Shakespeare and *A Doll's House,* by Henrik Ibsen.

We will continue to cut Torvald's lines, while maintaining his presence in the performance. It is important to maintain the convention that Nora is in a dialogue with Torvald, leaving pause space for her to "listen" to his lines. However, we will cut some of Nora's direct responses to Torvald's questions so that the pause-and-listen technique is not overused. Read the following edited passage of Nora's speech with a copy of the original text to see what been cut.

Nora: You have never understood me. A great wrong has been done to me, Torvald. First by Papa, and then by you. *(pause)* You have never loved me. You just thought it was fun to be in love with me. When I lived with Papa, he used to tell me what he thought about everything, so that I never had any opinions but his. And if I did have any of my own, I kept them quiet, because he wouldn't have liked them. He called me his little doll, and he played with me just the way I played with my dolls. Then I came here to live in your house — *(pause)*

I mean, then I passed from Papa's hands into yours. You arranged everything the way you wanted it, so that I simply took over your taste in everything — or pretended I did — I don't really know — I think it was a little of both — first one and then the other. Now I look back on it, it's as if I've been living here like a pauper, from hand to mouth. I performed tricks for you, and you gave me food and drink. But that was how you wanted it. You and Papa have done me a great wrong. It's your fault that I have done nothing with my life. I — *(pause)*

You've always been very kind to me. But our home has never been anything but a playroom. I've been your doll-wife, just as I used to be Papa's doll-child. And the children have been my dolls. I used to think it was fun when you came in and played with me, just as they think it's fun when I go in and play games with them. That's all our marriage has been, Torvald.

With that statement, Nora hits the most important beat in the play. It is delivered with a finality later echoed in the sound of a door slamming as Nora leaves the house. In the text, Torvald and Nora now enter into a faster-paced dialogue — a series of questions and answers that cannot effectively be cut down into a monologue without sacrificing the integrity of the play. Torvald, in a state of shock at Nora's unthinkable announcement, struggles with her intention to leave the marriage. He asks her how she can think of neglecting her most sacred duties — those of being wife and mother. Nora asserts that she has another duty, even more sacred — her duty toward herself. This is where we resume our adaptation.

> **Nora:** I believe that I am first and foremost a human being, like you — or anyway that I must try to become one. I know most people think as you do, Torvald, and I know there's something of the sort to be found in books. But I'm no longer prepared to accept what people say and what's written in books. I must think things out for myself, and try to find my own answer. *(pause)*
>
> I don't really know what religion means. I only know what Pastor Hensen told me when I went to confirmation. He explained that religion meant this and that. When I get away from all this and can think things out on my own, that's one of the questions I want to look into. I want to find out whether what Pastor Hensen said was right — or anyway, whether it's right for me. *(pause)* I don't know where I am in these matters. I only know that these things mean something quite different to me from what they do to you. I've learned now that certain laws are different from what I'd imagined them to be; but I can't accept that such laws can be right. Has a woman really not the right to spare her dying father pain, or save her husband's life? I can't believe that. *(pause)*
>
> Oh, Torvald, it hurts me terribly to have to say it, because you've always been kind to me. But I can't help it. I don't love you any longer. That's why I can't go on living here any longer.

There are more questions and answers. Torvald asks Nora to explain herself, since he cannot understand her frame of reference. Nora then makes specific mention of Krogstad's letter — an event which occurred earlier in the play and served as catalyst for her decision. We do not have the time to go back and fill the audience in on the details of that action, so it must be left out. We resume with Nora's final parting remarks.

> **Nora:** . . . I realized that for eight years I had been living here with a complete stranger, and had borne him three children —
>
> Oh, I can't bear to think of it! I could tear myself to pieces! As I am now, I am no wife for you. *(pause)* I can't spend the night in a strange man's house. Goodbye, Torvald. I don't want to see the children. I know they're in better hands than mine. As I

am now, I can be nothing to them. *(pause)* When a wife leaves her husband's house, as I'm doing now, I'm told that according to the law he is freed of any obligations toward her. In any case, I release you from any such obligations. You mustn't feel bound to me in any way, however small, just as I shall not feel bound to you. We must both be quite free.

The few remaining lines are again a dialogue between Torvald and Nora, and cannot be effectively cut into a single speech. Besides, after the statement, "we must both be quite free," there is, thematically, little else to say. Now let's turn to Katharina in *The Taming of the Shrew*.

The plot is simple. Baptista cannot marry off his younger daughter Bianca until his older daughter Katharina can find a husband. There is only one problem. "Kate" does not relish the idea of being married off, and much prefers her independence. At least, that is how a modern audience is likely to interpret her scathing rejection of the poor fellows who try to win her hand. Along comes Petruchio. Through trickery, incarceration and starvation, Petruchio "subdues the unbroken-in coltish jade" that is Katharina.[3] Of course, the play would not work if Kate and Petruchio were not truly attracted to one another, so love wins out in the end. Love, however, is greatly aided by the fact that Petruchio's behavior modification tactics are effective, and Kate comes around to his way of thinking. In her final speech, she astonishes her listeners with her dramatic change of heart. We will use this monologue in its entirety as we now construct our program.

The next step is to decide how the program will be edited. Will each passage stand alone? Should the performance of Kate and Nora be separated by a transition? The best way to answer these concerns is to, once again, review the purpose of the program. Since each character represents differing — and evolving — viewpoints, we want to highlight the contrast. This suggests a "parallel" performance. After the introduction, Kate and Nora are laid out side by side, e.g., the performer will shift back and forth between characters to emphasize their differences in thinking. A single page turn between characters establishes the convention of such a parallel performance.

The final editing might look something like this:

Teaser

Nora: Sit down here, Torvald, You and I have a lot to talk about. *(pause)* Sit down. It's going to take a long time. I've got a lot to say to you. *(pause)* No, that's just it. You don't understand me. And I've never understood you — until this evening. No, don't interrupt me. Just listen to what I have to say. You and I have got to face facts, Tor-

---

3 A. L. Rouse, *The Annotated Shakespeare* (New York: Clarkson N. Potter, 1978) 120.

vald. *(pause)* Doesn't anything strike you about the way we're sitting here? We've been married for eight years. Does it occur to you that this is the first time that we two, you and I, man and wife, have ever had a serious talk together?

Introduction

In 1879, Norwegian playwright Henrick Ibsen shocked conservative audiences when he created Nora — a character who leaves behind her husband, her children, and the conventional mores of the day with a "door slam heard 'round the world." In contrast, in The Taming of the Shrew, *William Shakespeare's irrepressible Katharina makes the opposite choice as she knuckles under to the demands of her husband Petruchio, proclaiming, "thy husband is thy lord, thy life, thy keeper, thy head, thy sovereign"... well, you get the picture! As war rages between men and women — he won't clean the house, she won't mow the lawn, he won't do windows, she won't take out the garbage — gender diplomacy begins with understanding how we reached this impasse. And as with most things in life, we can turn to literature to better know ourselves.* The Taming of the Shrew, *by William Shakespeare, and* A Doll's House, *by Henrik Ibsen.*

Katharina: Fie, fie! Unknit that threatening unkind brow,
And dart not scornful glances from those eyes,
To wound thy lord, thy king, thy governor:
It blots thy beauty as frosts do bite the meads,
Confounds thy fame as whirlwinds shake fair buds,
And in no sense is meet or amiable.
A woman moved is like a fountain troubled,
Muddy, ill-seeming, thick, bereft of beauty;
And while it is so, none so dry or thirsty
Will deign to sip or touch one drop of it.
Thy husband is thy lord, thy life, thy keeper,
Thy head, thy sovereign; one that cares for thee,
And for thy maintenance, commits his body
To painful labour, both by sea and land,
To watch the night in storms, the day in cold,
Whilst thou liest warm at home, secure and safe;
And craves no other tribute at thy hands
But love, fair looks and true obedience;
Too little payment for so great a debt.

Nora: You have never understood me. A great wrong has been done to me, Torvald. First by Papa, and then by you. *(Pause)* You have never loved me. You just thought it was fun to be in love with me. When I lived with Papa, he used to tell me what he thought about everything, so that I never had any opinions but his. And if I did have any of my own, I kept them quiet, because he wouldn't have liked them. He called me his little doll, and he played with me just the way I played with my dolls. Then I came here to live in your house — *(pause)*

I mean, then I passed from Papa's hands into yours. You arranged everything the way you wanted it, so that I simply took over your taste in everything — or pretended I did — I don't really know — I think it was a little of both — first one and then the other. Now I look back on it, it's as if I've been living here like a pauper, from hand to mouth. I performed tricks for you, and you gave me food and drink. But that was how you wanted it. You and Papa have done me a great wrong. It's your fault that I have done nothing with my life. I — *(pause)*

You've always been very kind to me. But our home has never been anything but a playroom. I've been your doll-wife, just as I used to be Papa's doll-child. And the children have been my dolls. I used to think it was fun when you came in and played with me, just as they think it's fun when I go in and play games with them. That's all our marriage has been, Torvald.

Katharina: Such duty as the subject owes the prince
Even such a woman oweth to her husband;
And when she is forward, peevish, sullen, sour,
And not obedient to his honest will,
What is she but a foul contending rebel
And graceless traitor to her loving lord?
I am ashamed that women are so simple
To offer war where they should kneel for peace,
Or seek for rule supremacy and sway,
When they are bound to serve, love and obey.

Nora: I believe that I am first and foremost a human being, like you — or anyway that I must try to become one. I know most people think as you do, Torvald, and I know there's something of the sort to be found in books. but I'm no longer prepared to accept what people say and what's written in books. I must think things out for myself, and try to find my own answer. *(pause)*

Oh, Torvald, it hurts me terribly to have to say it, because you've always been kind to me. But I can't help it. I don't love you any longer. That's why I can't go on living here any longer.

(Notice here, that the passage about Pastor Hensen was removed in the final editing of the program. It didn't advance the program thesis and referred back to other elements in the play outside the time limits of this program. Also, as the program progresses, it's important to build a sense of momentum — to highlight the contrast between the opposing points of view.)

Katharina: Why are our bodies soft and weak and smooth,
Unapt to toil or trouble in the world,
But that our soft conditions and our hearts
Should well agree with our external parts?
Come, come you forward and unable worms!
My mind hath been as big as one of yours,
My heart as great, my reason haply more,
To bandy word for word and frown for frown;
But now I see our lances are but straws,
Our strength as weak, our weakness past compare,
That seeming to be most which we indeed least are.
Then vail your stomachs, for it is no boot,
And place your hands below your husband's foot:
In token of which duty, if he please,
My hand is ready, may it do him ease.

Nora: . . . I realized that for eight years I had been living here with a complete stranger, and had borne him three children —

Oh, I can't bear to think of it! I could tear myself to pieces! As I am now, I am no wife for you. *(pause)* I can't spend the night in a strange man's house. Goodbye, Torvald. I don't want to see the children. I know they're in better hands than mine. As I am now, I can be nothing to them. *(pause)* When a wife leaves her husband's house, as I'm doing now, I'm told that according to the law he is freed of any obligations toward her. In any case, I release you from any such obligations. You mustn't feel bound to me in any way, however small, just as I shall not feel bound to you. We must both be quite free.

With those words, Nora is given the final say in the program, and makes its thematic point. Structurally, the performance is "bookended" — that is, opened and closed with the same character. Nora's parting words have more dramatic impact than Katharina's statement of submission, and make a better closing moment. Finally, a program should always end with text, never with the performer's own closing observations. As Shakespeare himself said, "no epilogue, I pray you, for your play needs no excuse."

"Speak the Speech, I Pray You, as I Pronounced it to You, Trippingly on the Tongue"

Each character must be physically distinguished from the others through voice, dialect, posture, gesture and focus. Think, for a moment, about the visual impact of a closeup in a film. The actor's face fills the screen, and the audience is focused upon her larger-than-life face. In contrast, on a stage, the actor's physical vocabulary is one that incorporates the entire body. The theatrical effect of a sweeping gesture of the arm and grand exit is whittled down to a shift of focus and lowering of the head in both the movies and the solo performance of dramatic interpretation. Think of your upper torso, arms and face as your "screen." All eyes are focused on this zone of communication which stretches from your open manuscript to your eyes. As you step forward and open your text, the movement of the script draws the audiences' focus first to your binder, then upward to your face as you begin performance. In subtle fashion, you establish first, the primacy of the text and second, the importance of the individual interpretation of the text.

In rehearsal, actors study the text, learn their blocking and integrate the isolated elements of the play into a cohesive whole. Rehearsal for the interpreter is much the same. Your "stage" is that space between you and your audience. Your "set pieces" are placed out of your head and in that space. In other words, visualize the elements referred to in the text — furniture, trees, windows...whatever — and place these invisible elements in that space between you and your audience. Keep the elements consistent, and in the same place, throughout your performance.

If your character is speaking to others, make the audience work as those other characters in the play. Katharina is speaking to a small group of people, so you can look around the room, making eye contact with everyone. Nora is speaking directly to Torvald, so choose one listener in a central position and make that person Torvald. Do not look over anyone's head to a back wall. Don't place another character off to the side and spend your performance time looking at empty space. Establishing eye contact with your audience is crucial to the success of your program. It makes us all a part of the action of the play and creates an interactive connection between performer and listener — in effect — transforming the listener into an active participant. That is what *off-stage focus* is all about. In summary — work in front of a mirror to establish focus points, study film close-ups and concentrate on your zone of communication in performance.

"They are the Books, the Arts, the Academes, that Show, Contain and Nourish all the World."

The following is a list of dramatic resource materials which would be nice to have on hand for reference. Between your university library and theatre department, most of the reference works probably can be found on your campus. The list includes phone numbers and addresses for ordering catalogues from various play services .

Reference Works

Ball, David. *Backwards and Forwards: A Technical Manual for Reading Plays.* Carbondale: Southern Illinois University Press, 1983

Benet's Reader's Encyclopedia. New York: Harper and Row, 1987.

Boyce, Charles. *Shakespeare: The Essential Reference.* New York: Dell Publishing (Laurel

Ottemiller, John. *Ottermiller's Index to Plays in Collections.* Metuchen, NJ: Scarecrow Press, 1988.

Rouse, A. L. *The Annotated Shakespeare.* New York: Clarkson N. Potter, 1978.

Yaakov, Juliette and John Greenfieldt, eds. *Play Index, 1983-1987.* New York: H. W. Wilson, 1988.

Play Services

American Theatre. A monthly publication of the Theatre Communications Group. TCG also publishes many new plays, so ask for a catalogue. Phone (212 697-5230, or write to:
Theatre Communications Group
355 Lexington Ave.
New York, NY 10017

Basic Catalogue of Plays and Musicals. A publication of the Samuel French play service. Phone the New York office at (212) 206-8990, the Hollywood office at (213) 876-0570, or write to:
Samuel French, Inc.
7623 Sunset Blvd.
Hollywood, CA 90046

Complete Catalogue of Plays. A publication of the Dramatists Play Service. Phone (212) 683-8960, or write to:
Dramatists Play Service, Inc.
440 Park Avenue South
New York, NY 10016

Duo Interpretation

Jan McKissick

Duo Interpretation is a unique and challenging forensics event in which you and another student perform a collaborative interpretation of literature. While some invitational tournaments do not restrict the genre of literature from which your draw your program, the AFA, NFA, and Phi Rho Pi national tournaments require that your interpretation program be drawn from a play (stage play, photoplay, teleplay or radio play). In either case, your cutting must involve dialogue between two characters, and you must perform from a manuscript rather than act out the scene. Although there are many similarities between interpretation and acting, the interpreter's burden is decidedly the more challenging. In interpretation, your task is to create fully fleshed-out characters within a recognizable scene without the use of costumes, props, scenery, or significant stage blocking. In this discussion, I will try to help you meet this challenge by answering several basic questions about the Duo Interpretation event.

How do we decide what literature to do?

One of your first considerations in choosing material for any interpretation event is the issue of literary merit. While the fact that an author is published may be some indication of merit, it is by no means an assurance. Generally speaking, "literary merit" refers to the perceived calibre, quality, or stature of a piece of literature. For some, the standard of merit may be higher than for others. Perhaps the point to be made here is that, while the fact that a particular piece of literature is published may be enough to prove merit for some critics (given the time and energy publishing houses give to screening), to others the standard means much more. Charlotte Lee and Timothy Gura assess literary merit in terms of the three touchstones of *universality, individuality* and *suggestion*. They define universal literature as material that is "potentially interesting to all people because it touches on a common experience."[1] Individuality involves "the writer's own fresh approach to a universal subject."[2] Finally, suggestion is defined as a characteristic of "the subtlest and most rewarding" literature, in which an audience is "left with something to do: they are not told everything on an immediate, purely logical level."[3]

Professor McKissick is currently Director of Forensics at Butte College.

1 Charlotte I. Lee and Timothy Gura, *Oral Interpretation* 7th Edition (Houghton Mifflin: Boston, 1987) 10.

2 Lee and Gura 10.

3 Lee and Gura 10.

Most successful interpreters will readily agree that a second important concern is the frequency with prospective material has been used in competition. Just because something is "overdone" does not necessarily make it a poor choice. However, when you choose to perform such material you confront a number of obstacles. First, your judge may well have heard other interpretations of this piece, and you may find yourself competing not only with the other performers in the round, but with all those whom the judge has heard interpret the piece before. Second, the novelty of less familiar material is rarely a handicap, and often an asset. If, however, you feel either that you are uniquely suited to a particular piece, or that you have a fresh and unique approach to interpreting it, the fact that it is overdone should not deter you. (I feel compelled to add that there are judges who equate "overdone" with "poor choice of literature." One can only hope they are a vanishing breed.)

A concern often overlooked in choosing material is whether or not it is suited to your interpretation situation. This encompasses concerns as obvious as physical characteristics, and as basic (albeit difficult to assess) as individual ability. Choose material to which you can relate on some level. This is not to suggest that you should not "stretch" or explore, but that you do so within reason. There is nothing intrinsically wrong with a female presenting an interpretation of a male character (or vice versa), or an 18 year-old doing an octogenarian; however, some judges find such "liberties" difficult to accept.

Perhaps the most important considerations in choosing literature have to do with constraints imposed by the event itself. The ten minute format raises an immediate question of whether your material involves too much or too little dialogue. While some pieces cut very easily into ten minute segments, others are unintelligible by the time they are edited to an appropriate length. Contrarily, piecing together shorter scenes makes it difficult to sustain a cohesive program. Also, since event rules deny you the use of theatrical blocking and the physical trappings of the theatre, you must be wary of staging requirements which make a scene unsuitable. For instance, a scene which requires a knock-down, drag-out fight or an all-out foot race would be difficult to perform effectively as interpreters. By the same token, a script with indispensable prop or costume requirements would be a poor choice.

A final concern in choosing material is the fact that you ordinarily will be performing in a small classroom before a captive audience. It probably is not a good idea to choose a scene which physically or verbally abuses your audience. There was a period when judges cringed when cuttings from the play *Equus* were performed. Screams of "Eq! Eq! Eq!" echoed through many a hall (and ear). Be wary of cuttings which encourage a volume that would be abusive in your physical setting. Also, some judges consider any kind of profanity to be verbally abusive, despite the fact that the author chose to be profane, not you. You also should be concerned about the amount of verbally graphic violence and explicit sex in your cutting. Some judges prefer that you edit out objectionable passages, others subscribe to a hands-off policy regarding the tone of the original text. Whether you decide to leave a passage in, delete it, or change it will depend upon your own preferences, your coach's preferences, and the integrity of your material. Use your own judgment when deciding how to edit your material. However, when in doubt, err on the side of conservatism, and always seek advice from your coach.

Where can we find appropriate literature?

Material suited to Duo Interpretation programs is available from a variety of sources, many of which you will find in your college or university library. The following is just a sample of standard references for dramatic literature.

Chicorel, Marietta. *Theatre Index to Plays in Anthologies and Collections.* New York: Chicorel Library, 1977.

Dramatists Play Service, Inc. 440 Park Avenue North. New York, NY., 10016.

Greenfieldt, John and Juliette Yaakov, eds. *Play Index, 1983-1987.* New York: H. W. Wilson, 1988.

______________. *Short Story Index.* New York: H. W. Wilson, 1989.

Handman, Wynn, ed. *Modern American Scenes for Student Actors.* New York: Bantam Books, 1978.

Keller, Dean, ed. *Index to Plays in a Selected List of Periodicals.* Kent, OH: Kent State University Library, 1960.

National Council of Teachers of English. *Guide to Play Selection.* 3rd edition. Urbana, IL: National Council of Teachers of English, 1975.

Ottemiller, John. *Ottermiller's Index to Plays in Collections.* Metuchen, NJ: Scarecrow Press, 1988.

Price, Jonathan, ed. *Classic Scenes.* Mentor: New American Library, 1979.

Samuel French, Inc. (Play Service). 7623 Sunset Blvd., Hollywood, CA., 90046.

Collectively, these resources cover a vast quantity of potential material for Duo Interpretation. They will not only help you avoid the "overdone literature" criticism, they may also help you find precisely the "right" scene for you.

How do we cut our selection?

Once you have selected material to interpret, your next task is to mold it (usually by cutting it down) into a nine-to-ten minute scene (or series of shorter scenes). The art of molding material into a ten minute performance, while still retaining all the elements that made it appealing in the first place, is exactly that — an art. Some interpreters tend to be better at it than others, but everyone strives to follow the same principles. The first principle is to try and maintain a sense of dramatic anticipation. There is little less satisfying than a scene which reaches an emotional climax after three minutes, and then spends seven minutes filling time. A second principle is to maintain balance in the cutting. Does the cutting divide the lines fairly equally between the characters in terms of numbers of lines and the dramatic impact of the dialogue? Since this is a duet event, the two of you should strive to achieve a balanced performance. Finally, and perhaps most importantly, be sure that in cutting the scene you have not compromised the integrity of the material by ignoring context or the author's intent. In general, adding dialogue is considered unacceptable, and you should carefully consider the integrity of a scene before you make any deletions.

What about introductions and transitions?

Despite the fact that event rules do not require introductions, most Duo Interpretation programs benefit from some sort of introductory material. An introduction serves two basic functions — it orients the audience to your voices and visual presence, and it "sets the scene" by providing information necessary for the audience to understand the program. Your introduction should include the title and author of the material you will perform, and should orient the audience to the characters, setting and plot.

The introduction is normally the first thing the audience hears from the interpreters, but sometimes it is very effective to "tease" the audience with a bit of monologue or dialogue. The "teaser" is currently a popular approach to introducing interpretation programs.

Most successful interpreters agree that introductions are best delivered in a conversational tone of voice, or normal persona, with manuscripts closed. However, it is sometimes appropriate (i.e., when teasing the audience) to deliver parts of the introduction "in character."

Now do we start rehearsing?

Not yet. A large portion of the work required for a good program occurs before any actual rehearsal begins. The first step in preparation should be to read the entire play, not just the scene you have chosen to perform. Carefully analyzing the setting, plot, and characters in the context of the entire play will help you become more aware of the logical and emotional content of the scene. To assist in the development and evolution of your character, it is helpful to prepare a character sketch. Begin by writing down everything the author has given you about a character — posture, attitude, size, physique, etc. Now you are ready to go beyond what the author tells you and flesh-out your character by bringing your own insights and experiences into the role. Use your character sketch journal as a place to keep adding new insights.

Another technique for creating a fuller, more believable character is to decide how the character would behave, feel, believe, etc., in a variety of situations which do not necessarily relate to the scene or scenes being used. For example, how would this character react to being involved in an auto accident on the freeway, being accused of shoplifting, hearing about the death of someone close or receiving unexpected gifts or compliments? Be sure to share all of the above information with your partner and director. In this way the interrelationship of characters will take on a cleaner focus.

How do we rehearse and develop our program?

Following a period of analysis and discussion, you and your partner should begin a schedule of regular rehearsals, ideally under the watchful eye of a director. A number of concerns need to be addressed in this phase of development. The first is focus. Duo Interpretation is not an acting event, and your focus (for the most part) should be offstage. This means that little or no eye contact is made between interpreters. Instead you should each focus on an imaginary mirror at the back of the room, and play the scene to the characters in the mirror. Offstage focus is difficult to master, and requires both a great deal of practice and a third party to observe and give feedback.

Another challenge is script management. Script size should be considered in terms of its relation to the your physical size. A very small woman might have difficulty managing a heavy 8½ x 11 manuscript binder, and a 6'8" male might look silly with a tiny binder. In general, the manuscript should be unobtrusive. However, I have seen them used on occasion as tables, baseball bats, hats, and various other items (sometimes effectively — sometimes not). Make such a decision carefully, as many judges will penalize such literalism in an interpretation event.

Another area of concern has to do with the interaction of the characters. All too often, individual interpreters are so concerned with their own lines that any true reaction to their partner's lines is lost. Try to be aware not only of your own lines but of the statements that elicited them. In many scripts, reaction is the key to a really believable performance.

Finally, you must pay attention to pacing your performance. Many people believe that a good sense of timing is inborn. But if you do not happen to be blessed with a natural sense of timing, try to listen to films, television, or even simple conversations with a more critical ear. Hear how lines interrupt and overlap each other. Listen for the pauses, their length and intensity. Try to find their meaning. Never underestimate the value of a pause. Again, according to Lee and Gura:

> Beginning interpreters are often afraid to hold the pause long enough for its dramatic effect to register with a listener. If a pause is motivated by real understanding, by identification with the feeling suggested, it may be sustained for a much longer time and with greater effect than you might realize. You need only be sure that during the pause something relevant to the material is going on in your own mind and consequently in the minds of your listeners.[4]

Also give thought to the pace of the entire cutting. Few scripts lend themselves to one pace throughout an extended scene. Look for the natural highs and lows in a scene, and work on developing climatic and anticlimactic pacing.

---

4 Lee and Gura 85.

Once you feel confident with the lines, movement, interpretation, etc., the next step is to test the scene on others. Oral interpretation, theater, and forensics classes are good sources for constructive feedback. Allow your scene to evolve. Experiment by trying it in different approaches and styles. Try to bring something new to your performance each time you rehearse.

Conclusion

Duo Interpretation requires that you collaborate with another student in performing an oral interpretation program. As with other interpretation events, you are seeking good literature, which is adaptable both to the event and to the competitive environment. The special challenge of this event is that you must mold the material into a balanced, cohesive ten minute exchange between two characters, and to work together to bring the audience to a deeper understanding of your material. It is this collaborative dimension of Duo Interpretation which makes it a uniquely attractive forensics event.

Poetry Interpretation

Janet Brehe

Bear, dirt, fur, eye and *fire*. Simple, straight-forward words, but in the hand of a competent poet, they can become magical. It is this magic that has drawn people to poetry for centuries. It is also this magic that confuses, scares, and frustrates many — usually because they just do not understand poetry and do not think they can.

I believe that Poetry Interpretation is one of the least understood and most feared events in forensics. Hopefully, after reading this article you will see that poetry is not something to be afraid of and that the performance of poetry can give you a grasp of how to use language that the other oral interpretation events do not quite accomplish.

What is a Poem?

To truly understand the art of oral interpretation of poetry, it is essential to first understand what poetry is all about. So, what is a poem? I like the definition given in *Webster's New World Dictionary*: "an arrangement of words . . . expressing experiences, ideas, or emotions in a style more concentrated, imaginative, and powerful than that of ordinary speech or prose. . . ." The following descriptions of the general characteristics of poetry may help you further understand this form of literature.

Cumulation. One plus one may equal two, but with poetry it more likely equals three, four, five or more. Because poetry is such a concise, intense literary form, the sum of its parts (the overall feeling or message conveyed) can far outweigh its individual pieces (words). The cumulative effect of words in poetry can be enticingly powerful.

Figurative language. All quality poetry uses figurative language, using words in a non-literal manner. The use of figurative language brings beauty, vividness and originality to poetry. My biggest gripe with poetic choices for forensic interpretation programs is that performers often choose literature without figurative language — literature that belongs on greeting cards or backs of cereal boxes.

Multiple meanings. Poems often have layers of meanings. Do not let this scare you. The truth is that any good writing — poetry, prose or drama — has multiple meanings. Choose the main meaning you desire to get across to your audience, and go with it.

Varied form. Poems can be written in many different forms. There are short poems like Haiku, long, novel-length epic poems, and just about everything in between. Poetry can be rhymed or unrhymed. it can use all lower case letters and no punctuation or ALL UPPER

Professor Brehe is currently Director of Forensics at Las Positas College. Except where otherwise noted, the poetic illustrations in this discussion are the original work of Professor Brehe.

CASE LETTERS AND,, LOTS! OF: PUN;CTU"ATI?ON. Truly, poetry is the imaginative mind's canvas.

Genres of Poetry

So now that you have a little stronger grasp on what poetry is, let us consider the three main genres of poetry: *lyric, dramatic* and *narrative.* While there are many subdivisions of these genres, let us keep this simple. It is important to be aware of the types of poetry because they can help you decide who is speaking and whom the poem addresses. If you are compiling a multi-piece program, you can increase your program's variety by choosing poems from different genres.

Lyric poetry. Lyric poetry is highly personal, emotional poetry usually written from the poet's viewpoint. Lyric poetry has been likened to "a flash of lightening that illuminates some object with a moment of vividness, in this case emotional vividness."[1] See if "Flash fire" illuminates an emotion for you.

the fire
that consumed him
scorches my heart
his teddy bear
one staring eye
fur wearing thin
dirt- and soot-laden
reminds me to never ever ever
forget the joy the love the life
the immeasurable grief

Dramatic poetry. In dramatic poetry, the speaker is clearly not the poet. Often written from a first-person point of view, dramatic poetry focuses on a character who is immersed in an internal or external struggle. Keep these characteristics in mind while reading "The Protector."

Looking through the rubble,
I almost missed it.
His brown teddy bear
  one-eyed
  fur worn
  winking up at me
  more alive than its owner.

---

1 Charlotte I. Lee and Timothy Gura, *Oral Interpretation* 7th edition (Boston: Houghton-Mifflin, 1987) 354.

Why had the fire taken him
yet not this
moth-ridden
dirt-dragged
handkerchief pillow?
Paw in hand he used to stand
So young, yet so wise
Pretending he was the father
and his bear the son
And in the end, doing a better job
Of protecting his off-spring
Than I did of mine.

Narrative poetry. Narrative poetry tells a story. It is usually written from a third-person point of view, and often contains dialogue. Using audience focus for the narration and off-stage focal points for the character dialogue can help make this type of poetry come alive. Read "Final Return," and see how it fits the criteria of narrative poetry.

"Daddy, don't go!"
He heard his son cry
While locking the door before leaving
"Don't worry, I'll always come back."
And he always did
But he wished he had money for a sitter
So his son wouldn't have to be alone
Money for food and a roof was all there was
And his ex had her own concerns
Under another roof
In another town

"Daddy, don't go!"
His son pleaded
Dragging his stuffed toy behind
The only true constant in his small world
Of spit-stained floorboards
And fissure-veined walls
"I'll be back. And remember, don't answer the door."
So he waited for someone to knock
And when they did
He burrowed deep into the laundry pile
And fell asleep

"Daddy, don't go!"
The phrase ringing in his head
Looking down at the soot-singed bear
With its well-loved fur
And knowing glare
"The fire swept through the building like lightening
It's amazing more people didn't die."

He heard the fireman say
Then picking the bear out of the ashes and dirt
He placed it next to his heart
Zipping his jacket over it
And walked away to start a new life

Main Features of Poetry

Besides knowing the genres of poetry, it can be very helpful for the interpreter to know the main features of poetry — *sensory imagery, literary imagery, use of sound* and *rhythm*. You don't have to know all of the terminology, but if you are acquainted with the following concepts, you will be better equipped to choose poetry worthy of performance.

Sensory Imagery. Poetry, as does other literature, appeals to our many different senses. As an interpreter, it is your job to help us *see* the fire, *feel* the heat, *smell* the smoke, *hear* the sirens and *taste* the bile. Do everything you can to make the literature come alive in our minds. Imagine yourself experiencing all of the senses that your poems convey. If we hear you and see you experiencing them, we will experience them too.

Literary Imagery. It is mainly literary imagery, using words in a non-literal, creative manner, that sets poetry aside from prose and drama. Through literary imagery, a poet can address an abstract idea in very concrete, specific terms. Remember, if your poetry does not contain literary imagery, it is probably not worth performing. Literary imagery makes a poem fresh, vivid and more alive. Do not get bogged down by the terminology, but do get familiar with the following concepts:

Allusion. An allusion is a reference to a person, place, object or event. Often the allusion is to something historical, mythological, biblical or literary. It is for readers "in the know." The phrase, "She had a Cheshire cat-grin," alludes to Lewis Carroll's, *Alice's Adventures In Wonderland.*[2] As a performer, it is your duty to investigate any allusions in your poetry that you do not understand.

Apostrophe. An apostrophe is a direct address to an abstraction, an inanimate object, or someone who is not there. The person or object of the address is always unable to answer. In "My Lute, Awake!" Thomas Wyatt directly addresses his lute: *"Now is this song both sung and past/My lute, be still, for I have done."*[3]

---

2 Lewis Carroll, *Alice's Adventures in Wonderland* (1907; London: Chancellor Press, 1985).

3 Alexander W. Allison et al, eds., *The Norton Anthology of Poetry* 2nd ed. (New York: Notron, 1975) 117.

Hyperbole. Hyperbole is a statement of exaggeration. In her poem, "Ego Tripping," Nikki Giovanni uses hyperbole when she writes: *"The hair from my head thinned and gold was laid across three continents"*[4]

Litotes. Litotes, the opposite of hyperbole, is an understatement. If you smash your hand in a car door, but when asked if your hand hurts stoically reply, "A little," you have used litotes.

Metaphor. A metaphor compares two dissimilar things, calling them the same, to make one clearer and more vivid. Shakespeare's, "All the *world* is a *stage*," is an example of metaphor.

Simile. One of the most recognizable literary images is the simile, a comparison using *like, as* or *as if.* "The *fire* swept through the building like *lightening*," is an example of simile.

Metonymy. In metonymy, one word or abstraction is substituted for another that it suggests. "The note's signed in Frank's hand," would mean that the note is signed in Frank's handwriting.

Synecdoche. Closely related to metonymy, synecdoche uses a part to suggest the whole. When you say, "I'll lend you a hand," you mean that your whole person will help, not just your hand.

Oxymoron. An oxymoron is when opposite or contradictory terms or ideas are combined but not resolved. "Living death" and "hot ice" are oxymorons.

Paradox. Related to the oxymoron, a paradox is seemingly contradictory but nonetheless true. "Handkerchief pillow" is a paradox. A handkerchief is not a pillow, yet a young child may use a teddy bear as a handkerchief and a pillow.

Personification. Personification happens when human qualities are attributed to inanimate objects, animals or concepts. When the teddy bear is found "winking up at me," personification is being used.

Use of Sound. Besides sensory and literary imagery, use of sound is another very important aspect of poetry. Learning how to use poetry's sound can be a challenge for the interpreter, but once you have mastered it, you will have the ability to make anything sound great. Let us examine how poetry uses sound and how you, the interpreter, can make the most of it.

Onomatopoeia. Onomatopoeia refers to words that sound like their meanings. Say the words *ouch, break, toot, sizzle* and *buzz.* Do you hear how they can sound like what they refer to? When you say *buzz*, your teeth should vibrate, sounding like a bee. Making your words sound like what they are referring to is a standard technique for an interpreter. When saying the line, "She walks quietly out of the room," make the word *quietly* sound quiet. Your voice does not have to *be* quiet to *sound* quiet.

Repetition. Repeated sounds, words and lines are often used for effect in both rhymed and unrhymed poetry. Here are some tips on how to handle repetition:

---

4 Paul B. Janeczko, comp., *Poetspeak: In Their Work, About Their Work* (New York: Bradbury Press, 1983) 85.

Often a poem will repeat a line or a phrase. You have to decide why the author used repetition. In "Final Return," I repeated the line, "Daddy, don't go!" because I wanted the reader to hear the child's plea over and over. This let the reader know that the father often had to leave and that the child always hated him to go. It also contrasts with the fact that in the end it is the child who leaves. In performance, however, I would not want these repeated lines to sound the same. Most repeated phrases should go somewhere, build. The final "Daddy, don't go!" should be the most chilling. When performing repeated lines or phrases, analyze where the poem is going and then let them help you get there.

Poets use a lot of repetition of short sounds. The oral interpreter must learn to use this repetition to accentuate the beauty of the poem, while keeping the sounds under control. To practice this skill, I suggest reading aloud Dylan Thomas' "A Child's Christmas In Wales."[5] Three main types of repeated short sounds to look for are *alliteration, consonance* and *assonance*. Alliteration is the repetition of similar consonant sounds, usually at the beginning of words. "*Dirt-Dragged*" and "*Soot-Singed*" both use alliteration. Consonance also repeats similar consonant sounds, but this time they are usually internal or terminal consonants. The examples used for alliteration also have consonance. Another example is "*The tighTrope walker hopeD the neT helD tauT.*" Assonance is when similar vowel sounds are repeated. Do you hear the *ai* sound in the following lines? "*Of spit-stAIned floorboards/And fissure-vEIned walls.*" Can you also identify the use of alliteration and consonance in the preceding lines?

Rhyme. Another feature of poetic sound is rhyme. What is rhyme? "*When similar short sounds repeat line to line/The critics all proclaim it's rhyme.*" Rhyme unifies a selection, making it a cohesive whole. Contrary to popular belief, however, poetry does not have to rhyme to be poetry. Also contrary to popular belief, rhyming poetry is not taboo in forensics. In multi-piece programs, I like to hear one rhymed selection. Rhymed poetry often gets a bad rap because it often is performed poorly. Here are a few performance tips.

- Don't punch the rhyme words.
- Don't pause after every rhyme word.
- Perform with the *thought* structure in mind. (Just because a line ends does not mean the thought does. Don't automatically put pauses at the ends of poetic lines.)
- Avoid a sing-song rhythm — PLEASE! (Unless you are doing it on purpose for some special effect.)

Rhythm. All poetry has rhythm, but conventional poetry has regular rhythmic patterns. Fear of these patterns can keep you browsing through only free verse poems for your program. Do not limit yourself.

---

5 Dylan Thomas, *A Child's Christmas in Wales* (N.p.: New Directions, 1954).

Poetic rhythm is the stress or emphasis within a word or phrase. Listen to the different rhythms in the following: *can't wait, tonight, substitute, Pandora, figurative.* Each of these words has a different rhythm, a different sound pattern, a different *meter*. The ancient Greeks gave specific names to each sound pattern. The most prevalent meter is *iambic*, when an unstressed syllable is followed by a stressed syllable. The words *again, convey, forgive, instill,* and *today* are all iambic.

Each sound pattern is called a *foot*, and the number of sound patterns repeated in one line will determine the number of *feet* in a line. If there are five repetitions of the same sound pattern in a line, the term *pentameter* is used. Notice the five repetitions of the iambic sound from Shakespeare's Sonnet 18: "*shall* I *com*PARE *you* TO *a* SUM*mer's* DAY*?*"

For brevity, I have only given you one example of each of the different meters in conventional poetry. It is most important that you know that there is a deliberate, discernible structure to poetry. If you are interested in learning more about meter, I suggest you read about it in Judy Yordan's, *Roles In Interpretation* or Charlotte Lee's and Timothy Gura's, *Oral Interpretation.*[6]

Program Preparation

So now that you have all this new-found wisdom about poetry, it is time to prepare a program. Let us begin by choosing poetry, then compiling a program and, finally, rehearsing it.

Choosing Poetry. When you choose poetry for your program, it is of utmost importance that you like the selection. You will perform it much better if it appeals to your creativity and emotions. Also keep in mind that not all poetry is meant to be read aloud. If you read a poem three or four times and you are still mind-boggled, leave it on the page. You may choose to perform song lyrics, but I do not advise it. If you know the melody, it will be hard for you to get it out of your head. If we know the melody, we will want to sway to the beat even though you are not singing. If you choose to do a one-piece program, make sure the poem has enough variety to support a 8-10 minute performance. If you are new to poetry and forensics, I suggest compiling a multi-piece program, relating all of the selections to one theme. Find one lengthy poem and then look for other shorter poems to go with it. (Starting with a short poem and looking for longer poems that relate to it can be very frustrating.) To find poems that link thematically, you might want to use *The Columbia Granger's Index to Poetry*, which lists poems according to author, first line and topic. You can find this index in the reference section of all libraries.

The best places to find quality poems are in the poetry sections of a good library or bookstore. I personally like to pick a spot on the floor, get comfy and start pulling volumes. Do not expect to find the perfect poem immediately. As you may know by now, forensics is a highly

---

6 Judy Yordan, *Roles in Interpretation*, 2nd edition (Dubuque: William C. Brown, 1989); Lee and Gura.

investigative activity, and you will read a lot of poems before you find one you want to perform. You might also want to look at literature anthologies, poetry magazines, and oral interpretation textbooks for ideas.

Compiling your program. One of the most important elements you should be concerned with when compiling a poetry program is *variety.* It bothers me when I hear a multi-piece program containing all sentimental, first-person, dramatic poems. There is so much out there to choose from! Try to combine poems from different genres, looking for selections with different points of view and which emphasize different poetic features.

As with other interpretation programs, you will need an introduction that may be given either before or after a poem. You will want your introduction to grab the audience's attention, discuss the theme of your selection(s), and state the author and title of the following poem (and the preceding poem if you open your program with a short poem to "tease" the audience). Usually poetry does not need any character or location set-up, but if you are doing an *author study,* a collection of poems by one author on one theme, you might give us some information about the particular poet. You may use transitions between your poems or splice them together for a MTV collage effect.

Because poetry is such a concise, intense form, every word a poet chooses has a purpose. *Do not edit poetry!* If you do, you will be messing with the poem's cohesive integrity. The only poetry you should cut, if you really need to reduce its length, is poetry written in stanzas. Edit *whole* stanzas, and be careful not to disrupt any rhyme scheme the poem may have.

You may want to mark up the script you will be performing from, highlighting important words to emphasize or using stress marks to help you with the poem's rhythm. You may also be tempted to write your poems out in paragraph form. If you need to do this to help you learn the poem, fine, but please do not perform from a script written in this manner. Challenge yourself. Learn to read a poem in its original structure. You may find it awkward at first, but in no time you will be a pro. Besides, you may have a judge who wants to see the poem on paper as well as hear you interpret it.

Rehearsing your program. When rehearsing your poetry, make sure you make good use of all the oral interpretation techniques. Use off-stage, internal and audience focus when appropriate. Use the sounds of the words for their greatest impact. Visualize the images in your poems — they are usually abundant.

I suggest listening to a taped recording of your poems while driving in your car, getting ready for school . . . whenever. Some people like to type or write their poems over and over to learn them. Whatever memorization method you choose, it is best to memorize over a long period of time. Practicing one hour a day for five days is more effective than practicing for five straight hours. To truly give the best performance possible, you need to have your poems well rehearsed.

Conclusion

The art of poetry interpretation is a very special skill to acquire. Poetry's magical use of sound and rhythm offer the interpreter a chance to become truly in tune with language and the voice's ability to handle it. Becoming skilled at poetry interpretation will help you become the very best interpreter you can be.

The time is here
Go forth and search
For what you find
May show in you
    So defined
    So refined
A gift
You'll travel with
Forever

Prose Interpretation in Intercollegiate Forensics

Janene Whitesell

In attempting to define Prose Interpretation, I frequently start with what is *not* prose. The explanation goes something like this: If it appears "stylized" on a page (e.g., not in standard paragraph form), or if character names are punctuated by a colon (Mary: or Father:) and action is described between parentheses (she moves toward the table), it is *NOT* prose. Otherwise, literature is prose. The American Forensic Association national tournament rules specifically prohibit play cuttings and poetry, but refer to acceptable literature merely as "prose material." The National Forensic Association national tournament rules are similar, using the phrase "program of prose literature" to describe the literature used in this event. Phi Rho Pi describes the material simply as "literature printed mainly in paragraph form." Thus, textbooks are prose, as are diaries, newspapers, biographies, essays, short stories and novels. Plays, and scripts for photoplays, radio plays, and teleplays are not prose. Poems are not prose.

Prose is a general label for a genre of literature which can be divided into two sub-categories. *Fiction* is "narrative literature that creates an imaginary reality in the form of a story written in sentences and paragraphs with no strong rhythmic base. . . ."[1] *Non-fiction* literature involves "works of fact or theory. . . ."[2] Perhaps an easier clue to distinguishing between fiction and non-fiction is to keep in mind that works of fiction are essentially not real-life occurrences — Stephen King's *Christine*, for example. Non-fiction works are based on real-life accounts — Jonathan Kozol's "Rachel and Her Children," for example.

Preparing Your Program

Step One: Selecting your literature. This is probably the most difficult task for a student or coach. Questions such as, "Has this been performed before?" or "Is this a winning piece?" or "Is this quality literature?" tend to get in the way of choosing pieces. The first rule of thumb is to read . . . read . . . read! Short story anthologies and collections of larger literary works are standard places to start. Smaller anthologies, such as *Stories by Latin American Women* and *Canadian Writers*, should not be overlooked. Similarly, autobiographies and works about contemporary issues can focus on specific experiences.

Professor Whitesell is currently Director of Forensics at Solano Community College.

1 Judy E. Yordon, *Roles in Interpretation*, 2nd ed. (Dubuque, Iowa: William C. Brown, 1982) 44.

2 Yordon 44.

The second rule of thumb is to *choose something you really like.* I say this for two reasons. First, you have to "live with the piece." If you dislike a piece, or perform it merely because you think it will "win," you probably will become bored with the selection. Second, as with relationships, you will continually discover new things about the piece (and about yourself) if you genuinely *like* the content, the writer, or the writing style.

Step Two: Analyzing your selections. The analysis of a selection is an important step prior to the performance. Listed below are the main concerns facing you in Prose Interpretation:

Point of view. The narrator is the central character is a story, and generally relates events that happened in the past. Since narrators are the connection between the audience and the text, it is important to understand their point of view. In *first-person* point of view, the narrator uses the pronoun "I" to tell the story. Thus, first-person narrators are rarely objective when telling a story, and the narration sounds much like a monologue in a play. In *second-person* point of view, the narrator used the pronoun "you" to tell the story. The most common point of view is *third-person*, in which the narrator uses "he" or "she" to identify the central character. Some third-person narrators describe the thoughts and feelings of a character, and are considered *omniscient.* Other narrators, called *observers*, are more removed from the scene and never enter the minds of the characters. What is most important to keep in mind about narrators is that, regardless of point of view, every narrator has a personality and lets the audience know *how they feel about the story they are telling.* The following example illustrates the various points of view:

> As I walked into the cemetery the air became still and cool and the birds stopped their chatter. The sudden silence unnerved me, and the chill in the air was out of place for the blow-dryer conditions that prevailed in May *(first-person).*
>
> As you walk into the cemetery the air becomes still and cool and the birds stop their chatter. The sudden silence unnerves you, and the air is out of place for the blow-dryer conditions that prevail in May *(second-person).*
>
> As Jan walked into the cemetery, the air became cool and still and the birds stopped their chatter. The sudden chatter unnerved her and the chill was out of place for the blow-dryer conditions that prevailed in May *(third-person omniscient).*
>
> As Jan walked into the cemetery, the air became still and cool and the birds stopped their chatter. The chill in the air was out of place for the blow-dryer conditions that prevailed in May *(third-person observer).*

Rhythm. Selections from plays have one speed — dialogue. Prose selections have three speeds — description, dialogue and summary. Distinguishing between rhythms is important because it gives clues on what the narrator feels is important in the story. *Description* is the slowest-moving rhythm because of the detail involved. For example, if a selection takes several paragraphs to describe a baby, the description would take longer than actually looking at the baby. In this sense, "story time" is slower than "real time." *Dialogue* is considered an average speed rhythm since story time is equal to real time. If a character in a story said "Get out of here," the dialogue would take the same amount of time as it would take to actually say "Get out of here." *Summary* is the fastest moving rhythm. For example, in real time it might take a character an hour to get ready for a date, while the narrator could summarize it in one or two sentences. When narrators summarize, story time can be much faster than real time.

Imagery and visualization. Imagery involves phrases which affect your senses in a way which elicits internal or external responses. Visualization involves recalling those images in performance. Narrators and characters can recall images they say, heard, felt, tasted or smelled. Consider the following passage: "Jan noticed that her footfalls made no sound (*hearing*), yet she could feel (*feeling*) the ground underneath her — the swirling softness of the grass cushioning her walk (*seeing and feeling*). What makes a performance powerful is the ability to recreate those images for the audience so they also can see, hear, feel, touch and taste for themselves.

Step Three: Editing your program. Few prose selections can be performed in their entirety, so the next step is to edit the material. Two general guidelines should be followed: First, stay consistent with the "author's intent." In other words, you do not want to change the meaning of the literature by the way you edit it. Second, edit content that does not seem to be an integral part of the theme. There are two general guidelines for editing most literature. Here are some specific recommendations for prose fiction:

Edit tag lines. After establishing who is speaking, lines like "he said" are not important for the audience. You can indicate who is speaking through posture and focus. In addition, emotions such as "she said angrily" can be suggested through tone of voice, facial expression and posture.

Edit excessive description. While description provides an excellent opportunity to display sensory images, it is the slowest-moving style of writing. Just as a platform speaker needs to weigh the worth of a story in a speech, you need to weigh the impact of the description versus the time it takes to perform it. In addition, the beginnings of prose selections often contain insignificant expository material which can be edited out. If the exposition helps to set the scene, refer to in your introduction.

Edit unnecessary dialogue. When people speak in "real-life," they frequently discuss several topics at the same time. In an 8-10 minute selection, you may not have that luxury. Dialogue can be "streamlined" by editing repetitions of certain lines and unnecessary interjections such as "Can I get you more coffee?" Keep in mind that dialogue can be edited as long as the repetitions and interjections are not important to the theme or the flow of the material.

Edit unnecessary characters. If you feel that a character is not important to the theme, the character and his or her lines may be edited. The questions to ask are "Have I changed the author's intent?" and "Does the *theme* remain intact?"

Editing non-fiction is somewhat different, since there may or may not be characters, and may or may not be dialogue. Generally speaking, edit non-fiction by cutting unnecessary description, and eliminating inconsequential episodes *in their entirety.* When a selection is unified and its theme is clear without an episode, it may be cut. Diaries, for example, could have certain dates cut out without affecting the author's intent.

Step Four: Preparing your introduction. The need for an introduction and transitions is one of the reasons why oral interpretation is a public speaking activity rather than a form of acting. When you perform a selection, the audience needs to know why the piece is being performed and how it relates to them. The following should ordinarily be included in an introduction:

Title and author. The audience needs to know what is being performed and who wrote it.

Orientation to plot or upcoming scene. This is especially important when a performer does not start with the beginning of the story. When the action or setting is not self-explanatory, the audience will feel as if they "walked into the middle of something."

Personal application. The audience might ask "Why should I be listening to this?" You should consider why the literature is relevant to the audience and try to relate it to them.

Theme. Themes are based on the subject matter of the literature, and answer the question, "What is the literature saying?" It is important to read the *entire* selection before considering this question. Themes such as love, death and war are standard themes in writing, but are overused and vague when used in performance. It is best to take the theme further and look for a new angle. Less common, but equally challenging, are themes focusing on the author. In this approach, you focus on what an author feels or how the author is unique in expressing these feelings. For example, you could analyze how Stephen King expresses the torments of childhood by reading selections from *Carrie, Christine* and *It.*

The following is an example of a poor introduction. Notice how it fails to give the audience necessary information or create any sense of "urgency" for listening to the selection.

> We've all been depressed. Today I'm going to read a cutting from a John Steinbeck novel. The story is about a family during the depression that moves to California. The grandmother dies in the truck. Rosa-Sharon, who is pregnant, is deserted by her husband. Their travels are full of turmoil and stress.

The title of the selection is missing from this introduction. While there is a quick reference to a theme and to common experience, it could be much stronger. Too much of the plot is discussed, and the introduction contains extraneous description. Now consider an improved version of the same introduction.

> What would you do if you lost your job? What would you do if you were evicted from your apartment or lost your house? If you're like most of us, you'd probably do what it would take to survive. It is this desire to survive that keeps us going, and it is in times of crisis that we discover how strong we really are. Historically, there have been times when entire nations have had to rely on this inner strength. Our time came in the 1930s during the Great Depression. Let me introduce you to one family that rallied together and did whatever it took to survive. *The Grapes of Wrath* by John Steinbeck.

Not only is the improved introduction more informative, it is more compelling. An audience listening to this version of the introduction is far more likely to sense that they are interested in the performance which is about to follow.

Rehearsing Your Program

You may be asking "Isn't it like acting if I rehearse my performance?" No, it is not. Most of us have had the unpleasant task of being called upon to read a Shakespearian sonnet to an audience. This kind of "cold" reading involves recitation, not oral interpretation. Oral interpretation *feels like acting* since both the actor and the interpreter need to rehearse their material. A comprehensive rehearsal includes working on both the vocal and physical dimensions of a performance.

Vocal suggestion. Vocal aspects of a performance include vocal quality, volume, pitch and rate. Performers must make decisions regarding the vocal qualities of the narrator as well as those of the characters. Several guidelines should be kept in mind. First, avoid impersonations of the author. A common question asked by students is "Do I have to *sound* like Mark Twain when I read his work?" Definitely not. In fact, for many judges, the impersonation gets in the way of the overall performance. Second, attempt dialects *only* if you are proficient with them. You can interpret dialogue of regional or ethnic characters without sounding like them.

Physical suggestion. While forensics judges in some regions tend to downplay the role of the body in characterization, most judges recognize the need to project the physical qualities of the narrator and characters. While the importance of projecting physical qualities of characters in the literature should be obvious, many interpreters feel that the narrator is a boring, non-feeling person who speaks when the characters are not speaking. This is not the case. The narrator is the storyteller, and just as we get excited or angry when recounting events of the day, narrators have feelings about the stories they tell. In terms of physical suggestion, you need to decide how old the narrator is, whether the narrator is male or female, and how recently the described events took place. For example, a narrator who is older might gesture differently when reflecting on childhood events than a younger narrator retelling the events of the previous day. Some authors create narrators who are very involved with the story. Others create narrators who are somewhat removed from the experience. This distinction will influence the physical involvement on the part of the interpreter.

Character placement. During a performance, an interpreter may be speaking directly to an audience. This is called *open focus* and is used by first-person narrators. At other times, a narrator or a character might be reflecting on some experience and not talking directly to anyone or talking to an inanimate object. This is called *inner-closed* or *semi-closed* focus. Finally, there is *closed focus*, when characters talk directly to each other. The performer needs to suggest that more than one character is speaking and keep those characters distinct from one another. While voice and body can clarify the differences, character placement maintains the distinction.

This is a difficult technique which requires much practice. Judy Yordon lists several factors to remember when placing characters.[3]

- Imagine that your characters are out in the audience, just above eye level. Raise or lower placement when characters are not on the same level.
- In general, place the most important character in the center and less important characters to the sides. When there are only two characters in a scene, place them left and right of center.
- If you use a script, glance down at it while a character is speaking and not during shifts between characters. Avoid pregnant pauses between speeches as you search to find the next line.
- Keep the silent characters alive with appropriate reactions in the voice and body of the speaking character. If the speaker says, "Sit down and hand me the telephone," have the speaking character watch the silent character sit and then reach out to accept the telephone.
- Do not consistently stare at a fixed spot. Establish the speaking character's placement as the line begins and ends, but feel free to glance about naturally in between.
- Place characters according to speakers rather than listeners. If there are forty characters in your scene, but only three characters speak, you need only three placements.
- Do not give narrators placement unless they speak dialogue. Since narrators are usually speaking to the audience and not to characters, their focus is open and no placement is necessary.
- Once you have placed a character in a certain spot, keep the character in that same spot regardless of time or place shifts, and regardless of whom the character is addressing.
- Be wary of placing characters too far apart so that there is no dead space as you move from one speaking character to another. Place characters primarily with your eyes, not with large distracting movements of your head or body.

Ten Tips for Successful Prose Interpretation

1. **Think twice about stories that have been made into great movies.** If you perform *Gone With The Wind*, for example, you run the risk of competing (in the judge's mind) against famous actors. This may be a burden that you do not want. From another point of view, do you think a judge would not think about Joe Foster's interpretation of Detective Starling in *Silence of the Lambs*? While I would not automatically discard this literature, I would think about *why* I had chosen it.

---

3 Yordon 117.

2. Think twice about "pop" authors. Stephen King, Danielle Steele and Sydney Sheldon certain write popular books, but some judges carry preconceived ideas about literary quality. Again, do not automatically discard works by popular authors, but think of how they will compare with works by authors like Alice Walker, Virginia Woolfe and Mark Twain.

3. With non-fiction, think about the content. It is often trendy to perform graphic cuttings about issues such as the Vietnam War, abortion or child abuse. While these issues are topical, graphic material can be too uncomfortable for audiences and judges. Think about *why* you are drawn to material which is graphic or contains profanity. If your purpose is to shock, you can bet that someone else already thought of it.

4. Look for good beginning points and ending points. Sometimes stories and non-fiction pieces have two or more endings, depending on the length and plots. As you read through a piece, ask yourself the question, "Can I effectively begin/end my performance here?"

5. Edit backwards. This is a technique which I teach to my students. Start at the end of the selection and edit out lines. Then move to the middle, then to the beginning. Most people, as they go along, become more comfortable with the editing process and edit larger chunks at a time. As stated earlier, there is more exposition at the beginning. When you edit in reverse, it is not nearly so painful to edit out the excess exposition.

6. Consider editing excessive profanity. A "shit" or two probably will not cause a stir, but frequently used, they inhibit a judge's appreciation of the piece. While it would be ludicrous to have a serial killer saying "darn" or "shoot," most characters can have their profane expressions modified or cut completely.

7. Avoid impersonations. The interpretation of a narrator should be unique to the person performing the material. Unlike dramatic characters, there is no description of the physical and vocal qualities of the narrator.

8. Avoid "false" voices. Males performing female lines should not raise their pitch artificially; females performing male lines should not lower their pitch artificially. It is possible to suggest gender differences through physical stance, vocal rate and general attitude. A male performer can suggest femininity without "acting girlish." It would be distracting, for example, to listen to a male performer read excerpts from *The Diary of Anne Frank* in falsetto.

9. Do not throw away narration or description. Frequently, performers feel that the impact lies in the characters' lines. However, there is also impact in describing a tractor destroying a house (John Steinbeck's *Grapes of Wrath*) or a skinned horse (Wallace Stegner's *Town Dump*).

10. Be innovative in your introduction. This is the time to display your own personality and unique writing style. Just as a platform speaker needs to grab an audience in the introduction, you need to get an audience's attention.

Program (Mixed Genre) Oral Interpretation

Jan McKissick

For a number of years, the American Forensic Association National Individual Events Tournament offered an experimental event called Program Oral Interpretation, a mixed genre interpretation event requiring you to perform literature from more than one literary genre (i.e., prose and poetry, poetry and drama, etc.). While this has become a standard AFA event, seeing a mixed genre interpretation event labeled "experimental" was a bit ironic to those of us who remember when such events were the only interpretation events around. On the other hand, it is nice to see that this kind of challenge has made a comeback on the four-year competitive circuit. (For some time, the Phi Rho Pi national tournament has offered the event under the name Oral Interpretation of Literature.) I say the event is a challenge because constructing a mixed genre program is just that — challenging and difficult. But, while two (or more) selections from two (or more) different genres may double (or triple) how hard you must work and what you risk, such a program also has double (or triple) the potential for success. Judges readily reward the program which can show not only interpretative ability but virtuosity, literary insight and creativity.

Constructing a Mixed Genre Program

Mixed genre interpretation requires that your material must be drawn from at least two distinct genres of literature. That is, one of the selections cannot be merely a portion of the other longer selection (e.g., a poem included in a short story and which appears only in that short story would not be a different genre).

In order to prepare a successful mixed genre program, you must consider a number of issues — theme, balance, choosing your material, order and placement of your selections, and introductions, transitions, and conclusions.

Tournament event rules generally require that your selections develop a theme. Although the rules from some invitational tournaments may fail to mention requiring a theme, it would be a mistake to think it is not a consideration. Avoid themes which are trite ("relationships"), vague ("love," "war," "peace in our time"), or overly simple ("food"). Strive for the unique or intriguing. Some programs which have done well in recent years include "Coming of Age," "Taking Risks" and "Flights of Fancy." More often than not, however, selecting your theme does not come first. It is more likely that you will find a particular piece of literature that you like, and will then be faced with finding another selection to match to it. This may mean long hours spent in the literature section of your library pouring through anthologies. Here, too, is where a

---

Professor McKissick is currently Director of Forensics at Butte College.

major thematic problem arises. Too many interpreters succumb to the temptation to *stretch* the theme of a particular piece to make it fit. (Like pairing Tennessee Williams' *A Streetcar Named Desire* with "Clang, Clang, Clang Went the Trolley" from *Meet Me In St. Louis*, for a program about *Trolleys*. Stretching a point? You'd be surprised!) Be sure when you are using a selection to illustrate a theme, that it is a major, not a minor, thematic element in the literature.

A second consideration of the mixed genre program is balance — of time, emotion, and strength or quality of the pieces. Balanced time simply means choosing selections which are approximately the same length. AFA rules require that "a substantial portion of the total time" be devoted to each selection. Although the Phi Rho Pi rules do not mention balance explicitly, you most likely will be penalized if one selection is eight minutes long and the other is a minute and a half. It is a substantial challenge to successfully cut two, and possibly three, pieces of literature into chunks of three to four minutes while maintaining all those literary elements that made the pieces desirable in the first place.

Balanced emotion means striving for a mix of emotional tones. If all of the pieces are too similar in this aspect, you create a couple of problems. Sustaining too narrow a range of emotions for ten minutes (e.g., jealousy and anger), can be tiring for both you and audience. In other words, two pieces which are too much alike are as troublesome as two pieces which are thematically mismatched. Also, if you create a program with a narrow range of emotion, you demonstrate no virtuosity.

Balancing the strength or quality of your material simply means choosing pieces that can hold their own in contrast to one another. A program made up of one very strong piece and one relatively weak one will feel unbalanced, and thus be less effective than a program in which the pieces are matched in strength and quality.

In selecting pieces for mixed genre programs, it is especially important that each cutting have a feeling of completeness. Be careful of cuttings which leave out too much essential information, or must be "butchered" to fit a particular time frame. In addition, *always* take selections from primary sources. A number of programs in recent years have been disqualified (or have come dangerously close) because a selection taken from a secondary source seemed to be prose, but turned out to be a play in paragraph form. Using primary sources in interpretation is every bit as important as it is in public speaking or the debate events.

Having selected and cut your material, you now must consider carefully how you will place the pieces in your program. Compare and contrast emotional tone and thematic elements to decide on the best arrangement. Consider where you want your program to begin and end emotionally (angry? happy? on a note of suspense? or fear?). Consider also whether the theme may require a definite ordering of the pieces to insure logical progression.

Introductions, transitions, and conclusions(should you choose to use a conclusion) are truly "the tie that binds" a mixed genre program. When you are linking pieces thematically, it is vitally important that the connections be clear and easy to follow. T is not the time for abstraction.

The introduction is where you begin your thematic development. Take time to fully present the theme. A rushed or overly brief introduction may mean important elements are missed by the program forward thematically and provide necessary information for a new piece of literature (setting, character, title, author, etc.), and yet you must be careful not to break the mood or overpower the literature just done or about to come.

Conclusions, as a rule rare in interpretation events, are sometimes appropriate. Carefully consider whether you want to "tie up" the theme with your words, or let the literature stand on its own with the author's words.

Conclusion

Mixed genre interpretation events present you with a unique opportunity to demonstrate your interpretation skills. Constructing a successful mixed genre program requires that you understand how to connect pieces of disparate literature into a cohesive, balanced arrangement of literary materials which sustain a particular theme. While putting such a program together is a substantially greater undertaking than selecting a cutting from a single piece of literature, the personal reward for having met the challenge makes the event worth the effort.

Readers Theatre
Patti Keeling

A few years ago, I was asked to write an article for a Southern California publication about Readers Theatre (sometimes called Chamber Reading or Interpreters' Theatre). In this article, I referred to such dramatic presentation as the "bastard child" of theatre, and indeed the history of Readers Theatre supports this view. Modern theatre, with the advent of the proscenium arch, decided long ago that the audience might observe, but certainly never participate, in the theatrical process. Thus, the Greek tradition, which really gave us Readers Theatre with its appreciation of audience participation, was abandoned. It wasn't until this century that there was a resurgence of interest in the audience as participants in the theatrical process, and in theatre of the voice in general. Certainly, Dylan Thomas' "Under Milkwood" debut on Broadway and, more recently, the advent of one-person shows and thrust stages, shows that the tide has been steadily shifting.

This is not intended as a lesson in theatre history, but rather as a way to set up a solid definition of Readers Theatre. It is a theatrical art form in which the audience must use its imagination, must not be afraid to share emotion, and must be actively involved. That is about as good a definition as I can come up with. Is that it? No discussion of scripts? Time limits? Blocking? Focus? I will discuss those elements, but they are not really the things that *define* the event. They are only prescriptions given to an already existing art form for the purpose of competitive unity. And I think it is crucial to always remember that this is a legitimate theatrical form; it was not created by the forensics community. Consequently, Readers Theatre should do what all good theatre does — change the audience's perception for a period of time.

With that in mind, how do you keep your artistic ego intact and still survive competition? Unfortunately, there are not three easy lessons for success. but I do think there are three crucial areas that need discussing: scripts, staging and focus (and I've thrown in some extras for good measures).

Scripting for Readers Theatre

The best scripts, in terms of success in competition, follow the traditional dramatic concepts of *balance* and *unity,* and generally take one of three forms: *compilations, single story/drama adaptations*, and *original scripts*. In drama, balance means the distribution of emotional peaks, character development, motivation, etc. In other words, all the elements in a script that grasp and hold our attention coming together in a unified fashion. The same holds true for Readers Theatre; it must have peaks and valleys, motivation, unity and an overall sense of balance. Bal-

---

Professor Keeling is a former Director of Forensics at Chabot College.

ance might be even more essential to this form of theatre given the event's twenty-five minute time limit. Remember, it takes a hardy soul to handle twenty-five minutes of pathos. By the same token, continuous laugh lines make one suspect that there is not much depth. Now let us look at the various kinds of scripting:

Single Story/Drama Adaptation. In selecting a single work for adaptation, you must consider several factors:

Can it be done effectively within the time limit and in the acting area provided? The question of time is always a problem and there are obvious shows that will never be adapted to this medium because of it (shows, for example, that are dependent on complex psychological development, such as *Cat on A Hot Tin Roof,* or most of the prose of John Fowles). These works need much more time to develop the themes and characters that make them so special to begin.

In some cases, however, scenes or episodes from single works can be used effectively. I had success with a cutting from Michael Lynch's *Sister Gloria's Pentecostal Baby,* by selecting only the scenes that could stand by themselves, and by limiting the main character's point of view. In *Sister Gloria's* case, the mother's obsession with her son becoming a leader in the Pentecostal church is what I chose to emphasize. I have also seen treatments of D. H. Lawrence's mammoth short story, "Rocking Horse Winner," in which different characters were chosen to tell the story, and yet Lawrence's overall point of view regarding human greed remained intact. Another excellent example was an adaptation of "A Rose For Emily" performed by students from Diablo Valley College. The story was cut to a reasonable a length, yet Faulkner's narrative was beautifully preserved.

The acting area provided at most competitions is not conducive to a show with a large cast or large set pieces. Keep in mind that most of the time you will be competing in classrooms, and for community college theatres, even hotel rooms at the state and national tournaments. I saw an attempt to do the Broadway show, *Barnum* at a national tournament a few years ago, as well as a hard-rock version of *Wings*. Both had very talented performers, but were doomed by being entirely too big for the acting area.

Do you have the talent available to produce the show? When I first started to direct Readers Theatre, I had a show I desperately wanted to do. It was terribly miscast and, consequently, never enjoyed the success the script deserved. It is very hard to want to do a show and not have the right talent, but sometimes you have to wait until the right actors show up. Face it, *Amadeus* wouldn't be much without a pretty hot musician or two.

Is there an even distribution of lines for the characters? Granted, there is usually a features protagonist in a single work, but certainly the supporting cast must have enough to do, or the script will seem terribly unbalanced. This does not mean that you should count lines to make sure everything is evenly distributed, but if there is a balance problem in the script, you had best be prepared as a director to do something creative to fix it. Sometimes it is simply a problem of keeping everyone involved even when they have no speaking lines. This can be achieved through focus or facial response. In my theatre, "Scoundrel Time," there was a long scene in the courtroom where only the Lillian Hellman and Joseph McCarthy characters had lines, but the presence of the entire cast and their responses was essential in making the scene work. It was not until the cast committed themselves to the characters of courtroom observers that the scene actually worked (and comments regarding balance disappeared from the ballots).

Another technique is to use your players to create atmosphere. I incorporate this even in scripts that are well-balanced, mainly because I am not particularly fond of backs to the audience or bowed heads to indicate performers are "out of character." I prefer freezes, where you can create the effect of suspended action rather than stopped action. Another technique is simultaneous scene action, where background characters continue a voice-under conversation, giving the illusion of continued action.

Compilations. John Lennon said it best, "Imagine." Imagine a show that can teach, illustrate, argue, indict, praise, or all of these things, with a clear rhetorical point. Imagine using literature to provide dramatic commentary on (to list just a few):

- Justice
- History
- AIDS
- Family unity
- Admirable people
- Political issues
- Significant social events
- Solutions to world problems

Then imagine having all the ideas and the expression of those ideas available for you to weave into a tapestry of dramatic life. That is what is so exciting about a compilation script.

For me, compilation theatres give a truly creative challenge. To a degree, it is more problematic in terms of unifying all the selections — the range of material to choose from is mind-boggling: poetry, drama, songs, prose, dance. But, creatively speaking, you get the best of all worlds. And, *you* are in control of expressing a point of view.

After you have thought about a theme for your theatre, the problem is how to compile the material. Here are some guidelines:

Ask yourself, "What's the point?" Does your idea have integrity? Is it truly relevant to the audience, or is it trite or patronizing? Have you chosen "quality" literature? There is a lot of literary distance between Lillian Hellman and Erma Bombeck, which is not meant to imply that they might not work beautifully separately. But in choosing material for a compilation, choose the author who not only best supports your theme, but who also says it best.

Do all the selections work together to unify the theme? I have, for example, sat in rounds listening to beautiful singers, wondering what their songs had to do with the theatre as a whole. Do not get me wrong, I love music in theatre — when it is properly integrated. The same holds true for poetry, scenes from plays, whatever you choose — they must all work together. Unity, however, does not mean repetition. Many scenes seem to say the same thing over and over without varying perspectives. Consequently, the action of the theatre stops.

How do you compile the script? It is never easy and again, there are no hard, fast rules. I have had success using poetry as a framework ("Storms Begin Far Back" and "Walking To Sleep" come to mind). A poem, or portions of a poem, can provide a compelling way of introducing the theme, as well as effective transitional material. The same effect can be achieved by "weaving" portions of a play throughout the script. The 1988 Huffer-Goldman winner, "Rhythm of Life," used scenes from "Tambourines For Glory," by Langston Hughes, to focus on religious exploitation. "And Justice For All," a stunning production performed by students from Mt. San Antonio College, threaded the compelling story of a man wrongly accused of a crime throughout a biting look at American justice. Songs can also be used in this manner and, of course, cast members simply narrating their perspectives also works well.

Transitions come easier if you first decide how you are going to arrange the material. Once I have collected all the pieces I want to use, I try to structure the script like a novel — it is very rare for a novel to start with the dramatic climax. I tend to put the more powerful pieces toward the middle or the last of the show, because I feel this gives the theatre forward energy.

Original Scripts. This encompasses a whole additional creative area — the world of creative writing. I think good writing is governed by specific rules and techniques that are outside the scope of this article. I do feel, however, that until you master some of the more traditional methods of scripting Readers Theatre, you should wait before attempting an original script. There are, of course, always exceptions and my hat is off to them.

Staging Readers Theatre

Along with speaking the first four words, most performers would agree that getting on the stage is the hardest thing they do. Entrances are especially problematic in Readers Theatre since performers have no wings to hide in, or proscenium to hide behind. One way to make your entrances effective is to integrate them somehow into the action of the show. I felt this was beautifully achieved by a theatre performed by students from San Francisco State University, "What Have You Got To Lose?" The song they used to enter from the audience was clever, fun and relevant to the show, and it immediately captured the audience's attention. Likewise, a show I directed a few years ago, "Voices of the Other World," used the characters Zeus and Hera to "summon" the other players from the audience to the stage. In the show "Vote for Me," all the actors entered from the audience carrying ladders and stools and actually set-up the "campaign headquarters" in which the majority of the show took place.

Entering the acting area as a cast before starting the actual performance is traditional and acceptable, but make sure your entrance is polished. Staging is where judges really look for technical expertise, so concentrate on a unified look and be aware of good script management.

Generally speaking, scripts should open and close together or at least in some organized fashion. Scripts, while they certainly don't "define" Readers Theatre, are an expected part of competitive theatre. I suppose this is something we can all live with, but I think while living with it, we should also work toward either making the script as unobtrusive as possible or, conversely, as integrated as possible. Overall, the cast should work toward smooth and controlled script management.

Set blocks can be the key to effective staging. The kinds of creative set pieces used in the last few years have really lessened the problems blocking used to pose. The witness stand designed for "Scoundrel Time" is an excellent example of how a set block can take on symbolic importance for the entire show. Blocks can become boats, or mountains, or buses, or just about anything your imagination can see them be. Stools, music stands, ladders, stairs, risers — all are simple but effective aids to creative blocking. Blocks, like traditional set pieces, can enhance the artistic look of your show. Gone are the days of four black stools, or even plain black blocks. Set pieces can "house" important theatrical elements of your show. In "The Photo Album," a theatre performed by students from Las Positas College, blocks were constructed with beveled edges that later were removed to become picture frames which the actors used in various and creative ways throughout the show. From a practical point of view, use set pieces that the cast can carry easily, and that will stack to make various shapes and levels.

It is almost impossible to write about how to block a theatre because every script calls for a different look. I also think anyone attempting to direct a theatre should have at least some basic knowledge of stage movement (power positions, problems with upstaging, etc.). Here are a few basics to remember:

Keep in mind at all times the overall look of your theatre. Does the stage look balanced? Are subordinate characters placed properly? Is anyone "pulling focus" (calling attention to themselves at inappropriate moments)?

Make sure that the movement onstage is motivated by the literature. Remember, the spoken word is the thing in theatre of the voice, so do not be tempted to rely on too much gimmickry. On the other hand, a little choreography and visual razzle-dazzle is fine, if it enhances the message and the audience's pleasure.

Does the blocking make good dramatic sense? For example, does the proximity of the characters to each other create the necessary kind of tension needed for a dramatic scene? An intimate scene? A power struggle? Think for a moment how you would stage moments like these. A scene involving intense anger, for example, might best be served with both characters downstage a bit using crossed focus to further enhance the tension. Intimate scenes might play nicely with some "onstage" moments.

As a beginning directors, you usually have only your intuition to depend upon. Take heart, we all started at that point, and that which is thoughtfully intuited usually turns out right.

Focus

Trying to explain how focus works is like trying to teach someone to swim without a swimming pool. Still, it is such a crucial part of Readers Theatre that I have to touch upon it as best I can.

Remember the role the audience plays in Readers Theatre. The choices and uses of focus probably emphasize audience involvement more than any other aspect of Readers Theatre. Open general focus, when the audience is directly addressed by the performer, illustrates the intimacy and imagination inherent in this form of theatre. Offstage focus depends entirely on the audience's imaginative involvement, as it literally creates an acting area in the minds of the audience. While these are traditionally the predominant focuses used, I think there are moments when onstage focus is also necessary. Onstage focus enhances moments of intimacy, for example, much like an onstage touch does. Many judges see the use of onstage focus as a breach of Readers Theatre criteria. Nonsense. If the audience is still intimately involved, if onstage focus is crucial to the scene (providing the entire show is not done with onstage focus), there is no earthly reason why it should not be used. I particularly like theatres that incorporate a variety of focuses, because each type produces an entirely unique dramatic effect, and each demands something different from the audience.

One of the major problems performers have in Readers Theatre is holding focus. Once committed to an offstage focal point, sustaining it is everything (especially in a scene involving dialogue). If you break focus, looking down at your script for example, the entire illusion is destroyed. This also applies to reading along when you are not directly involved in the scene; it not only looks sloppy but it also can pull focus from the main scene. Learning to deal with offstage focus and the problems it presents can only come with practice. I often encourage my students to work with mirrors in order to perfect their focus (which also works well for practicing facial responses).

Random Thoughts

With a wonderful script, a talented cast and a sound staging plan, there is not much else a beginning director should need. However, there are a couple of loose ends I would like to touch upon. One involves costuming. Ensemble costuming has long been permissible in Readers Theatre, and yet I am amazed at the teams that show up for rounds looking like they're dressed for a flea market. I do not think it is necessary to spend a fortune on costumes (most teams could come up with a unified look out of their own closets), but do I think it is necessary to have an overall, pulled-together look to your show. As communication students, you all know the importance of first impressions. Your theatre should provide an impression of unity and of pride in your production. Ensemble dress often is visually enhancing to the whole presentation. "The Victorians," performed by students from Santa Rosa Junior College, had a stylish look that transported the audience back a hundred years. The parochial school outfits of "Growing Up

Catholic," performed by students from Diablo Valley College, and the sweet dream pastels of my own theatre, "Walking to Sleep," each incorporated an ensemble look that supported the overall aura of the theatre.

Keep in mind that Readers Theatre isn't easy — successful theatres require hours of rehearsal, patience, energy, commitment, and confident, competent direction. Nothing can guarantee a "winning" theatre. Sometimes you just have to be satisfied with a job well done and wait till next year. Still, it would be nice to peek into the minds of real live forensic judges and find out exactly what they look for. Since this article is based on my perspective and my opinion, you already have a good idea what I look for. But, I do not propose to have all the answers, however. So, I asked some of my colleagues to identify briefly what they look for when they judge rounds of competition. From Bill Poschman, Diablo Valley College:

> I look for the following: A script that is coherent, has continuity and contains quality material; direction that reflects energy and imagination; breaking new ground as opposed to repeating the same old formula; performers who read intelligently and with emotional commitment.

From Susan Stathas Houlihan, Santa Rosa Junior College:

> There are four general areas that I examine when judging Readers Theatre: Script, Interpretation, Blocking, and Stylistic Unity. The following questions are a few that I ask about these aspects as criteria for judgment: Does the script possess a clear sense of dramatic shape? Are parts equally balanced among the readers? Are interpretation techniques used unique and/or traditional to Readers Theatre (i.e. choral reading)? Is blocking imaginative, fluid, and exhibiting a sense of symmetry, depth, and height? Do movements, set pieces, and costuming blend for a unified thematic and visual effect?

And, from Janet Brehe, Las Positas College:

> When I have the happy privilege of judging a Reader's Theatre round, I look for a script that is intelligent, cohesive and creative, one that somehow touches or moves me, whether to laughter or tears, without being overtly manipulative. I look for a cast that works as a unified team, is technically sharp and, above all, knows how to bring literature to life through oral interpretation. Finally, I look for imaginative blocking that used the literature and performers to their fullest creative potential.

Let me conclude by saying that nobody has all the answers, nor is there any guaranteed formula for success in competitive Readers Theatre. However, closely looking at some of the expectations that the forensics community has for Readers Theatre, and clarifying some basic theatre techniques should have helped those of you who want to produce a solid theatre and be proud of the result.

So here's to a successful season. Good luck!

Demystifying Debate

T. C. Winebrenner

Debate is the oldest and best known of the various forensic events. It also is the most intimidating to beginning forensics students. When you listen to your first debate, most of what transpires might seem incomprehensible. The debate will progress through a long series of rapid-fire speeches in which the participants make dispassionate pleas for you to accept their opinions regarding some complex contemporary issue. From time to time they will stop and ask each other ominous questions. Many in the audience will appear to be engrossed by the debate, as they listen intently and take copious notes. To you, however, the debate event remains a mystery. You would not be the first beginning forensics student to wonder how people can understand debates, much less enjoy them.

Oddly enough, thousands of forensics students do understand and are excited about debating. Most of them were, at one time, as mystified by debate as you. They discovered, however, that there really is no mystery. You can make the same discovery. In short order you can learn to understand the debates you observe. Before long, you will be ready to participate. And, with time and effort you can become a knowledgeable and enthusiastic college debater. My modest intention is to help you take the first step, to whisk back the shroud of mystery and introduce you to intercollegiate debate.

What Is Academic Debate?

Technically speaking, a debate is any formal dialogue conducted between persons taking opposite sides of a controversy. Such dialogues take many forms. You are probably familiar with political debates, such as the Presidential debates, and may have participated in less formal debates is some of your classes. Academic (forensic) debate lies somewhere between the formal structure of political debates and the relative informality of classroom debates. It is a kind of contest in which you engage in dialogue about significant contemporary issues as a way of developing and honing valuable argumentation skills. While any number of argumentation skills might be attributed to debating, they can be reduced to a list of three: (1) *Debate promotes information processing skills.* Debating requires that you learn the difference between informed and uninformed opinions. Effective arguing presumes knowledge, and debate is an exercise in learning to discover, scrutinize and assimilate the information upon which you should base your opinions. (2) *Debate promotes critical thinking skills.* Debating requires that you subject your opinions to public scrutiny. You will learn to analyze information, to carefully reason your way

---

Dr. Winebrenner is currently Director of Forensics at California Polytechnic State University, San Luis Obispo.

to opinions, and to defend those opinions when publicly attacked. (3) *Debate promotes communication skills.* Debating is an exercise in effective oral communication, requiring you to present your opinions clearly and concisely. Debates take place before and are judged by audiences, which means that you must learn to become a persuasive communicator. In short, academic debate is forensics competition in which students argue about contemporary events. Debaters are expected to be knowledgeable about the topics they argue, to critically examine their own opinions and the opinions of others, and to effectively communicate their arguments to audiences. Students do not participate in debate in order to become better debaters, they participate in order to become more informed, clearer thinking, better communicating citizens.

What Happens In A Debate?

In order to understand the way debate competition proceeds, you must first understand the kinds of controversies which may be resolved through debate. First, people disagree about facts.[1] Did Babe Ruth hit 714 home runs or did he hit 712? Did Richard Nixon resign the Presidency or was he impeached? Does smoking contribute to ill health? While we assume facts are indisputable, they are frequently subject to controversy. Things and events are more and less observable and more and less verifiable — the less observable or the less verifiable a fact the more likely it is to be disputed. Since we generally *know* to be true less than we *presume* to be true, what we assume to be certain may really be quite controversial. When our "facts" conflict with other people's "facts," disputes are likely.

People also disagree about value judgments.[2] Is Barry Bonds a more dangerous hitter than Frank Thomas? Was George Bush an effective President? Is good grammar really important? Even when we agree on a set of facts, we are likely to disagree in the meanings we assign to them. Just as we find it difficult to distinguish between what we know to be true and what we believe to be true, we often have trouble separating facts from opinions. We assume that the qualities we value are valued by others and expect them to share our judgments. When the value judgments we express conflict with the value judgments expressed by others, disputes are likely.

Finally, people disagree about policies.[3] Should the National League use designated hitters? Should the President be elected by popular vote? Should the Constitution be amended to

---

1 *Facts* are things or events which have been, could have been, or could be observed and verified.

2 *Value judgments* are assessments of the quality or worth of persons, places, things, events or ideas.

3 *Policies* are courses of action undertaken by individuals or institutions.

require a balanced Federal budget? *Should* probably ignites more controversy than any other concept in the English language. What we believe ought to be inevitably conflicts with what others believe ought to be, and this conflict breeds controversy.

Disputed facts, disputed value judgments and disputed policies are related to each other. Arguments about policy cannot be resolved without making value judgments about the disputed policies. Arguments about value judgments cannot be resolved without examining the facts which support the disputed opinions. Thus, policy disputes are likely to involve arguments about policies, value judgments and facts, value disputes are likely to involve arguments about value judgments and facts, and factual disputes may escalate to disputes about values and policies.

The principles. The first principle of academic debate is that a designated topic for debate is agreed upon in advance.[4] This topic is expressed in the form of a resolution which is a disputable statement of fact, value or policy. Debaters are obliged to discover the specific arguments which make up the dispute, to critically examine those arguments and to present cases for and against the resolution. What you observe when you listen to a debate is the clash between those cases.

The second principle of academic debate is that the dispute is resolved by a third party critic. The object of debate is to present a case which persuades the critic to decide the dispute in your favor. This means that debaters must use their information processing, critical thinking and communication skills to discover, construct and present strong cases and to critically examine and refute the cases presented by their opponents.

The third principle of academic debate is that the critic resolves the dispute according to how well the debaters have argued their cases rather than according to the critic's personal beliefs about the topic. Debaters, in turn, are expected to demonstrate a faculty for effective public argument. While evaluating this faculty is somewhat subjective, there are a number of argumentative techniques critics regularly look for in resolving the dispute. In general, these techniques relate to recognizing and fulfilling argumentative burdens.

The procedures. There are three debate events offered in intercollegiate forensics tournaments — team policy topic debate, team non-policy (fact/value) topic debate, and Lincoln-

---

4 Debaters must research a topic in considerable depth to analyze and argue it well. Thus, topics for academic debates are announced well in advance and are used for a number of tournaments. The Committee for Intercollegiate Debate and Discussion publishes a national topic for policy debating which is used for an entire academic year. The Cross Examination Debate Association publishes two national topics for non-policy debating; one is used for the first academic semester and the other for the second semester.

Douglas debate.[5] Team policy and non-policy topic events are what their names imply — debates between teams of students arguing about policy or non-policy resolutions. Lincoln-Douglas debate is an event for individual competitors arguing about either policy or non-policy resolutions. Since the team debate events are more common than Lincoln-Douglas debate, and since their procedures are similar, this section will be devoted primarily to the procedures of team debating. A limited discussion of the Lincoln-Douglas event will conclude the section.

A debate team consists of two students who have worked together in researching and analyzing the debate resolution. A debate round pairs two teams and arbitrarily assigns one team to argue in favor of (affirm) the resolution and the other to argue against (negate) it. A critic is assigned to evaluate the round and to resolve the dispute by voting for either the affirmative or the negative team (a debate round cannot end in a tie).

An academic debate progresses through two stages. The constructive stage initiates the debate and is used to lay out the cases the debaters have discovered for supporting or attacking the resolution. The rebuttal stage completes the debate and is reserved for re-examining the cases and summarizing arguments. Several cross-examination periods are integrated into the constructive stage. Cross-examination is used to clarify issues and lay a foundation for arguments which will be presented during the constructive and rebuttal speeches. In addition, each team is normally allowed a set amount of time (usually five to eight minutes) to prepare for their speeches.[6] During the debate, each debater will deliver a constructive speech and a rebuttal speech, will cross-examine an opponent and will be cross-examined by an opponent. By the end of the debate, each student will have had ample opportunity to demonstrate his or her information processing, critical thinking and communication skills.

The structure of an academic debate is less complex than it appears. Basically, a debate is laid out in a manner that gives each team an opportunity to both construct a case (affirming or negating the resolution) and refute a case (constructed by the opponents). Additionally, a debate is structured to encourage a logical "flow" of issues from contention (constructing a case)

---

5 Policy topic debate is often called NDT debate, an acronym for the National Debate Tournament, the American Forensic Association sponsored national championship for AFA members, a tournament which uses the national policy topic. Non-policy topic debate is often called CEDA debate, an acronym for the Cross Examination Debate Association, the organization which selects and publishes national non-policy topics, computes national CEDA topic sweepstakes rankings, and sponsors a national championship for CEDA members.

6 Preparation time is used in lieu of beginning a speech as soon as the previous speaker finishes. Rather than allowing speakers a predetermined amount of time to prepare for a speech, each team is allotted a *total elapsed preparation time* to be divided as they see fit.

to refutation (refuting a case) to rebuttal (defending a case). While the structure gives the affirmative team the advantage of presenting both the first speech and the last speech in the debate, the negative team has the advantage of a "negative block," back-to-back speeches in the transition between the constructive and rebuttal stages. The order of the speeches and traditional duties of the speakers are: (1) The first affirmative speaker presents a constructive speech. In this speech, the speaker presents the arguments which make up the case supporting the resolution. (2) The first affirmative speaker is cross-examined by a negative speaker. The questions focus on the case constructed during the affirmative speech and/or lay a foundation for the case the negative will present. (3) The first negative speaker presents a constructive speech. In this speech, the speaker analyzes the case presented by the affirmative and tries to find its weaknesses. (4) The first negative speaker is cross-examined by an affirmative speaker. The questions focus on the arguments presented during the negative speech and/or lay a foundation for defending the affirmative case. (5) The second affirmative speaker presents a constructive speech. In this speech, the speaker analyzes and attacks the arguments presented by the negative and attempts to defend the case presented in the first affirmative speech. (6) The second affirmative speaker is cross-examined by a negative speaker. The questions focus on the arguments presented during the affirmative speech and/or lay a foundation for re-examining the affirmative case. (7) The second negative speaker presents a constructive speech. In this speech, the speaker constructs a case against the resolution. (8) The second negative speaker is cross-examined by an affirmative speaker. The questions focus on the case constructed during the negative speech and/or lay a foundation for defending the affirmative case. (9) The first negative speaker presents a rebuttal speech. In this speech, the speaker summarizes the arguments against the affirmative case and defends the first negative constructive speech. (10) The first affirmative speaker presents a rebuttal speech. In this speech, the speaker analyzes the case against the resolution presented by the negative and defends the case presented by the affirmative. (11) The second negative speaker presents a rebuttal speech. In this speech, the speaker summarizes and defends the arguments against the affirmative case and those against the resolution. (12) The second affirmative speaker presents a rebuttal speech. In this speech, the speaker summarizes and defends the arguments against the negative case as well as the arguments supporting the resolution.

The Lincoln-Douglas event adjusts the debate format for individual competition, reducing the round to 5 speeches and two cross-examination periods. The debate follows this pattern: affirmative constructive speech, cross-examination period, negative constructive speech, cross-examination period, affirmative rebuttal speech, negative rebuttal speech, affirmative rebuttal speech. In Lincoln-Douglas debate, the affirmative has the advantage of giving an additional speech while the negative has the advantage of giving longer speeches.

The burdens. When critics evaluate debates they expect that debaters will try to satisfy three basic debate burdens. The first of these is the *burden to argue the issues of the resolution.* In general, this burden means that debaters are expected to have discovered the arguments which comprise the dispute over the resolution and to present cases which reveal those arguments. These cases attempt to resolve questions which are known as *stock issues*. Stock issues are general concerns related to the nature of the dispute rather than the content of the topic disputed, and are tools for discovering the differences of opinion which make-up a dispute. The primary difference between NDT and CEDA debate relates to the concerns which become stock issues. In NDT debate, you are given a policy resolution and the dispute focuses on the wisdom of pursuing such a policy. A sample policy resolution might be "Resolved: that the United States should devote greater resources to higher education." In CEDA debate, you are given a resolution which involves a matter of judgment, and the dispute focuses on whether that judgment is sound. A sample non-policy resolution might be "Resolved: that the U.S. space program has been an unwise investment." Quite naturally, opinions about policies do not generate the same sets of questions as do opinions about facts or value judgments.

Policy disputes are concerned with five stock issues. The first of these is the *problem* issue. This stock issue asks "Are there significant problems with the current condition?" For our sample policy resolution, this would be rephrased to ask "What is wrong with the level of resources now devoted to higher education?" The second stock issue is an *inherency* issue. This issue asks "Are the problems a fundamental part of current policies?" For our sample resolution, this would be rephrased to ask "Why aren't current resources adequate?" The third issue is a *solvency* issue. This stock issue asks "Would a new policy avoid these problems?" For our sample resolution, this would be rephrased to ask "Would increasing resources solve the problems of higher education?" The fourth stock issue is an issue of *disadvantages*. This issue asks "Would a new policy promote new or greater evils?" For our sample resolution, this would be rephrased to ask "Would increasing education resources lead to new or intensified problems for the nation?" The final issue is the *counterplan* issue. This stock issue asks "Are there better ways to solve the problems?" For our sample resolution, this would be rephrased to ask "Are there better ways to solve the problems of higher education?" The reason these are called stock issues should be readily apparent. When people argue about policies, they are concerned with whether there are fundamental problems to be solved and how best go about solving them. The five stock issues are the natural questions born of these concerns.

The stock issues for non-policy disputes are not so clearly defined. This is due primarily to the fact that CEDA resolutions take many different forms, and that this relatively new debate event has not developed terminology as familiar as the policy event. In general, however there are three issues which inevitably crop up in CEDA topic debate.[7] The first stock issue is one of

---

[7] These issues reflect stock concerns and thus may be addressed in any non-policy topic debate. However, the *names* for the issues vary from textbook to textbook.

interpretation. Even common words can mean different things to different people. Before a meaningful discussion can take place, the debaters must ascertain that they are interpreting the resolution in reasonably similar ways. The "intended" meaning of a resolution is always a matter of opinion, and often a subject of dispute. Debaters provide definitions for the ambiguous terms of the resolution, and should a definition be disputed, they are expected to defend their interpretation. While matters of definition are important to any debate, they are of particular concern to CEDA debate, which generally focuses on such abstract concepts as wisdom, justice, beneficence and relative importance. Our sample non-policy resolution states that the U.S. space program has been an unwise investment. The interpretation issue focuses on what that statement means by asking the questions: "What all is encompassed by the U.S. space program?" "What is meant in this context by investment?" "What does it mean to be unwise?"

A related stock issue is one of *perspective.* The general nature of CEDA resolutions is that they masquerade as factual statements. Judgment is implied in the way resolutions use subjective or evaluative terms. With our sample resolution, establishing the "fact" that the U.S. space program has been an unwise investment requires both observing and verifying the events of the space program, and making a specific judgment about those events. People generally find such subjective or evaluative judgments difficult to argue because they are sound only when examined from a particular perspective. Whether an event possesses a particular quality is potentially observable and verifiable. How that quality is judged depends upon what the arguer believes to be valuable. Thus, a subjective dispute cannot be resolved until the disputants settle on a common perspective. Debaters present criteria which identify the grounds upon which their particular judgment will be made. As with definitions, debaters are expected to defend disputed criteria. For our sample resolution this issue would ask "Under what circumstances is an investment *unwise*?"

The final non-policy topic stock issue is one of *opinion*. Once the debaters have defined the scope of the debate, discovered the implied judgment and established criteria for assessing that judgment, the actual judging must take place. This stock issue asks "What are the arguments supporting and disputing this judgment?" The issue of opinion really takes two forms. The affirmative team constructs and defends *contentions* (commonly called "case" arguments) intended to support the claim that the judgment expressed in the resolution is sound. For our sample resolution, the affirmative team would ask "In what ways has this investment been unwise?" The negative team constructs and defends *objections* (commonly called "off-case" arguments) intended to support the claim that the judgment is unsound. For our sample resolution, the negative team would ask the contrary question, "In what ways has this investment been wise?" Of course, the negative speakers will spend a considerable amount of time refuting the affirmative team's case arguments, just as the affirmative speakers will spend time refuting the negative team's off-case arguments.

As with policy stock issues, non-policy stock issues come from the questions which inevitably arise when subjective or evaluative judgments are disputed. Recognizing the judgment to be made, identifying how it is to be made, and determining the product of that judgment are the natural stages of resolving any non-policy dispute.

The second debate burden is the *burden of proof.* This means that debaters are expected to convince the critic that their opinions are believable. There are two qualities generally associated with believable opinions. The first quality is that they are based on experiences which can be confirmed. When debaters confirm experiences they normally rely upon *evidence*, or verified facts and opinions. For instance, if I argued that Barry Bonds is a more dangerous hitter than Frank Thomas, I might base my opinion on career batting averages or statements made by professional baseball players. However, I would need to verify those facts and opinions. For evidence, I might cite statistics published in *The Sporting News*, or the published opinions of Major League pitchers. The point is, even when opinions are based on valid information, that information must be verified before the argument has been supported. Verification is not absolute. Using evidence *persuades* rather than *requires* a critic to accept an argument; "strong" evidence is persuasive and "weak" evidence is not. Critics are concerned with four qualities of evidence — the authority of the source, the recency of the statement, the force of the statement and the accuracy of the statement. Thus, when debaters use evidence to support their arguments they qualify the evidence by indicating who made the statement, why the source ought to be believed, when the statement was made and where it was published, and by quoting the source verbatim. The second quality of believable opinions is that they are grounded in *sound reasoning*. When I argue that Bond's higher lifetime batting average means that he is the more dangerous hitter, or that he must be more dangerous because he is more respected by the pitchers he faces, you have the right to ask "Why?" Why does a higher batting average prove that Bonds is more dangerous? Why are pitchers particularly good judges of dangerous hitters? When arguments are effectively supported, the answers to these questions are readily evident. Sometimes quoted evidence will explain the reasoning behind a particular opinion. This is the most valuable kind of evidence you can find to support your arguments. Other times, quoted evidence does no more than verify a particular fact. In these circumstances, you should take care to make sure that your own reasoning is understood clearly.

The final burden is the *burden of rebuttal.* Debate is a valuable critical thinking activity because it exposes opinions to scrutiny. When an opponent attempts to refute your arguments, it is on the grounds that your facts and reasons are wrong or misleading. Were you to ignore such criticism, your opinions would be dogmatic and your aguments unlikely to persuade. You are expected not only to argue the issues of the resolution and to prove your arguments, you are expected to *defend* those arguments which are disputed. Remaining silent in the face of criticism, or failing to defend your arguments adequately, admits that your opinions cannot hold up to scrutiny. The ability to rebut arguments is just as important as the ability to construct them.

Where's The Mystery?

Academic debate is less complicated than it first appears. Think about what you now know about the event. You know that the debaters have spent time researching the topic so that they may argue intelligently. It is not surprising that they have a lot to say. You know that the debaters are trying to make a case for or against a particular resolution, and that the dispute will be decided by a critic rather than by the participants. This means that the debaters are arguing *to* someone as well as *with* someone. You know that the critic is evaluating argument skills. The debaters are trying to use the appropriate stock issues to discover the fundamental questions to be resolved, they are trying to prove their arguments with both evidence and reasoning, and they are trying to defend their arguments against the criticism levied by their opponents. Finally, you know that the debate will involve a set number of speeches and take a set amount of time. You even know a lot about what the debaters are trying to accomplish in each of the speeches.

Try a simple experiment. Spend some time in a library reading about the current CEDA or NDT debate topic. Using the appropriate set of stock issues, think about the questions which are fundamental to the topic and make a list of important arguments for and against the resolution. Now, listen to a debate. What did you notice? The debate you heard probably examined many of the same issues you examined, and may very well have involved some of the arguments on your list. The debate ought to have progressed pretty much as you expected, and you should have understood much of what each speaker was trying to accomplish. By the end of the debate, you probably had an "informed opinion" about who "won" the competition. Approached this way, debate is not a mystical experience. Don't be put off by first impressions. Give debate a try and you are likely to become a convert.

Figure One
Sample CEDA Debate Flow Sheet

1AC	1NC	2AC	1NR	1AR	2NR	2AR
Definition of term 1	→ Counter definition	→ Defense	→ Rebuttal	→ Rebuttal	→ Rebuttal-Summary	→ Rebuttal-Summary
Definition of term 2	→ Counter definition	→ Defense	→ Rebuttal	→ Rebuttal	→ Rebuttal-Summary	→ Rebuttal-Summary
Definitions etc.	→ Counter definition	→ Defense	→ Rebuttal	→ Rebuttal	→ Rebuttal-Summary	→ Rebuttal-Summary
Criteria for judgment	→ Counter criteria	→ Defense	→ Rebuttal	→ Rebuttal	→ Rebuttal-Summary	→ Rebuttal-Summary
Contention 1	→ Refutation	→ Defense	→ Rebuttal	→ Rebuttal	→ Rebuttal-Summary	→ Rebuttal-Summary
Subpoint 1	→ Refutation	→ Defense	→ Rebuttal	→ Rebuttal	→ Rebuttal-Summary	→ Rebuttal-Summary
Subpoint 2	→ Refutation	→ Defense	→ Rebuttal	→ Rebuttal	→ Rebuttal-Summary	→ Rebuttal-Summary
Subpoints etc.	→ Refutation	→ Defense	→ Rebuttal	→ Rebuttal	→ Rebuttal-Summary	→ Rebuttal-Summary
Contention 2	→ Refutation	→ Defense	→ Rebuttal	→ Rebuttal	→ Rebuttal-Summary	→ Rebuttal-Summary
Subpoints etc.	→ Refutation	→ Defense	→ Rebuttal	→ Rebuttal	→ Rebuttal-Summary	→ Rebuttal-Summary
Contentions etc.	→ Refutation	→ Defense	→ Rebuttal	→ Rebuttal	→ Rebuttal-Summary	→ Rebuttal-Summary
Subpoints etc.	→ Refutation	→ Defense	→ Rebuttal	→ Rebuttal	→ Rebuttal-Summary	→ Rebuttal-Summary

2NC	1AR	2NR	2AR
Off-case Objection 1	→ Refutation	→ Defense-Summary	→ Rebuttal-Summary
Subpoint 1	→ Refutation	→ Defense-Summary	→ Rebuttal-Summary
Subpoint 2	→ Refutation	→ Defense-Summary	→ Rebuttal-Summary
Subpoints etc.	→ Refutation	→ Defense-Summary	→ Rebuttal-Summary
Off-case Objection 2	→ Refutation	→ Defense-Summary	→ Rebuttal-Summary
Subpoints etc.	→ Refutation	→ Defense-Summary	→ Rebuttal-Summary
Off-case Objections etc.	→ Refutation	→ Defense-Summary	→ Rebuttal-Summary
Subpoints etc.	→ Refutation	→ Defense-Summary	→ Rebuttal-Summary

This illustrates a potential flow of arguments. In practice, negative debaters rarely dispute every point made by the affirmative, choosing instead to bypass some opportunities for refutation. Generally, the arguments will sift down to a few important issues by the rebuttal stage of the debate. Pay particular attention to the way the negative speakers coordinate their arguing in the 2nd Negative Constructive and 1st Negative Rebuttal, avoiding duplication in order to maximize the advantage of the "negative block." While the division may not be along the lines of "case" and "off-case" arguments (as illustrated here), the first negative rebuttalist should always avoid rehashing ground covered by the second negative constructive speaker.

Figure Two
Sample NDT Debate Flow Sheet

1AC	1NC	2AC	1NC	1AR	2NC	2AR
Definition of term 1	→ Counter definition	→ Defense	→ Rebuttal	→ Rebuttal	→ Rebuttal-Summary	→ Rebuttal-Summary
Definition of term 2	→ Counter definition	→ Defense	→ Rebuttal	→ Rebuttal	→ Rebuttal-Summary	→ Rebuttal-Summary
Definitions etc.	→ Counter definition	→ Defense	→ Rebuttal	→ Rebuttal	→ Rebuttal-Summary	→ Rebuttal-Summary
Problem Contention	→ Refutation	→ Defense	→ Rebuttal	→ Rebuttal	→ Rebuttal-Summary	→ Rebuttal-Summary
Subpoint 1	→ Refutation	→ Defense	→ Rebuttal	→ Rebuttal	→ Rebuttal-Summary	→ Rebuttal-Summary
Subpoint 2	→ Refutation	→ Defense	→ Rebuttal	→ Rebuttal	→ Rebuttal-Summary	→ Rebuttal-Summary
Subpoints etc.	→ Refutation	→ Defense	→ Rebuttal	→ Rebuttal	→ Rebuttal-Summary	→ Rebuttal-Summary
Inherency Contention	→ Refutation	→ Defense	→ Rebuttal	→ Rebuttal	→ Rebuttal-Summary	→ Rebuttal-Summary
Subpoints etc.	→ Refutation	→ Defense	→ Rebuttal	→ Rebuttal	→ Rebuttal-Summary	→ Rebuttal-Summary
Solvency Contention	→ Refutation	→ Defense	→ Rebuttal	→ Rebuttal	→ Rebuttal-Summary	→ Rebuttal-Summary
Subpoints etc.	→ Refutation	→ Defense	→ Rebuttal	→ Rebuttal	→ Rebuttal-Summary	→ Rebuttal-Summary

2NC	1AR	2NC	2AR
Solvency Attack 1	→ Refutation	→ Defense-Summary	→ Rebuttal-Summary
Subpoints etc.	→ Refutation	→ Defense-Summary	→ Rebuttal-Summary
Solvency Attack 2	→ Refutation	→ Defense-Summary	→ Rebuttal-Summary
Subpoints etc.	→ Refutation	→ Defense-Summary	→ Rebuttal-Summary
Solvency etc.	→ Refutation	→ Defense-Summary	→ Rebuttal-Summary
Subpoints etc.	→ Refutation	→ Defense-Summary	→ Rebuttal-Summary
Disadvantage 1	→ Refutation	→ Defense-Summary	→ Rebuttal-Summary
Subpoints etc.	→ Refutation	→ Defense-Summary	→ Rebuttal-Summary
Disadvantage 2	→ Refutation	→ Defense-Summary	→ Rebuttal-Summary
Subpoints etc.	→ Refutation	→ Defense-Summary	→ Rebuttal-Summary
Disadvantages etc.	→ Refutation	→ Defense-Summary	→ Rebuttal-Summary
Subpoints etc.	→ Refutation	→ Defense-Summary	→ Rebuttal-Summary

For Additional Reading

American Forensic Association. *Argumentation and Advocacy* (formerly *Journal of the American Forensic Association*). Published quarterly.

Bartanen, Michael and David A. Frank. *Debating Values.* Scottsdale, Arizona: Gorsuch Scarisbrick, 1994.

Brownlee, Don (ed). *Contributions on the Philosophy and Practice of CEDA.* Long Beach, California: Cross-Examination Debate Association, 1981.

Brownlee, Don (ed). *Perspectives on Non-Policy Debate.* Long Beach, California: Cross-Examination Debate Association, 1980.

Chruch, Russell T. and Charles Wilbanks. *Values and Policies in Controversy: An Introduction to Argumentation and Debate.* Scottsdale, Arizona: Gorsuch Scarisbrick, 1986.

Cross-Examination Debate Association. *CEDA Yearbook.* (Published annually).

Copeland, James C. *Cross-Examination in Debate.* Skokie, Illinois: National Textbook Company, 1981.

Corcoran, Joseph. *An Introduction to Non-Policy Debating.* Dubuque, Iowa: Kendall Hunt, 1988.

Ericson, Jon, James J. Murphy and Raymond F. Zeuschner. *The Debaters' Guide.* Carbondale, Illinois: Southern Illinois University Press, 1987.

Freeley, Austin J. *Argumentation and Debate: Critical Thinking for Reasoned Discourse.* Belmont, California: Wadsworth, 1990.

Goodnight, Lynn. *Getting Started in Debate.* Skokie, Illinois: National Textbook Company, 1988.

Kemp, Robert L. *Lincoln-Douglas Debating.* Clayton, Missouri: The Study Group, 1985.

Klopf, Donald F. *A Programmed Introduction to Debate.* Portland, Maine: J. Weston Walsh, 1974.

Klopf, Donald W. and Cambra, Ronald W. *Academic Debate: Practicing Argumentative Theory.* Denver, Colorado: Morton, 1979.

Patterson, J. W. and Zarefsky, David. *Contemporary Debate.* Boston: Hougton Mifflin, 1983.

Perrella, Jack. *The Debate Method of Critical Thinking.* Dubuque, Iowa: Kendall Hunt, 1987.

Pfau, Michael, David A. Thomas and Walter Ulrich. *Debate and Argument: A Systems Approach to Advocacy.* Glenview, Illinois: Scott-Foresman, 1987.

Pollard, Tom and Prentice, Diana (eds). *Lincoln-Douglas Debate: Theory and Practice.* Lawrence, Kansas: University of Kansas, 1981.

Sheckels, Theodore F. Jr. *Debating: Applied Rhetorical Theory.* New York: Longman, 1984.

Thomas, David A. (ed). *Advanced Debate: Readings in Theory, Practice and Teaching.* Skokie, Illinois: National Textbook Company, 1979.

Thomas, David A. *Lincoln-Douglas Debate.* Kansas City, Missouri: National Federation of State High School Associations, 1981.

Ziegelmueller, George W. and Dause, Charles. *Argumentation: Inquiry and Advocacy.* Inglewood Cliffs, New Jersey: Prentice-Hall, 1975.

Wood, Stephen and John Midgley. *Prima Facie: A Guide to Value Debate.* Dubuque, Iowa: Kendall/Hunt, 1989.

Non-Policy (CEDA) Debate
Nicholas F. Burnett

When you first begin to debate, the task of gaining even a basic understanding of the substance, procedures and vocabulary of the event may seem a bit overwhelming. In addition to the work it takes to acquire a working knowledge of the specific topic you will debate, you may well find the conventions and jargon of debate difficult to master. The purpose of this discussion is to introduce you to the basic procedures and "language" of debate in order to make your entry into the activity a bit less painful. No one feels entirely comfortable venturing into the unknown; hopefully this introduction will be useful in reducing your anxiety level, and making your first tournament experience a memorable one.

Analyzing Debate Resolutions

The controlling feature of any academic debate is the proposition being debated. More than simply a statement of the topic under consideration, the debate proposition, or resolution as it is sometimes called, is a specifically worded sentence that will be the focus of the debate. The affirmative team in a debate attempts to prove that the resolution is true while the negative team in a debate tries to counter the affirmative's arguments by proving that they are wrong.

In advocating the affirmative side of a debate proposition, you will assume a burden of proof — that is, you will have the responsibility of proving your side of the resolution is true. Conversely, when you defend the negative side of a proposition, you have the advantage of presumption — you only have to prevent the affirmative from fulfilling their burden of proving the resolution true, not prove that it is untrue. While you refute the affirmative by offering arguments that the resolution is false, you also may accomplish your goal by refuting or contradicting the arguments offered by the affirmative team. These complementary notions of burden of proof and presumption are similar in operation to the legal concepts of burden of proof and presumption of innocence. A prosecutor needs to fulfill a burden of proof to convict someone accused of a crime, while a defendant in a criminal case maintains a presumption of innocence. Rather than "proving" a defendant's innocence, a defense attorney merely needs to create a reasonable doubt as to the defendant's guilt. In much the same way, a negative team need not prove the resolution false, but merely provide a basis for doubting that the affirmative has fulfilled their burden of proof.

Debate propositions usually focus on a single subject with the wording being very important. Figure 1 lists some of the propositions debated or considered for debate by CEDA in past few years.

Dr. Burnett is currently Director of Forensics at California State University, Sacramento.

Figure 1

Sample CEDA Resolutions

Resolved: that restriction of the private ownership of handguns in the United States would be justified.

Resolved: that violence is a justified response to political oppression.

Resolved: that the trend toward increased foreign investment in the United States is detrimental to this nation.

Resolved: that the US constitution should be amended to prohibit the purposeful mistreatment of the flag.

Debate textbooks generally recognize two different kinds of resolutions — policy and non-policy propositions. Simply put, policy propositions call for a change in some policy by including the word "should" before some described policy option (i.e., sample resolution number four). The more common kind of resolution debated in CEDA, and the focus of most of my discussion, is the non-policy proposition (i.e., sample resolutions one, two and three). Non-policy propositions (sometimes further categorized as value or fact propositions) generally feature an evaluative term that deserves special attention. For instance, in the first two sample propositions, the term "justified" needs additional discussion and elaboration. In the third resolution, determining when a particular effect would be "detrimental" is the key to evaluation. You need to ask yourself how you determine when something is justified or detrimental — is an action justified if it saves money or lives, or is an economic trend detrimental if it provokes ill will or threatens economic independence?

Because the affirmative team is responsible for proving the resolution true, one of your first responsibilities as an affirmative debater is to establish how the evaluative term will be debated. For instance if a debate were to be staged on the proposition, Resolved: that Stanford is a better university than USC, the key evaluative term would be "better." As affirmative, you would be responsible for offering criteria as to how the judge would know when a particular university was better than another. Absent a careful discussion of criteria, it is likely this debate would simply involve each team listing the positive characteristics of each university. Without establishing some sort of common ground, the debate would involve very little clash of ideas or arguments. In this sample debate, you might argue that a "better" university is one that offers students a wider choice of majors, or has a higher percentage of students going on to graduate or professional programs after their undergraduate careers. In defending Stanford as the better university, you would offer arguments to prove that these criteria were reliable measures of academic superiority, and that Stanford in fact meets these criteria.

As a negative team in this debate, you would have a number of different strategies available to you. You might argue that the criteria identified by the affirmative to discuss the evaluative term were inappropriate. For instance, you could argue that number of major choices is meaningless if the academic programs are inadequate, or that the number of students going on to graduate programs is not a reliable indicator of academic quality. As the negative team, you would then offer your own criteria for determining a "better" university — perhaps that more liberal financial aid policies or the overall quality of the faculty are better measures of academic quality. You would then go on to argue that USC meets these alternative criteria, or that Stanford simply does not measure up when examined in this fashion. Another possible strategy would be to accept the affirmative criteria, but to prove that, in fact, USC meets the criteria even better than Stanford does, or that Stanford does not even meet the criteria being offered by the affirmative. You might do this by indicting the affirmative's evidence or statistics. You may have more up-to-date evidence, indicating a shift in circumstances. It is important as a negative team that you have a clear idea of the approach or combination of approaches you will use in each particular debate, and that you and your partner each understand what the other will be attempting to prove.

To review then, the affirmative team in a debate on a non policy proposition needs to offer criteria for considering the evaluative term in the resolution, and then prove that they meet those criteria. The negative team has the option of accepting the criteria, proving that they meet them better than the affirmative, or rejecting the criteria altogether and offering some of their own.

Doing Debate Research

The foundation of any argument is the evidence upon which it is based. Sometimes the evidence for an argument will be common knowledge and not subject to much dispute between the teams in a debate, but more often, arguments in a debate are driven by statistics, examples, and the testimony of experts that can only be mobilized by doing library research on the topic. There is no substitute for going to the library and doing original research on the topic. As a novice debater, it may be a bit daunting to think that you have to master all of these debate concepts and then realize that your preparation has not even reached the halfway point. One of the advantages of being a member of a debate *team* however is that team members can pool their research burdens and share their ideas and evidence with one another.

After a preliminary analysis of the debate resolution, you must begin the sometimes arduous task of collecting information to be used as evidence. No resource should be ignored — books, magazines, scholarly journals, and newspapers should all be consulted. Perhaps one of the most important research skills you should seek to develop is the use of indexes. While you probably can find your way through a card catalog, you should pay attention to more specialized hard copy and computerized index systems. The *National Newspaper Index* and the *Magazine Index* are now found in most college libraries on a system called Infotrac. Searches are quite easy to do on this menu driven system. The attraction of the various computerized systems, however, should not deter you from the use of traditional indexes, including the *Social Science Index*, the

Public Affairs Information Service, the *Business Index*, and the *Index to Legal Periodicals*. Indexes to particular newspapers like the *New York Times*, the *Washington Post*, and the *Christian Science Monitor* are generally available in university libraries. You should use all available indexing resources to build a working bibliography of sources.

Once you have compiled a substantial list of available articles and books, you should begin the task of finding the specific resources and reviewing their contents for possible debate evidence. By skimming articles or reading introductory chapters in books, you will soon develop the ability to judge whether a particular resource will be helpful on a particular topic. Remember to keep an open mind, and tournaments will require you to debate on both the affirmative and negative side of a resolution. So, you will need evidence to support a variety of points of view. When you find relevant articles, photocopying the complete article and save it in case there questions arise about the context of a piece of evidence or the author's intent; in the end, it will save you a good deal of time and trouble.

Evidence is generally recorded verbatim, that is, word for word, on index cards. You should always include a full source citation for each piece of evidence; that includes the name of the author, his or her qualifications, the source of the information (the name of the book or journal), the date, and the page number. This information is critical for demonstrating the credibility of the evidence and the reliability of the judgment or statistics it provides. In addition, you may want to put a brief summary statement at the top of the card, called a "slug" or "tag," so you will know at a glance the point the evidence makes. This makes it easier to find a particular piece of evidence in the heat of a debate. Keeping track of your evidence is made easier if you design some type of filing system — keeping evidence that supports specific arguments or groups of arguments filed together. At a later time, you may want to bundle groups of arguments together in support of or refuting a particular issue. Called briefs, these bundles of arguments are often an efficient way for you to prepare for opposing arguments before a tournament takes place.

The danger, of course, to relying too much on briefs prepared for generic renderings of an argument is that you may be unable to adapt to the specific way your opposition argues a point.

A brief note about handbook or research service evidence is appropriate here. There are a number of services that provide, for a fee, fully researched briefs and evidence on the debate topic to debate programs around the country. Coaches disagree about the relative benefits of using these services — they may make available information that teams from small schools may not have access to, but they may so discourage students from engaging in original research that the commercial evidence has a negative effect on the educational benefits of debate. In general, coaches agree that handbook evidence should be used sparingly, if at all. It is far wiser to view handbooks as a kind of annotated bibliography from which you can get sources to research first hand. Researching the sources from which handbook evidence has been drawn will also help you understand the original context of the evidence, so you are better able to interpret what the statement was intended to mean. Be sure to check with your coach regarding his or her policy for using handbook evidence.

The Debate Process

In this final section, I would like to "walk you through" the responsibilities each debater faces in each of the speeches of a typical debate. Although there is likely to be a good deal of variation in the debates that you will be doing, short of actually observing a debate, this should give you an idea of what is expected of you in a typical novice intercollegiate debate. Figure 2 illustrates the traditional CEDA debate format.

Figure 2
Order and Length of Speeches

1st affirmative constructive	**8 minutes**
Cross-examination by the 2nd negative	**3 minutes**
1st negative constructive	**8 minutes**
Cross-examination by the 1st affirmative	**3 minutes**
2nd affirmative constructive	**8 minutes**
Cross-examination by the 1st negative	**3 minutes**
2nd negative constructive	**8 minutes**
Cross-examination by the 2nd affirmative	**3 minutes**
1st negative rebuttal	**5 minutes**
1st affirmative rebuttal	**5 minutes**
2nd negative rebuttal	**5 minutes**
2nd affirmative rebuttal	**5 minutes**

Each team is also allowed five-to-eight minutes of preparation time to be used between speeches to prepare for the upcoming speech. Use your preparation time wisely by reserving most of it for the rebuttals.

1st Affirmative Constructive Speech. From an organizational perspective, this is easily the most important speech of the debate. Constructive speeches are ones in which debaters *build* arguments. In this speech, the you have to provide the foundation for your support of the resolution being debated. Most first affirmative constructives (1ACs) follow a fairly standardized format. Keeping in mind that the affirmative assumes the burden of proof and is generally responsible for setting the specific topic of debate, most 1ACs begin with what's called an observation on Resolutional Analysis. Simply put, in this argument, the you defines important terms of the resolution, and establish the criteria for discussing the evaluative term in the resolution.

Definitions of the key terms in the proposition ensure that there will be no misunderstanding regarding exactly what does and does not fall within a particular topic. For instance in the sample topic about handgun control, a legal definition of handgun would probably exclude you (and your opposition) from talking about rifles or most automatic assault weapons. Definitions can be obtained from standard dictionaries, specialty dictionaries by discussing how experts in the topic area understand and use a word or phrase. For instance, a resolution which looks at the desirability of direct economic aid to Russia would force debaters to determine exactly what "direct economic aid" entails. Is it only money? Could it include goods as well as money? Is it credit for commercial goods? Obviously how you define this important term will have a controlling impact on the progress of the debate.

After the definitions and criteria have been made clear, you will generally make specific arguments (often called contentions) indicating that you meet the criteria you have established for the evaluative term. In the economic aid to Russia topic, having defined key terms and then offered criteria for determining the desirability of a particular policy option (Does it ensure world peace? Does it enhance international economic interdependence?), you might proceed to offer contentions to prove that direct economic aid to Russia would enhance world peace by strengthening Yeltsin political control and ensuring Russia's new democratic reforms.

Good 1ACs sound more like talking outlines than typical persuasive speeches. You should use explicit organizational devices (previews, summaries, tag lines, and standard outline sign-posting) to ensure that both the judge and the opposing team can follow easily the arguments you are making. What most clearly distinguishes good debate speeches from other speeches is the relative density of information. Debate speeches tend to be highly organized, with a great deal of information presented in a relatively short period of time. Because of this, your organizational skills are at a premium. Unlike any other speech in the debate, the 1AC is often a manuscripted, prepared speech. All subsequent speeches are generally delivered extemporaneously, relying on limited notes (although evidence is read verbatim!). Good debaters will continue to improve and re-work their 1ACs over the course of a semester, as they find better evidence or find a different strategic emphasis for their arguments.

Cross-examination. Rather than deal with each cross-examination (C-X) period separately, the comments in this section will apply to all four of the C-X periods.

Unlike the speeches, C-X allows for the direct interaction between affirmative and negative debaters. The questioner in each case asks the respondent a series of specific questions that can be designed to clarify a point made in a previous speech, probe a particular point for more information or the implications of advocating the particular position, or investigate the motives or qualifications of the source of a piece of evidence as a prelude to refuting or indicting of that evidence. As you become more experienced, you will find it easier to construct a series of questions that can be used as an effective weapon for crystallizing an opponent's position and unearthing flaws or contradictions within those positions. As a beginner, C-X is an opportunity for you to make sure that you understand the arguments made by the opposing team in the previous speech, and to be sure that you have recorded all of those arguments. You may want to begin to probe points you find illogical or farfetched by asking your opponent to elaborate on the position taken by their sources or whether the evidence is even appropriate for supporting a point at all.

Remember, practice is the key to developing a good C-X style. The idea of cross examination, contrary to the popular view provided by "L.A. Law," is not to humiliate, embarrass, or harass the competition — it is far more devastating to let them speak for themselves and then use their words against them. Most judges will want admissions gained or weaknesses exposed in C-X to be reiterated during the constructive or rebuttal speeches to demonstrate that you know you have elicited a damaging bit of information, and to give your opposition an opportunity to argue with the way you interpreted the answers to your question. Finally, politeness goes a long way in making a cross examination period and a debate far more pleasant — avoid an overly aggressive demeanor in asking or answering questions.

1st Negative Constructive. As the first negative speaker, it is your responsibility to set the broad scope of the negative attack, to initiate the attack on criteria and resolutional analysis issues, and to begin a refutation of the contentions argued in the 1AC. As I noted above, this speech (and all subsequent speeches in the debate) is delivered extemporaneously. Every first negative however should have a number of generic arguments which apply to a broad range of affirmative cases. For instance, resolutions will often set-up predictable confrontations between important values like the value of life and the value of rights. If it becomes clear that the negative, for strategic purposes, needs to advocate a value orientation different from the one advocated by the affirmative, then as first negative debater you need to have that attack briefed-out and ready for each round of debate. Once you hear a particular 1AC, you can decide whether or not it is to your advantage to run the brief.

It is possible that an affirmative team may take liberties with the definitions or manipulate its interpretation of the resolution in such a way as to include a discussion of issues that are seemingly outside the scope of the topic as you understand it. In these cases, as 1NC, you need to launch what is called a topicality argument. Topicality simply refers to questions about whether the affirmative's interpretation of the key terms of the topic is legitimate and reasonable. For instance, if in the resolution on handgun control an affirmative argued that we should have restrictions on semi-automatic assault rifles, you could effectively argue that the affirmative is not topical because assault rifles are not generally understood to be handguns. Had the affirmative argued that assault rifles were handguns because they have to be held with the hands to be fired, then you could claim that such an interpretation is illegitimate because it conforms to neither the legal nor the everyday common sense understanding of "handgun." Topicality arguments, by and large, should be advanced only if you believe that the affirmative's interpretation is a clear violation of the letter or spirit of the resolution. Topicality can be an important strategic argument because almost always award the decision to the negative team that wins a topicality issue, irrespective of how the substantive issues in the debate were resolved.

Your final responsibility as first negative is to refute the contentions brought up by the 1AC. Your 1NC should generally follow the organization of the 1AC, applying arguments or challenging the logic and evidence offered by the affirmative. It is important that you not merely ask questions of the affirmative, but rather make specific arguments while explaining to the judge how your arguments make the affirmative's arguments less believable. Because most debate topics offer a fair amount latitude to affirmatives, as first negative speaker, you need to be prepared to debate against a variety of affirmative cases. Your preparation, grounded in the research that you do in the library, should include attention to all those cases that you know are being debated by teams in your region. Most importantly, if you debate and lose to an affirmative case for which you were not prepared, get to the library and vow that they will not catch you unprepared again

Second Affirmative Constructive. This speech follows closely along the organizational pattern initiated in the 1AC. As 2AC, you have the dual responsibility of rebuilding the arguments offered by your partner, and attacking the arguments initiated by the 1NC. It is essential that you deal with *all* of these arguments, because once an argument goes unanswered (or is "dropped," as debaters say it), your opposition can claim that by your silence you have conceded the point to them.

As the second affirmative speaker, you should have a reasonable idea of what the strong and weak points of your affirmative case is, and be prepared to defend those positions and have arguments briefed and ready to go. A thorough research job on your part should mean that you will not be surprised by any argument the negative might make.

The critical skill that you need to develop to be a good second affirmative speaker is the ability to extend arguments. Extending an argument does not mean merely repeating what you or your partner said earlier in the debate, but rather taking the original argument, analyzing way your opponents dealt with it, and then defending your argument *in light of your opponent's response.* Good extensions of arguments show the evolution of a position rather than mere repetition. Novices are not generally very skilled at extending arguments; it is a skill that develops with time and practice.

Second Negative Constructive. As second negative speaker, you often have the difficult job of finishing up what your partner could not do in the 1NC, in addition to presenting arguments that explain why the affirmative's defense of their value or criteria is actually inconsistent or wrong.

In policy debates, the 2NC has the rather straightforward responsibility of presenting the negative consequences or disadvantages of adopting the affirmative's policy. In non-policy debate a similar type of argument (called a "value objection" of "off-case argument") allows you to argue the affirmative not only fails to meet the value or criteria they have advanced, but that they actually contradict it. For instance, in a debate on the proposition that military intervention is immoral, an affirmative might argue that we would know if an action is immoral by whether or not lives are lost as a result of it. Such an argument virtually begs for a negative value objection indicating that military intervention does not always cost lives, and often is used to preserve life. When military intervention is used to prevent a madman from using chemical or nuclear weapons, then you might argue that military intervention, even by the affirmative's own criteria, would be quite moral.

In addition to relating to the affirmative's criteria, value objections could be used to confirm any counter-criteria introduced in the 1NC. For instance in the debate over handgun control, an affirmative might take the position that with life as their paramount concern, handgun control is justified because it saves lives. As 2NC, could counter not only with an argument that handgun control may cost lives because it deprives people of the ability to defend themselves from criminals, but also that a more important concern might be the rights guaranteed to us under the Constitution, rights which gun control materially damages. In this strategy, you and your partner work in concert — 1NC presents a counter-criterion and argues when it is a superior measure of the key evaluative term in the resolution, and 2NC presents an argument which shows that the affirmative endangers the values intrinsic to the counter-criterion (e.g., 1NC would argue that Constitutional rights are the most important concern when judging restrictions on personal behavior because those rights are the foundation of our social and political tradition, and 2NC would argue that handgun control compromises the values implicit in the 2nd Amendment).

First Negative Rebuttal. Rebuttal speeches differ from constructive speeches in at least two important respects: first, they are considerably shorter, and second, you are prohibited from launching new lines of argument in these speeches. You may extend or answer arguments presented in the constructives, or read additional evidence in support of or attacking existing arguments, but it is inappropriate to introduce refutation you had every opportunity to present in an earlier speech.

Much like the 2AC, the 1NR extends arguments introduced earlier in the debate (1NC), while responding to the answers made by the previous speaker (2AC). Because of the limited time devoted to rebuttal speeches, you need to make decisions about what is important and what is not, which arguments you are winning, and which arguments are better left to die quietly. Arguments advanced in the 1NC but dropped in 1NR generally will not figure into a judge's decision. You have a brief amount of time, and you are expected to tell the judge which arguments you feel are most important and why you feel you are winning them. Crystallizing the key issues and making it clear to the judge what impact your arguments on the affirmative case are two important skills to be learned for the novice 1NR. Finally, be sure not to cover issues or arguments just discussed by the 2NC. Division of labor is an important factor in maximizing the strategic impact of these two consecutive negative speeches.

First Affirmative Rebuttal. The 1AR is arguably the most difficult speech in the debate. It follows a block of thirteen minutes of negative speeches, but is allowed slightly more than one-third that amount of time in which to fashion adequate responses. As 1AR, you have an absolute duty to respond to those arguments introduced by the 2NC, and most judges believe it is also necessary to answer all of the arguments extended by the 1NR as well.

The keys to a good 1AR are advanced preparation, solid organization, and the ability to answer arguments efficiently. Novice debates are often lost due the mistakes made in the 1AR, making it imperative that you prepare for all possible value objections, and practice as much as is feasible. As 1AR, you need to have outstanding strategic judgment and clear issue perception. This is a speech that make take a great deal of time to master, but if done well, it can be wielded as a powerful weapon against your opponents.

Second Negative Rebuttal. As the final negative speaker in the debate, it is your responsibility to summarize the debate from the negative point of view, and tell the judge why you believe you have won the debate. Arguments not mentioned in the 2NR generally will not factor into a judge's decision, so it is important to extend what you consider to be the important arguments in the debate. Even if you are clearly winning the debate up to this point, unless your 2NR effectively summarizes and extends the winning negative arguments, the judge generally will vote for the affirmative. Special attention should be paid to explaining the status of criteria and counter-criteria arguments, and to what negative arguments reveal about how well the affirmative case satisfies the various criteria.

In this speech, it is extremely important for you to have a sense of the debate as a whole, to understand the strategic implications of the arguments being made, and a notion of which arguments need to be clinched to ensure a victory. A good 2NR can clinch a debate; a poor one can grasp defeat from the jaws of victory.

Second Affirmative Rebuttal. As the final speaker in the debate, your responsibilities are similar to the responsibilities of the 2NR. As 2AR, you summarize the debate from the affirmative point of view, emphasizing why the your case has triumphed. As with the 2NR, a 2AR who fails to extend and summarize arguments may find the decision going to the opposition opponents even if the affirmative team has demonstrated superior skills to that point in the debate. A good 2AR also pays special attention to criteria arguments, and tries to view the debate as a whole — looking for the strategic implications of the entirety of affirmative arguments.

Conclusion

This has been a brief introduction to the challenging world of intercollegiate CEDA debate. Diligence, persistence and hard work will pay off, making your participation in debate one of the most valuable activities in your undergraduate education. Good luck!!

Policy (NDT) Debate

B. Christine Shea

Should public sector employees be required to take drug tests? Should government censor "obscene" popular rap music recordings? Should the United States send ground troops to act as a peacekeeping force in central Europe? Should the federal government guarantee every citizen access to affordable health care? These are the kind of political issues our nation continually faces, and the kind of issues you will address as a policy debater. Policy debate, commonly known as NDT debate, differs from non-policy debate in that you actually assume the role of a legislator, proposing and defending sample pieces of legislation. In non-policy debate, you might discuss whether drug tests would compromise implicit Constitutional guarantees of privacy, whether censoring obscene artistic expression violates the First Amendment, whether the United States has a moral obligation to protect fledgling democracies, or whether health care is more important than other national issues. What you will not have done as a non-policy debater, is discuss *how* to require drug tests, censor popular music, defend democracy in central Europe, or guarantee affordable health care, or the *effects* of particular pieces of legislation designed to accomplish those ends. Policy debate takes the next logical step in debating important political issues by requiring that affirmative teams construct and defend a particular *plan of action* designed to solve the problems they have identified. Requiring that you examine the policy dimension of a debate resolution opens a whole new world of debate issues. My purpose in this discussion is to introduce you to policy debate by distinguishing between policy and non-policy (fact or value) propositions, discussing the relevant stock issues raised by questions of policy and outlining the duties of each speaker in a policy debate. You should not view this discussion as a substitute for sound coaching, but as an introduction to debating policy resolutions.

The Nature of Policy Propositions

Propositions of policy suggest that some action *should* or *should not* be taken. Earlier in this text, you read about fact and value (non-policy) propositions, and the burdens associated with arguing about them. Policy propositions generally are more complex topics for debate in that they subsume questions of fact and value. For instance, if you argue a resolution that the federal government should ban abortion, then you would support the resolution with arguments about facts (i.e., "life begins at conception," and "an abortion kills an unborn child,") and arguments about value judgments (i.e., "abortion is the moral equivalent of murder," and "abortion is

---

Professor Shea is a former Associate Director of Forensics at California Polytechnic State University, San Luis Obispo.

detrimental to the health of women"). However, since this is a policy resolution, you also would be required to support your case with arguments about the policy dimension of the topic (i.e., "moral discourse cannot end abortion," "a federal law banning abortion would significantly reduce the numbers of abortions performed," "a federal ban would not lead to back-alley abortions," etc.). So, resolving policy disputes involves discussing facts and values as well as policies. Issues that are relevant when you examine non-policy propositions become a part of the discussion when you examine policy propositions.

Policy vs. Non-policy Propositions. Sometimes debaters confuse the burdens associated with advocating policy propositions with those of defending non-policy propositions. Many of the non-policy resolutions with which you are familiar are actually *quasi-policy* resolutions. Although these resolutions are not expressed in terms of *agents of action* and what these agents "should" do, they require you to evaluate broad policies by justifying the existence or arguing the desirability of a general course of action. Members of the Cross-Examination Debate Association (CEDA) have debated many quasi-policy propositions, including resolutions that the United States is justified in providing military assistance to nondemocratic governments (Fall 1985); that continued United States covert involvement in Central America would be undesirable (Fall 1987); that increasing restrictions on the civilian possession of handguns in the United States would be justified (Spring 1989); and that U.S. military intervention to foster democratic government is appropriate in the post-Cold War world (Spring 1994). These resolutions each examine implicit policies — military assistance to nondemocratic nations, covert involvement in Central America, handgun restrictions, and U.S. military intervention. Had you debated one of these quasi-policy resolutions, you might have operationally defined (defined by example) the implicit policy, but you would not have offered a specific plan for assisting nondemocratic governments, prohibiting covert involvement, restricting handguns, or militarily intervening to foster democratic government. Instead, you would have focused on evaluating the broad course of action suggested by the resolution without getting into specific plans and the implications of those plans. However, if you were to reframe one of the resolutions to identify an agent who "should" undertake one of these policies, then additional issues would be raised, and you would incur the burdens associated with debating a proposition of policy. You would not merely address the policy in broad terms, but would be required propose a specific plan of action, including what the policy would mandate (exactly what would be done), who would administer the policy, and how the plan would be funded and enforced. You would also have to present evidence suggesting that your specific plan would solve the problems you identified, and defend your plan against attacks made by the negative team.

There are two primary differences between the burdens imposed by quasi-policy and policy propositions. First, in addition to justifying a course of action, to support a policy resolution you must present a clear, specific plan or model piece of legislation. Second, you must defend the specifics of your plan as well as the general course of action proposed by the resolution. For example, when defending the policy resolution that the Federal Government should significantly restrict the possession and/or use of handguns by civilians in the United States, you would offer a clear, concrete plan that significantly restricts the possession and/or use of handguns by civilians in this country. Figure 1 illustrates a plan you could use for this resolution.

Figure 1

Sample Affirmative Plan

I. Administration: This plan will be administered by the Bureau of Alcohol, Tobacco, and Firearms of the U.S. Treasury Department.

II. Mandates: Establish a national law requiring a 14-day cool-off waiting period for all civilians wishing to purchase a handgun.

- **A. Any individual intending to purchase a handgun must file an application of intent with a retailer.**
- **B. A recent photograph and identification documentation must accompany each application.**
- **C. The retailer must forward the application to BATF within 24 hours of receipt.**
- **D. The consumer may purchase a handgun from that retailer no sooner than 14 days nor later than 28 days after filing the application.**

III. Enforcement: BATF will investigate and prosecute all violations of this plan.

- **A. Retailers convicted of selling handguns in lieu of processing an application, or before or after the 14-28 day cooling-off period, will lose their license to sell firearms.**
- **B. Retailers convicted of failing to process applications in accordance with these restrictions will be fined $1000 for a first offense, $5000 for a second offense, will lose their license to sell firearms upon a third conviction.**
- **B. Individuals who falsify applications or purchase handguns in violation of these restrictions will be fined $1000 and imprisoned for a period of 30 days.**

IV. Funding: Enforcement costs will appear as a specific expenditure in the BATF annual budget, and will be funded through general federal revenues.

Notice that the plan in Figure 1 is a bare-bones outline of legislation to restrict civilian possession of handguns. It identifies the specific restrictions which will be imposed, who is responsible for enforcing the restrictions, and how the plan will be funded. It is *not* a complete piece of legislation — there are many legal and legislative concerns which would be addressed in a complete legislative document that are missing from a policy resolution plan. The plan is a working outline which defines the essential nature of the real legislation, enabling the debaters to get at the fundamental issues surrounding this legislative action.

Stock Issues in Policy Debate

Debating the policy dimension of a resolution introduces a specific set of argumentative issues which act as a general framework for the debate. As a policy debater, you must address whether there is a problem to be resolved (need for action), why our current arsenal of policies is deficient (inherency), how the specific plan would relieve the problem (solvency), whether the specific plan would generate any undesirable side-effects (disadvantages), and whether there would be a better way to go about relieving the problem (counterplan). These five issues are called the *stock issues* of policy, because they outline the fundamental concerns which ought to accompany any legislative discussion. In a policy debate, a judge's decision is based on how well these issues are addressed by the debaters.

Need. Debaters use the term *status quo* to refer to the current state of affairs surrounding any policy discussion. What do you find objectionable about the status quo? Your need for action could be grounded in specific *harms* you might identify in the status quo, or in specific *advantages* which might result from a change in policy. In either event, you have created a basis for comparing the status quo with the policy you support. The presence of identifiable harms and the absence of particular advantages in the status quo become arguments supporting your contention that we need to improve our policies.

Inherency. Whatever the problem, agents of action probably have a vast arsenal of policies which they could draw upon to eliminate the harms or produce the advantages associated with the problem you have identified. What is wrong with those policies? Debaters search for *inherent barriers* to resolving a problem without changing policies. Are there fundamental structural flaws in the policies already at our disposal? Are there perverse attitudes which are allowed to affect the way problems are resolved? The inherency issue involves a search for the institutional causes of problems. If you cannot identify why status quo policies fail to resolve your problem, then you cannot know what policy changes to specify in your plan.

Solvency. Your plan details a specific course of action designed to resolve the problem you have identified in the status quo. What makes you think that your plan will diminish the harms or generate the advantages around which you have built your case? At a minimum, you must show that your plan eliminates the institutional causes by correcting the structural flaws or circumventing the perverse attitudes in the status quo. You also are expected to provide, by virtue of models, past experience, or expert testimony, evidence which supports your assumption that eliminating the institutional causes will eliminate the effects of status quo policies.

Disadvantages. Policies are never introduced in a vacuum. Action taken to produce one effect may well produce undesirable side-effects. When the cure is worse than the disease, it is better to leave the disease untreated. When you argue *against* a specific change in policy, you will want to search for possible side-effects in order to establish that the affirmative plan would be, on-balance, disadvantageous.

Counterplan. Often, people generally agree that there are problems which the status quo cannot reasonably be expected to resolve. However, they may well disagree on how to go about solving those problems. When you argue against a proposed policy, you may choose to do it on the grounds that there is a better way of dealing with the inabilities of the status quo, and so you propose an alternative to the affirmative plan. A counterplan is a specific policy supported by the negative in lieu of defending the status quo. Counterplans require that the negative establish three things in the debate: The negative plan is counter to the resolution (e.g., not merely a different restriction placed on civilian possession of handguns), the negative plan competes with the affirmative (you are arguing to reject the affirmative plan, not merely to add to it), and the negative plan is superior to the affirmative (you are claiming that your alternative is a better approach). Counterplan debates essentially boil down to a comparison of plan effects — the plan which does more good and less bad is the preferred plan.

Although the affirmative team has *the* burden of proof in a debate (burden to prove the resolution true), all debaters have *a* burden to prove their claims. As you examine the five stock issues, you will make a number of arguments about the status quo (or counterplan), the affirmative plan, and the effects of each. Each of these arguments will involve you making a claim about one of the policies, and it is your responsibility to provide adequate evidence and reasoning to support your claim. It makes no difference whether you are taking the affirmative or the negative side of a resolution, the basic rule of debate is "She who asserts must prove."

Speaker Duties

Policy debate is normally a cross-examination team event, which means that it uses the same general format as CEDA debate — four constructive speeches, interspersed with four cross-examination periods, and followed by four rebuttal speeches reserved for extending and summarizing arguments introduced during constructives. The primary difference is the relative length of the speeches. Figure 2 illustrates the structure of a typical NDT debate.

Figure 2
Order and Length of Speeches

1st affirmative constructive	**9 minutes**
Cross-examination by the 2nd negative	**3 minutes**
1st negative constructive	**9 minutes**
Cross-examination by the 1st affirmative	**3 minutes**
2nd affirmative constructive	**9 minutes**
Cross-examination by the 1st negative	**3 minutes**

2nd negative constructive	**9 minutes**
Cross-examination by the 2nd affirmative	**3 minutes**
1st negative rebuttal	**6 minutes**
1st affirmative rebuttal	**6 minutes**
2nd negative rebuttal	**6 minutes**
2nd affirmative rebuttal	**6 minutes**

Policy debate tournaments also allow debaters time to prepare for speeches, generally 10 minutes per team, which they are allowed to divide as they wish.

The cross-examination periods in NDT debate serve the same general function as in CEDA debate: to clarify issues, expose weaknesses in existing arguments, and to set-up subsequent arguments. However, since policy resolutions make different demands on you than do non-policy resolutions, the responsibilities of individual speakers are somewhat different. The following is a basic discussion of the speaker duties in a typical policy debate.

First Affirmative Constructive (1AC). Since your affirmative case is unlikely to change in the midst of a tournament, the 1AC is the one speech which can be scripted in advance of a debate. In this speech, you must identify the resolution being debated and construct a *prima facie* case which supports that resolution. Technically, prima facie means "at first glance," which means that this speech must make a case against the status quo which is sufficient to support the resolution absent any negative response. In practical terms, this means that you must present your plan of action, and support that plan by identifying a problem with the status quo, pinpointing the inherent barriers which prevent the status quo from resolving the problem, and providing reasons to believe that your plan will resolve the problem. Notice that the disadvantage and counterplan issues are absent from this speech. You cannot be expected to defend against claims that your plan would create particular disadvantages, or compare your plan to particular counterplans, until the negative identifies the disadvantages or proposes a counterplan.

First Negative Constructive (1NC). As the first negative speaker in a policy debate, you must decide whether you are willing to accept that the particular plan presented by the affirmative is "topical," that is, whether or not it is an example of the kind of policy proposed by the resolution. For example, you might not be willing to accept CIA paramilitary operations as an example of military intervention. When an affirmative plan is not topical, it is because they have misinterpreted or equivocated some term in the resolution. What is that term? How should that term be defined in this context? Topicality arguments are very powerful because they are sufficient to win the debate on procedural grounds, irrespective of what happens with the stock issues. However, since disputes about definitions are as likely to be grounded in differences in interpretation as in mistaken interpretation, judges generally are reluctant to rule that an affirmative plan is not topical. Your second duty as 1NC is to decide what policy you will compare with the proposed plan — will it be the status quo (programs and policies as they now exist), a modified status quo (existing programs and policies modified in some minor way to make them more effective), or a counterplan. If you choose to defend a counterplan, you normally are expected to present it sometime during this speech, preferably near the beginning of the speech. If you choose to defend the status quo or to modify the status quo, you probably will want to make a number of inherency arguments in which you show how existing programs or policies could go about solving the problem. Finally, it is your responsibility to attack the affirmative case by making arguments which refute the problem, inherency, and solvency arguments introduced by the affirmative. You need not attack every argument in the affirmative case (you need only win one stock issue to win the debate), but judges generally assume that you agree to those arguments which you are unable to refute.

Second Affirmative Constructive (2AC). As the second affirmative speaker, you are responsible for defending your case against the attacks introduced by the 1NC. If the 1NC argues that you are not topical, you must defend the way you have interpreted the disputed terms in the resolution. If the 1NC proposes a counterplan, you should consider arguing that it is topical (not counter to the resolution) or that it could be added to the affirmative plan (not competitive with the plan). You should definitely attack the ability of the counterplan to solve the problems identified in the 1AC, identify disadvantages the counterplan would produce, and refute any the 1NC claims about why the counterplan would be better than the affirmative plan. Finally, you must defend your problem, inherency, and solvency arguments against any attacks levied by 1NC. Unlike the negative, as the affirmative you cannot choose to leave opposing arguments unanswered — you have to win *all* of the stock issues in the debate, and failing to answer some of the negative arguments places this in jeopardy.

Second Negative Constructive (2NC). As the second negative speaker, your primary duty is to make constructive arguments addressing the two plan-oriented issues in the debate — solvency and disadvantages. Constructive solvency arguments are proactive rather than reactive. That is, rather than refuting the solvency proofs offered by the affirmative (a reaction which ought to have been pursued in the 1NC), you should introduce arguments which demonstrate barriers which will hamper the ability of the specific affirmative plan to solve the problems identified in the 1AC. Disadvantages are cause-and-effect kinds of arguments in which provisions of the affirmative plan, or effects of the affirmative plan, act as causes of undesirable side-effects. Disadvantages must be unique, either in the sense that the status quo (or counterplan) do not produce these side-effects, or do not produce them to as great a degree as the affirmative plan. It is *not* legitimate to argue that the affirmative plan will not or cannot be adopted, because the debate focuses on what *ought* to be, not what *will* be. Thus, such arguments as "Congress will never pass this plan," or "The courts will reject it as unconstitutional" are illegitimate. In this speech, you assume that the plan has been adopted and focus on the probable effects of its adoption. If your partner proposed a counterplan, you might want to take time in this speech to defend it against the attacks made by the 1AC. This will make the job of the 1NR substantially easier. Finally, if 2AC added anything new to the affirmative case, you will want to take this opportunity to refute these new arguments.

First Negative Rebuttal (1NR). In this speech, you are completing the negative block, 15 minutes of negative arguments interrupted only by a cross-examination period. What you do *not* want to do in this speech is waste time covering arguments addressed by the 2NC. Instead, you defend and extend the arguments you made during your constructive speech. Ordinarily, you will not be able to cover as much ground in your rebuttal as you were able to cover in your constructive speech. This means that you must choose which arguments to defend and extend. Which of your constructive arguments do you still think you can win? If you win those arguments, will they help you win the problem, inherency, solvency, or counterplan issues? Do not waste time defending inconsequential arguments or arguments you will not win. Instead, concentrate your defense on those arguments which can determine the outcome of the debate.

First Affirmative Rebuttal (1AR). This speech can be the most stressful speech in the debate. Following 15 minutes of negative arguments, you must defend your case against any and all outstanding attacks in only 6 minutes. Thus, time is your most precious commodity. Your first duty is to refute the solvency and disadvantage arguments presented by the 2NC. You do not have time to thoroughly analyze each argument, so you are looking for fundamental flaws to attack. You are not trying to get in as many blows as possible, but to make those you do have time to get in disabling blows. Your second duty is to defend your case against the arguments extended by the 1NR. Your job has probably been made easier by the fact that the 1NR did not try to carry through every possible argument. Do not waste valuable time dealing with arguments the 1NR decided to drop.

Second Negative Rebuttal (2NR). In this speech, you will summarize the negative position in the debate. For the first time, you will be defending the arguments your partner has been making about the problem, inherency, and solvency issues. Also, you must defend and extend the solvency and disadvantage arguments you introduced in your constructive speech. Like the 1NR, you must choose which arguments to defend and which to let die. However, make sure that you do not drop any arguments which could win the debate. Even if the 1AR ignored or did a poor job of answering an argument, dropping it means that you have conceded it to the affirmative.

Second Affirmative Rebuttal (2AR). As the final speaker in the debate, your job is to summarize the debate from the perspective of the affirmative. How does your case now stand? Which of your arguments did the negative stop disputing? Where has the negative failed to adequately defend the arguments they continued to extend? Your basic duty is to defend each of the stock issues against all remaining negative arguments. However, you want to do this in a way which emphasizes the "big picture," a comparison between your plan and the status quo (or counterplan) which demonstrates why the judge should prefer your course of action.

This discussion has been limited to the basic duties associated with debating policy propositions. There are any number of common policy debate strategies which may affect the way these duties are fulfilled — choosing between harms, comparative advantages, and goals cases, using plan spikes, introducing add-on advantages, using argument shells, making circumvention arguments, constructing extra-topicality arguments, etc. Many of these strategies are used effectively in novice level debates, and they are matters you will want to take up with your coach.

Conclusion

As a policy debater, you will develop many of the same skills as you would debating non-policy topics. You will learn how to support your arguments with evidence and reasoning, to recognize weaknesses in evidence and reasoning, to ask and answer probing questions, to think on your feet, and to express yourself clearly and cogently. As with non-policy debate, you also will learn a great deal about the issues involved in topics of national and international importance. The difference in policy debate is that you will take these topics to another level — the policy dimension. In non-policy debate, you can learn about how to analyze facts and value judgments, and how facts and values affect the decision making process. In policy debate, as you search for problems in the status quo, you also will learn about judging facts and values. In addition, you will learn about how practical issues such as inherency, solvency, disadvantages and counterplans influence policy decision making. Policy debating will open up to you an entirely new range of argumentation experiences.

Lincoln-Douglas Debate
Mark Woolsey

The 1858 Illinois senatorial debates between Abraham Lincoln and Stephen Douglas are firmly entrenched as one of the most celebrated campaign events in American history. The 1960 presidential debate between John F. Kennedy and Richard Nixon is regarded by many experts as the pivotal event in one of the closest presidential elections of all time. Televised debates between major presidential (and vice-presidential) candidates are now an established feature of the presidential campaign process. In fact, few political events draw more media attention than modern day presidential debates, with the number of people tuning in rivaling the audience for the Superbowl.

Today, with an ever growing number of tournaments offering individual debate, you have the opportunity to participate in a similar forum. The event is Lincoln-Douglas (L-D) debate, named after the famous 19th Century debates. Since most seasoned intercollegiate debaters have little trouble switching between debate events, the purpose of this discussion is to introduce incoming high school debaters and ambitious individual events competitors to intercollegiate L-D debate. It may also serve to inspire an experienced team debater to give L-D a try, or intrigue a forensics coach or tournament director to experiment with the event.

The Lincoln-Douglas Format

College tournament Lincoln-Douglas debate uses a conventional five speech, one-on-one, cross-examination framework, with the length of individual speeches depending upon the particular tournament. Figures 1 and 2 illustrate the standard L-D formats.

Figure 1

Order and Length of Speeches (Long Format)

Affirmative Constructive Speech	**8 minutes**
Negative Cross-Examination of Affirmative	**3 minutes**
Negative Constructive Speech	**12 minutes**
Affirmative Cross-Examination of Negative	**3 minutes**
Affirmative Rebuttal	**6 minutes**
Negative Rebuttal	**6 minutes**
Affirmative Rebuttal	**4 minutes**

Professor Woolsey is currently Director of Forensics at Fresno City College.

Figure 2

Order and Length of Speeches (Short Format)

Affirmative Constructive Speech	**6 minutes**
Negative Cross-Examination of Affirmative	**3 minutes**
Negative Constructive Speech	**7 minutes**
Affirmative Cross-Examination of Negative	**3 minutes**
Affirmative Rebuttal	**4 minutes**
Negative Rebuttal	**6 minutes**
Affirmative Rebuttal	**3 minutes**

Tournaments using the long format usually allow each debater five minutes of total preparation time, while those using the short format usually allow four minutes to each debater.

Speaker Duties. Your responsibilities in each speech are drawn from a common sense adaptation of team debate. The affirmative constructive speech must introduce a *prima facie* case, the stock issues of which will depend upon whether the topic takes the form of a proposition of fact, value or policy. The negative constructive speech combines the case/off-case or case/plan duties assigned to the two constructive speeches in team debate. The first of the affirmative rebuttals is similar to the team 1AR, the negative rebuttal is similar to the team 2NR, and the remaining affirmative rebuttal is similar to the team 2AR. As in any cross-examination debate, the C-X periods are used to clarify issues, probe for weaknesses, or set-up arguments.

Differences Between College and High School Lincoln-Douglas Debate

While Lincoln-Douglas debate is a relatively recent addition to many college tournaments, it has been a regular part of high school forensics competition for almost 15 years. In 1980, the National Forensic League sanctioned the event for the first time. Since then, the number of students who have competed in L-D probably runs into six figures. The growth of L-D at the secondary level stemmed from a desire to offer an alternative to more traditional two-person debate. L-D was seen both as an escape from the abuses of team debate (over reliance on evidence and rapid delivery), and as a forum for examining value resolutions. Lincoln-Douglas debates at the secondary level stress the public speaking side of debate. As Maridell Fryar and David Thomas have explained, high school L-D debate "is founded on the principle that debate can be an oral communication event in which students learn how to speak, as well as how to do research and apply critical thinking."[1] The topics almost always take the form of value propositions, which are used only for a few tournaments before changing to a new topic.

---

1 Maridell Fryar and David A. Thomas, *Student Congress and Lincoln-Douglas Debate* (Lincolnwood, Illinois: National Textbook Company, 1985).

At the college level, the event often borrows the current NDT or CEDA team debate topic, although some tournaments frame a resolution especially for L-D debate. Depending upon the traditions of a particular region, L-D topics are as likely to be policy as to be non-policy resolutions, and the event draws its conventions of topic analysis and argumentation strategies from both the NDT and CEDA debate communities. If there is a similarity between high school and college L-D debate, it is that there generally is greater emphasis placed on presentation skills than in the team debate. As the rules for the National Forensic Association national tournament remind, "Rapid fire delivery . . . is considered antithetical to the purpose and intent of this event."[2]

Despite a similar focus on presentation skills, college L-D is far less likely to be confused with "dueling oratories." College L-D is, first and foremost, a debate event. Lincoln-Douglas debates are expected to be centered around the same notions of stock issues and burdens of proof as CEDA and NDT team debates. You are expected to display a firm knowledge of the topic area, be well researched, to understand how to use evidence and reasoning to support your claims, to be prepared to effectively refute your opponent's arguments, and to defend your own arguments. Debaters who ignore traditional stock issues, who use the negative constructive to present a prepared generic negative case, and who use rebuttals solely for summary, are unlikely to succeed in college competition. Debate is, by its nature, an extemporaneous interactive event. Choosing to ignore either dimension inevitably dooms you to failure.

Differences Between Lincoln-Douglas Debate and Platform Speaking

Lincoln-Douglas debate can be viewed as a combination of the Persuasive Speaking, Extemporaneous Speaking, and Impromptu Speaking events. At the same time, it is significantly different than any of the three.

Lincoln-Douglas is like the persuasive event in that it involves a substantial commitment to research. Just as persuasive speeches are expected to be well documented, debating requires that you assume a burden to prove the claims you make. Debate carries this expectation to an extreme. In competitive debate, all facts and opinions are suspicious. Where you might have asserted what you considered to be common knowledge or an inconsequential fact in a persuasive speech, you probably will be expected to provide documentation in L-D debate (if not by the judge, then by your opponent). Also, it is common in persuasive speaking to paraphrase sources, so long as the information is properly attributed. In debate, all of your information should be presented verbatim so that your opponent has an opportunity to critique your interpretation of the original text. A second major difference is that L-D debate focuses more heavily on *logos*

---

2 National Forensic Association, "Rules of Competition for NFA L-D Debate," 1994 National Forensic Association National Tournament Invitation, 6.

oriented appeals. While debate flirts with *ethos* (source qualifications) and *pathos* (impacts), the focus is concentrated on the quality of your documentation and the sufficiency of your reasoning rather than your ability demonstrate a grasp of persuasive appeals.

Lincoln-Douglas is similar to the extemporaneous and impromptu events in its modes of delivery. Despite the importance of good delivery skills, debate speeches are not scripted, practiced presentations. You cannot effectively interact with your opponent's arguments when you work from a script. The affirmative constructive, which can be scripted, is *interpreted* less in its presentation than is the case with persuasive speeches. L-D debaters are expected to be effective communicators, but judges are not looking for oratorical magnificence. Like the extemporaneous event, your topics will be drawn from significant contemporary issues, and your speeches are expected to be argumentative in nature. However, extemporaneous topics usually are framed in a fashion which allows you to choose which side of a controversy to support. In debate events, you are assigned to a particular side (except in elimination rounds), and are expected to be able to defend effectively either side of the controversy. Also, since you will use the same topic throughout a tournament (and probably for several tournaments), you have an opportunity to research prior to the tournament, and so you are expected to be far more knowledgeable, and your documentation far more complete, that in an extemporaneous speech.

The most important difference between Lincoln-Douglas debate and the platform speaking events is that debate involves an interactive series of speeches. By its nature, debate places your ego at greater risk. As an analogy, imagine how you would feel if, following your persuasive speech, the next contestant spent seven-to-twelve minutes explaining to the judge just how poorly argued your speech really was. In platform speaking, you do not experience critical feedback until the end of the tournament, and even then it will involve only a few lines on a ballot and will (hopefully) balance discouraging observations with encouraging comments. In debate, criticism is immediate and wholly negative. What makes debate exciting is that you are given an opportunity to defend yourself, and to critique your opponent in return.

Closing Thoughts

In the past, college level Lincoln-Douglas debaters tended to come from team debaters who were, for one reason or another, without a partner. This has been changing, particularly in the eastern regions where individual events tournaments are increasingly offering an L-D event. In the western regions, L-D is no longer an uncommon event, as more tournaments are beginning to accommodate small forensics programs which have few students interested in debate and little time or expertise for debate coaching. The greater focus on speaking skills, and the somewhat less demanding environment of Lincoln-Douglas debate, means that these programs can make debate experiences available to students who would otherwise have been restricted to platform speaking events. At the same time, many students have found a home in Lincoln-Douglas debate. They see the L-D environment as more conducive to developing the kinds of skills which attracted them to forensics in the first place, and more relevant to their post-collegiate careers.

For traditional debate programs, L-D can be a unique way to get new students involved. Given the shorter time frame and less complex division of responsibilities, L-D can be far less intimidating than team debate. Without the difficulties of trying to coordinate partners, intramural L-D competitions are easy to administer. Recently, the argumentation instructors on our campus had tremendous success bringing non-forensics students together for a one day Lincoln-Douglas tournament. With this modest experience under their belts, students who enjoyed their initial debates are more likely to be willing to try tournament debating when they can compete in a familiar environment. In this fashion, L-D can serve as a practical way of funneling beginning students into the mainstream program.

College level Lincoln-Douglas debate is unlikely to challenge the predominance of team debate events as it has at the secondary level. However, L-D has been a welcome addition to the slate of events at those tournaments which have embraced it. If you are a beginning debater, particularly in a program which does not have an established support system to facilitate your transition into debate competition, give L-D a try. Irrespective of whether you move on to the more demanding environment of CEDA or NDT team debate, your experiences in Lincoln-Douglas will help you understand why most college debaters think that debate is the ultimate forensics activity.

Appendix One
Sample Statement of Ethical Principles

[Editor's Note: Intercollegiate forensics is an activity which involves a great deal of unregulated student, educator, judge and tournament administrator behavior. Nonetheless, it is an activity in which all parties are expected to act in accordance with high ethical principles. Various national and regional forensics organizations have attempted to capture those principles in aspirational statements and/or codes of ethics. The following statement of ethical principles was selected for inclusion in this text because it clearly and cogently expresses the ethical standards to which the forensics community aspires. Although the statement is framed in terms of CEDA debate events, the principles contained therein are applicable to the full range of forensics activities. As indicated in the Epilogue, this document is not intended as a series of rules subject to adjudication (although such rules may appear in other documents). Rather, it is a statement of the ethical behavior to which all students, educators, judges and tournament administrators should aspire.]

Preamble

The Cross Examination Debate Association is committed to promoting ethical communication behavior. Its members recognize that the adversarial and competitive nature of academic debate places participants — students, educators, judges, and tournament administrators — in the position of having to weigh the merits of competing strategies that may have ethical implications. This document attempts to set forth the aspirations of the Association for ethical and educational debate activity. It is hoped that this statement of ethical principles will promote behavior and discussion which ensure the long-term growth and survival of intercollegiate debate.

Competitor Practices

Students competing in CEDA debate contests share a unique opportunity to develop their abilities to analyze, research, organize, evaluate, and communicate ideas and to experience personal growth. This opportunity is maximized when participants recognize their responsibility to preserve and promote the educational benefits of intercollegiate debate.

Participation. Participants in CEDA debate should recognize that their academic program is more important than their competitive success. Minimally, students who compete in CEDA debate should be in good standing at and be making normal progress toward a degree from the

---

Taken from "Statement of Ethical Principles," Constitution and By-Laws of the Cross Examination Debate Association, 15-18. Used by permission of the Cross Examination Debate Association.

institution which they represent in competition. Maximally, students who compete in CEDA debate will apply their developing abilities in such a way as to achieve the very best academic standing of which they are capable. Sacrificing one's academic progress for competitive success, or extending one's college career to excessive length in order to go on debating are behaviors contrary to the goals of this organization.

While there are exceptional occasions in which a student with a baccalaureate degree wishes to participate in debate (e.g., a non-traditional student seeking certification to teach), CEDA debate is designed to be primarily an undergraduate activity.

Competitive fairness is best maintained for all students when eligibility standards and division definitions are respected by all participants. Students should be familiar with the eligibility provisions and division definitions of the CEDA constitution and by-laws, and of individual tournaments, and should abide by those limits.

Competitive Behavior. Students engaging in CEDA debate are obligated to adhere to high ethical standards. Such an ethical commitment by debaters is essential because the value of tournament activity is directly dependent upon the integrity of those involved. For that reason, it is the duty of each debater to participate honestly and fairly.

Furthermore, students should remember that debate is an oral, interactive process. It is the debater's duty to aspire to the objective of effective oral expression of ideas. Behaviors which belittle, degrade, demean, or otherwise dehumanize others are not in the best interest of the activity because they interfere with the goals of education and personal growth. The ethical CEDA debater recognizes the rights of others and communicates with respect for opponents, colleagues, critics, and audience members. Communication which engenders ill-will and disrespect for forensics ultimately reduces the utility of forensics for all who participate in it and should, therefore, be avoided.

Students should recognize the importance of judges to the debate activity. Students should be willing to listen to judges' statements regarding conduct of rounds, suggestions for improvement, and reasons for decisions. While debaters should feel free to ask questions of judges, they should be wary of badgering judges for decisions and comments during the course of a tournament; they should recognize that the written ballot is the primary means of communicating reasons for decision and that tournament rules often prohibit revelation of decisions.

Use of Debate Materials. The primary creation of argument and the primary research effort in CEDA debate must be the student's. Students who rely on briefs written or evidence researched by faculty or graduate assistants, on handbook evidence rather than library research, or materials and evidence traded among programs fall short of the goal of maximizing their development as competent arguers and users of evidence.

Evidence plays a key role in debate. It is important, therefore, that debaters use evidence responsibly. Responsible use of evidence includes accurate recording and documenting of material, as well as avoidance of plagiarism, misrepresentation, distortion, or fabrication. Debaters are responsible for the integrity of all the evidence they use.

Debaters should clearly identify and qualify, during their speeches, the source of all the evidence they use. Omitting the source of evidence denies opponents, judges, and the audience the opportunity to evaluate the quality of the information. Claiming another's written or spoken words as one's own is plagiarism, a very serious offense against responsible scholarship. Debaters should use only evidence which is in the public domain and, hence, open to critical evaluation by others.

Debaters should not fabricate, distort, or misrepresent evidence. If evidence is misrepresented, distorted, or fabricated, the conclusions drawn from it are meaningless and ethically suspect. Fabrication of evidence refers to falsely representing a cited fact or statement of opinion as evidence when the material in question is not authentic. Distorted evidence refers to misrepresenting the actual or implied content of the factual or opinion evidence. In determining whether evidence has been distorted, debaters should ask if the evidence deviates from the quality, quantity, probability, or degree of force of the author's position on the particular point in question. Any such deviation should be avoided because such alteration can give undue rhetorical force to an advocate's argument. Distortions include, but are not limited to:

1. quoting out of context;
2. misinterpreting the evidence so as to alter its meaning;
3. omitting salient information from quotations or paraphrases;
4. adding words to a quotation which were not present in the original source of the evidence without identifying such as addition;
5. failure to provide within a reasonable time complete documentation of the evidence (name of author(s), source of publication, full date, page numbers and author(s) credentials when available in the original) when challenged.

Commitment to Program. Debaters should recognize that when they join a forensics program, that program commits substantial teaching and monetary resources to their education and personal growth. Consequently, transferring from one CEDA debate program to another is not encouraged. A student who is considering transferring to another debate program should notify his or her current coach as soon as possible. The student should consult with his or her coach about the desirability of the transfer prior to making the final decision, and should notify the former coach as soon as possible after the final decision is made.

Educator Practices

Because CEDA debate is primarily an educational activity, forensics educators should emphasize learning before competitive success and should try to pass on this view to their students. It is the responsibility of the forensics educator to maximize the opportunity for ethical development and behavior among all debate participants.

Ethical principles for forensics educators participating in CEDA debate include:

A. Forensics educators should enter student competitors in accordance with national, regional, and individual tournament regulations for eligibility.

B. Forensics educators should encourage their students to compete honestly, fairly, and ethically in each and every competitive debate round in which they participate.

C. Because students differ in talent, experience, motivation, and purpose, forensics educators should adapt pedagogical methods to student needs. In all cases, however, coaching efforts should supplement, not substitute for, student efforts. The primary creation of argument and the primary research effort in debate must be the student's. Forensics educators may engage in limited research designed to teach students research techniques, demonstrate model evidence or briefs, or identify key areas of argument while teaching scholarly techniques in debate, but the fundamental arguments, cases, briefs, and research must be the students' own.

D. Forensics educators should maintain, and teach their students to maintain, the highest ethical principles of logic and reasoning, evidence, and behavior in debate. Forensics educators should teach students the principles and objectives of sound reasoning and the value of rigorous scholarship.

E. Forensics educators should encourage behavior that will insure ordinary progress towards the completion of students' undergraduate degrees. Forensics educators should also recognize the importance of students' development as whole persons, including positive relationships with family, friends, employers, and community.

F. Because all students can benefit from debate experience at some level, and because all students, at whatever level, require and deserve coaches' attention and efforts, forensics educators should all treat students fairly and promote equality of opportunity for appropriate and challenging learning experiences for all students.

G. Forensics educators should recognize that the recruiting and transfer issues in collegiate debate are sensitive ones. The standard in recruiting and transfer should always be the overall best interests of the student. CEDA endorses the following guidelines for forensics educators:

   1. Forensics educators should be honest with students concerning the educational opportunities of their schools and of their forensics programs, and of the educational opportunities and forensics programs of other institutions.
   2. Forensics educators should avoid unduly influencing students from another program. When transfer between programs becomes a serious possibility, the student's new coach should seek professional contact with the student's current coach to discuss the matter.
   3. Forensics educators should avoid conflict of interest vis a vis their recruiting efforts when running a workshop or tournament (e.g., granting potential recruits special

jobs or opportunities), or when judging (e.g., rewarding decisions or high points to promote recruiting goals).

Judge Practices

Judges are important to the debate activity. In addition to supplying decisions as judges, they educate the student participants through their reasons for decisions and suggestions for improvement. CEDA recognizes the inherent tension and potential conflict between these two roles. In an attempt to facilitate both functions, CEDA encourages judge-educators to acknowledge their two-fold responsibility and act with competence, integrity, fairness, and courtesy before, during, and after each debate round.

Debate seeks to be a full, free testing of ideas, yet as educators, some feel a responsibility to discourage student behavior they find to be counterproductive. Often judges must delicately balance these two considerations: the need for rigorous examination of any and all views, however unpopular or unrealistic, and the guidance and direction of student behavior. If undesirable behavior is discourages in a positive, fair, and courteous manner, the judge/éducator roles can be simultaneously satisfied.

Ethical principles for judges participating in CEDA include:

A. Judges should strive at all times to render impartial decisions. Judges should excuse themselves from rounds they do not feel they could judge fairly.

B. Judges should be willing to inform debaters, either through a statement of philosophy or through response to student questions, of strongly held beliefs or standards that could affect the outcome of the debate round.

C. Judges should evaluate debate rounds on the arguments as they are presented by the debaters, rather than on personal knowledge of or opinion about particular substantive arguments. Judges need not be "tabula rasa," but do need to be fair.

D. Judges should provide detailed and constructive criticism of any and all rounds of debate they evaluate. Reasons for decision should be in accordance with any beliefs or standards announced at the outset of the round. Judges are expected to provide written comments on the ballots provided by the tournament, even if they also provide an oral critique. These written comments should be made available to all the debaters a judge has heard by the conclusion of the tournament.

E. Judges have an ethical obligation to uphold without exception the tournament rules. Judges should inform the tournament director of any conflicts which could prevent them from carrying out this duty.

F. Judges who have the misfortune of witnessing fraudulent behavior on the part of competitors they are judging should:
   1. conform to tournament rules (if any), and
   2. act in accordance with their consciences in assessing appropriate sanctions.

Tournament Administration

In administering tournaments, educators should strive to insure that all students have an equal opportunity to excel. Educators should be particularly cognizant of the issues involved in scheduling and judge assignment. Tournament administration should seek to promote high quality and fair learning experiences for all debaters. Tournaments should be hosted for educational, not profit-making, reasons.

A. In order to give all participants equal information about tournament procedures, tournament invitations should include clear definitions of events and division, clear explanations of matching and judge assignment systems, clear explanations of criteria for advancement to elimination rounds and for awards, clear announcements of fees and schedules, and a clear statement of tournament rules.

B. In order to provide a fair and educational tournament, administrators matching debate rounds should attempt to allow students an equal number of rounds on each side of the resolution and should maximize insofar as possible the range of opponents encountered by each team.

C. In order to provide a fair and educational tournament, judge assignment insofar as possible should be random. Debaters should have equal opportunity to be heard by a range of judges and to be protected from judges who might have a conflict of interest.

D. In order to maximize the educational function of tournaments, administrators should make results and ballots available to all participants as soon as possible at the end of competition.

Epilogue

Provisions of this document are not subject to adjudication. For specific standards regarding eligibility and their adjudication, participants should consult the CEDA by-laws.

Appendix Two
Descriptions of Individual Events

American Forensic Association

All materials used in competition shall not have been used by the student in interscholastic competition prior to September 1 [of the current academic year].

A contestant may not use the same cutting/content or any portion of that cutting/content in more than one prepared event at any given tournament.

After-Dinner Speaking. An original, humorous speech by the student, designed to exhibit sound speech composition, thematic coherence, direct communicative public speaking skills, and good taste. The speech should not resemble a night club act, an impersonation, or comic dialogue. Audio-visual aids may or may not be used to supplement and reinforce the message. Minimal notes are permitted. Maximum time limit is 10 minutes.

Communication Analysis. An original speech by the student designed to offer an explanation and/or evaluation of a communication event such as a speech, speaker, movement, poem, poster, film, campaign, etc., through the use of rhetorical principles. Audio-visual aids may or may not be used to supplement and reinforce the message. Manuscripts are permitted. Maximum time limit is 10 minutes.

Drama Interpretation. A cutting which represents one or more characters from a play or plays of literary merit. This material may be drawn from stage, screen or radio. Use of manuscript is required. Maximum time limit is 10 minutes including introduction.

Dramatic Duo. A cutting from a play, humorous or serious, involving the portrayal of two or more characters presented by two individuals. This material may be drawn from stage, screen, or radio. This is not an acting event; thus, no costumes, props, lighting, etc., are to be used. Presentation is from the manuscript and the focus should be off-stage and not to each other. Maximum time limit is 10 minutes including introduction.

Extemporaneous Speaking. Contestants will be given three topics in the general area of current events, choose one, and have 30 minutes to prepare a speech that is the original work of the student. Maximum time limit for the speech is 7 minutes. Limited notes are permitted. Students will speak in listed order. Posting of topics will be staggered.

Impromptu Speaking. An impromptu speech, serious in nature, with topic selections varied by round and by section. Topics will be of a proverb nature. Speakers will have a total of 7 minutes for both preparation and speaking. Timing commences with the acceptance of the topic

---

Taken from "Description of Events," 1994 AFA-NIET Invitation, 9. Used by permission of the American Forensic Association.

sheet. Limited notes are permitted. Each speaker in a given section will choose to speak from one of the same two topics offered.

Informative Speaking. An original, factual speech by the student on a realistic subject to fulfill the general aim to inform the audience. Audio-visuals may or may not be used to supplement and reinforce the message. Multiple sources should be used and cited in the development of the speech. Minimal notes are permitted. Maximum time is 10 minutes including introduction.

Persuasive Speaking. An original speech by the student designed to inspire, reinforce or change the beliefs, attitudes, values or actions of the audience. Audio-visual aids may or may not be used to supplement and reinforce the message. Multiple sources should be used and cited in the development of the speech. Minimal notes are permitted. Maximum time limit is 10 minutes.

Poetry Interpretation. A selection or selections of poetry of literary merit which may be drawn from more than one source. Play cuttings and prose works are prohibited. Use of manuscript is required. Maximum time limit is 10 minutes, including introduction.

Program Oral Interpretation. A program of thematically-linked selections of literary merit, chosen from two or three of the recognized genres of competitive interpretation (prose-poetry-drama). A substantial portion of the total time must be devoted to each of the genres used in the program. Different genre means that material must appear in separate pieces of literature (e.g., a poem included in a short story that appears only in that short story does not constitute a poetry genre.) Use of manuscript is required. Maximum time limit is 10 minutes including original introduction and/or transitions.

Prose Interpretation. A selection or selections of prose material of literary merit, which may be drawn from more than one source. Play cuttings and poetry are prohibited. Use of manuscript is required. Maximum time is 10 minutes including introduction.

National Forensic Association

After-Dinner. Each contestant will present an original speech whose purpose is to make a serious point through the use of humor. The speech should reflect the development of a humorous comedic effort, not a stand-up comedy routine. The speech must be memorized. Maximum 10 minutes.

Dramatic Duo. A cutting from a play, humorous or serious, involving the portrayal of two characters presented by two individuals. This is not an acting event. Thus, costumes, props, etc., are not permitted. Presentation must be from manuscript and focus should be off stage. Maximum 10 minutes.

Extemporaneous. For each round, contestants will select one of three topics on current national and international events. The contestant will have thirty minutes to prepare a five to seven minute speech on the topic selected. Notes are permissible, but should be at a minimum. Maximum 7 minutes.

Impromptu. Contestants will receive short excerpts dealing with items of general interest, political, economic, and social issues. The contestant will have a total of seven minutes to divide between preparation and speaking. Students should speak for at least three minutes. All contestants in the same section shall speak on the same topic. Maximum 7 minutes.

Informative. The contestant will deliver an original factual speech on a realistic subject to fulfill a general information need of the audience. Visual aids that supplement/reinforce the message are permitted. The speech must be delivered from memory. Maximum 10 minutes.

Persuasion. A speech to convince, to move to action, or to inspire on a significant issue. Delivered from memory. Maximum 10 minutes.

Poetry. The contestant will present a program of poetic literature. Original introductory comments and transitional remarks are permitted. Programs may consist of single or multiple selections. Manuscripts are required. Maximum 10 minutes.

Prose. The contestant will present a program of prose literature. Original introductory comments and transitional remarks are permitted. Programs may consist of single or multiple selections. Plays are not permitted. Manuscripts are required. Maximum 10 minutes.

Rhetorical Criticism. Contestants will deliver an original critical analysis of any significant rhetorical artifact. The speaker should limit the quotation of, paraphrasing of, or summary of the analyzed artifact to a minimum. Any legitimate critical methodology is permissible as long as it serves to open up the artifact for the audience. The speech must be delivered from memory. Maximum 10 minutes.

Taken from "Description of Events," 1994 NFA National Individual Events Tournament Invitation, 5. Used by permission of the National Forensic Association.

Phi Rho Pi

Unlimited Preparation Events.

These rules apply to the events of Persuasion, Informative, Oral Interpretation, Interpretation of Prose, Interpretation of Poetry, Duo Interpretation, Speech to Entertain, Communication Analysis and Dramatic Interpretation. (NOTE: All interpretation events, other than Interpreters' Theatre, shall be required to use only published material available to everyone through normal research methods.)

The persuasion, informative, speech to entertain, interpretation programs, duo interpretation scenes, or speech(es) or communication act selected for criticism, may be on any subject the speaker may desire.

The speeches and programs in these events should be the work of the student.

No portion of the speeches and programs in these events shall be identical material used in competition prior to the preceding September.

The time limits in these events shall be ten (10) minutes maximum, with no minimum time limit specified. A thirty (30) second grace period will be allowed with the judge having the discretion to determine if the overtime is due to audience response. Timing of the event shall begin with the performance, however, set-up time is to be kept to a minimum.

With the exception of Oral Interpretation, Interpretation of Prose, Interpretation of Poetry, and Dramatic Interpretation which require an extemporized introduction and transitions and the reading of selections from manuscripts, the speaker may use, as a means of presentation, memorized or extemporaneous delivery, with or without notes.

Each contestant shall have available a bibliography, footnotes outline, or manuscript for examination by the Tournament Committee or at its request. The intent of this rule is to prevent plagiarism.

No contestant may use any portion of speech or program in more than *one* event.

Persuasion. The purpose of the persuasive speech shall be to convince, stimulate, or actuate (to win belief, to reinforce conviction, or to ask for or move to action speeches of eulogy, condemnation, inspiration, and problem-solving are equally acceptable). Not more than 10% of speech may be direct quotation.

Informative Speaking. The purposes of the informative speech are to describe, clarify, explain and/or define an object, idea, concept or process. (A speech explaining the nuclear test ban treaty would classify as an informative speech, while a speech giving a value judgment or advocating a position concerning the treaty would classify as a persuasive speech). Audio-visual

---

Taken from "Event Rules," Phi Rho Pi Handbook, *Part III, Document A, Section 3, 19-23. Used by permission of Phi Rho Pi.*

aids may be used so long as they do not interfere with the speaker's ability to communicate effectively with the audience. Contestants are advised that the Tournament Committee will not supply special features for the use of aids.

Interpretation of Poetry. Poetry shall include one or more selections written in rhymed or unrhymed meter or cadence of some regularity excluding drama. If more than one selection is used, these selections should be linked by a thematic transition. All programs must include an introduction.

Interpretation of Prose. Prose shall consist of single or multiple selections of literature printed mainly in paragraph form, excluding drama. If more than one selection is used, these selections should be linked by a thematic transition. All programs must include an introduction.

Dramatic Interpretation. This event shall consist of a cutting or cuttings from a play, teleplay or screen play, featuring monologue or dialogue. If more than one selection is used, these selections should be linked by a thematic transition. All programs must include an introduction. *NOTE: If material has appeared in more than one form (i.e., novel and play, play and essay, etc.) the classification of literature shall be determined by the source from which the cutting was taken. The source should be provided by the coach. In cases of confusion as to which genre best encompasses a selection, the Library of Congress system shall be the basis for final arbitration.*

Oral Interpretation of Literature. This event is to consist of a unified presentation made up of at least two selections of different genre (i.e. prose, poetry, dramatic literature, plays). A contestant may use the works of one or more authors. The selections should develop a theme.

Communication Analysis. Speeches of Communication Analysis may be a spoken event (i.e. speech, speaker, movement, etc.) or of other Communication events (i.e. songs, posters, cartoons, slogans, symbols, etc.). The analysis should be critical rather than descriptive in nature — strictly historical or biographical analysis is not acceptable. The speaker is to apply principles of rhetorical and/or communication theory to the event in order to contribute to a better understanding of that event.

Entertainment Speaking. The Speech to Entertain shall be an original speech, the primary purpose of which is to entertain. Just as in any other speech, there should be a central topic sentence or thesis statement which the speaker develops. This event is not merely a series of jokes or a "stand-up" routine.

Duo Interpretation. A cutting from a play, humorous or serious, involving the portrayal of two or more characters presented by two individuals. This material may be drawn from stage, screen, or radio. This is not an acting event; thus, no costumes, props, lighting, etc., are to be used. Presentation is from the manuscript and the focus should be off-stage and not to each other. Maximum time limit is 10 minutes including introduction.

Limited Preparation Events

Extemporaneous Speaking. The general topics shall be National and International Events in the areas of Politics, economics and International Relations of the three months preceding the National Tournament.

At least thirty (30) minutes before time of speaking, each contestant will be given a choice of three topics. Drawing will be posted at seven minute intervals. The speech should be the work of the student, but notes, books, and magazines may be used in preparation.

The time limit for speaking is seven (7) minutes maximum, with no specified minimum. The speaker may use, for reference while speaking, a maximum of one note card, not to exceed 5" x 8" in size.

Impromptu Speaking. The topics for all rounds shall be drawn from a variety of slogans, maxims, objects, lyrics or other creative topics exclusive of areas covered by extemporaneous speaking. Notes may not be used. One note card, not to exceed 3"x5", may be used by the speaker for reference.

Speakers will be given three (3) topics as outlined above from which to select one topic on which to speak. The seven (7) minutes maximum time limit will begin when the topics are received by the speaker. The speaker may divide the seven (7) minutes between preparation and presentation as desired. (The event will be held with all speakers in the room.)

Interpreters' Theatre

Interpreters Theatre is defined as interpretation of literature by a group of oral readers who act as a medium of expression for an audience.

While Interpreters Theatre is both aural and visual, the emphasis is on the oral interpretation of the printed word and its resultant effects on the minds, emotions and imaginations of the listeners/viewers. The audience should have the feeling of a unified whole in which each performer at all times contributes to the total effect desired.

The time limitation for the performance is twenty-five (25) minutes. An additional 2 minutes shall be allowed for set-up and take-down of material.

Interpreters Theatre is a team entry and is included in the six (6) teams per college limitation. A team is limited to a minimum of three (3) and a maximum of fourteen (14) participants.

Programs are not allowed in this event (handouts).

The audience must have a sense of production being interpreted from a manuscript. Director, performer, and judges should be allowed freedom to exercise artistic, interpretive judgment; however, manuscripts must be interpreted from during the presentation.

Suggestions in contemporary or ensemble dress may be used. The literature should determine the nature of this suggestion, although costuming should not be a focus of this presentation.

Reading stands, chairs, stools, ladders, platforms, steps props, lighting effects may be used. HOWEVER, facilities limitations (space equipment, time, etc.) should govern a director's choice. Readers may stand, sit, or both and may move from one reading stand or locale to another so long as the movement is consistent with the ideas or moods of the literature and the director's concept.

Music/sound effects recorded or live are acceptable as background accompaniment and part of the context. Since the emphasis of Interpreters Theatre is on oral interpreting, complicated musical arrangements that dominate or distract from the oral interpretation will be considered inappropriate. A performer whose sole function is to play a musical instrument on or off-stage will be counted in the 14 persons limit.

Northern California Forensics Association

After-Dinner Speaking. An original humorous speech by the student, designed to exhibit sound speech composition, thematic coherence, direct communicative public speaking skills, and good taste. The speech should not resemble a nightclub act, an impersonation, or a comic dialogue. Audio-visual aids may or may not be used to supplement and reinforce the message. Notes are permitted. Maximum time limit is ten minutes.

Argument Analysis. A maximum of seven minutes speaking time. The contestant must analyze the argumentative components of selected discourse and demonstrate an understanding of the theories of reasoning. A significant period before the round the participants will be given an argumentative statement. Students are free to select any argumentative method to analyze the rhetorical event. The speech should be extemporaneous and notes are allowed. Contestants will all analyze the same discourse, therefore, speakers can only enter the room one at a time. After the speech is given, students are encouraged to stay and hear the remaining contestants. Examples of the type of event we envision are the identification of different fallacies in a letter to the editor, or the discussion of a political campaign speech using Toulmin's argumentative scheme.

Communication Analysis. An original speech by the student designed to offer an explanation and/or evaluation of a communication event such as a speech, speaker, movement, poem, poster, film, campaign, etc., through the use of rhetorical principles. Audio-visual aids may or may not be used to supplement and reinforce the message. Manuscripts are permitted. Maximum time limit is ten minutes.

Dramatic Interpretation. A cutting or cuttings which represents one or more characters from a play or plays of literary merit. This material may be drawn from stage, screen or radio. Use of manuscript is required. Maximum time limit is ten minutes including introduction.

Dramatic Duo. A cutting or cuttings from a play, humorous or serious, involving the portrayal of two or more characters presented by two individuals. This material may be drawn from stage, screen or radio. This is not an acting event. Thus, no costumes, props, lighting, etc., are to be used. Presentation is from the manuscript and focus should be offstage and not to each other. Maximum time limit is ten minutes including introduction.

Extemporaneous Speaking. Contestants will be given three topics in the general area of current events from the ninety days preceding the tournament, choose one, and have thirty minutes to prepare a speech. Maximum time limit for the speech is seven minutes. Limited notes are permitted. Students will speak in listed order. Posting of topics will be staggered.

Impromptu Speaking. An impromptu speech in which the speaker will be provided with a choice of three topics. Topics may include maxims, quotations, lyrics, objects, or other creative topics. Speakers will have a total of seven minutes for both preparation and speaking beginning with receipt of topics. Minimal notes are permitted. Tournament bulletins will specify topic area(s). (It is recommended that if extemporaneous speaking is not offered, then there should be one general current events topic per round offered.)

Informative Speaking. An original factual speech by the student on a realistic subject to fulfill the general aim to inform the audience. Audio-visual aids may or may not be used to supplement and reinforce the message. Multiple sources should be used and cited in the development of the speech. Notes are permitted. Maximum time limit is ten minutes.

Oral Interpretation of Literature. This event is to consist of a unified presentation made up of at least two selections of different genres (i.e. prose, poetry, dramatic literature). A contestant may use the works of one or more authors. The selections should develop a theme. Maximum time limit is ten minutes including introduction.

Poetry Interpretation. A selection or selections of poetry of literary merit, which may be drawn from more that one source. Play cuttings are prohibited. Use of manuscript is required. Maximum time limit is ten minutes including introduction.

Persuasive Speaking. An original speech by the student designed to inspire, reinforce or change the beliefs, attitudes, values or actions of the audience. Audio-visual aids may or may not be used to supplement and reinforce the message. Multiple sources should be used and cited in the development of the speech. Notes are permitted. Maximum time limit is ten minutes.

Prose Interpretation. A selection or selections of prose material of literary merit, which may be drawn from more that one source. Play cuttings are prohibited. Use of manuscript is required. Maximum time limit is ten minutes including introduction.

Readers' Theatre. Total time limit including set-up and take-down is twenty-five minutes. Any literary form in permissible. Material may be published or original. Each Readers' Theatre group shall consist of 3 to 14 people. Recorded or live incidental music is permissible but any live musicians count in the company. Manuscripts must be psychologically present. No costumes beyond ensemble costumes are permitted. Reading stands, chairs, stools, ladders, platforms, steps, props, lighting effects may be used, however, facilities limitations should govern these choices.

Appendix Three
Eligibility Requirements

[Editor's Note: The various forensics associations establish eligibility requirements which ostensibly affect only the tournaments or awards they sponsor. However, in order that students who compete in invitational tournaments might qualify for association tournaments or awards, invitational tournaments generally subscribe to the rules and regulations of select regional and national associations. Most invitational tournaments abide by the AFA, NFA and CEDA eligibility requirements so that individual events contestants may qualify for the AFA and NFA National Tournaments, and debaters may earn CEDA sweepstakes points. In addition, many tournaments subscribe to more restrictive eligibility requirements prescribed by regional or local forensic associations. For instance, all tournaments sanctioned by the Northern California Forensics Association agree to abide by the NCFA eligibility requirements unless otherwise noted in their tournament invitations. *In some cases, the various association rules conflict with each other, as in the case of Novice Division eligibility. Have your coach check the tournament invitation to ascertain which specific eligibility requirements will be in effect in a particular invitational tournament.*]

American Forensic Association National Individual Events Tournament

Contestant Eligibility

Participants in the AFA-NIET must be full or part-time undergraduate students. Students possessing a bachelor's degree WHO HAVE NO forensics experience may request a one year waiver of the undergraduate rule. Request should be made to the NIET chair.

An undergraduate is defined by the AFA-NIET Committee as an individual who has not received a bachelor's degree. *(A student is considered as possessing a baccalaureate degree upon completion of requirements toward that degree and having been approved for graduation by her/his respective school.)*

No student shall be allowed to participate in more than four AFA-NIETs as a contestant.

No student who has competed in eight or more six-month periods (July 1- December 31, or January 1-June 30) in three or more tournaments per period of time will be eligible to compete in the AFA-NIET.

Taken from "AFA-NIET Eligibility," and "Qualification Procedures," 1994 AFA-NIET Invitation, 3-6. Used by permission of the American Forensic Association.

If a student qualifies for the AFA-NIET while eligible under the above requirements and then graduates during the academic year, he/she will be permitted to compete in the AFA-NIET for that year. (Mid-year graduates may not compete at District Qualifiers.)

A student may not pursue at-large qualification after the final day of the term in which he/she has met the requirements for graduation and has been approved for graduation by the student's respective school.

Qualifying Procedures

District Qualifier. A student participant may qualify for the AFA-NIET if he/she finishes in the top ten percent in a particular event at the District Qualifier.

The top three individuals in each event, regardless of total entries, will be advanced to the National Tournament.

The total number of persons in an event at the District Qualifier will be rounded off to the next highest interval of ten (e.g., if 31 students compete, 4 students would be advanced to Nationals under the 10 percent provision).

In order to hold a District Qualifier tournament, a minimum of three schools must participate.

At-Large Qualification. One may advance to the National Tournament by superior performance in three tournaments during the regular tournament season within the following provisions:

Each of the tournaments must have had at least ten schools competing in individual events.

The three tournament placements may not exceed a cumulative total of eight (8), based on the following formula: Up to six legs may be awarded in a final round, but no more than 50% of the competitors may earn legs in an event. The total number of entries will be rounded down.

Number of entries in the event	Number of legs earned	Places that earn legs
1	0	0
2-3	1	1st
4-5	2	1st, 2nd
6-7	3	1st, 2nd, 3rd
8-9	4	1st, 2nd, 3rd, 4th
10-11	5	1st, 2nd, 3rd, 4th, 5th
12+	6	1st, 2nd, 3rd, 4th, 5th, 6th

When determining the number of students entered in an event, the number must be based on the total number of participants competing in ALL preliminary rounds of competition in the given event. However, if a student does not actually compete in a round, but the tournament director determines that this was due to circumstances beyond the student's control and, *therefore, averages the score,* that student shall be deemed to have competed in all preliminary rounds.

Students competing in a collapsed division must be eligible for *and* advance (if they earn the right to do so) to the open division final before the numbers in a collapsed division may be counted for the at-large process. When students from a host school participate in a tournament in order for t heir numbers to count for at-large qualification totals, they must be eligible for open final placing and must advance if they earn the right to do so.

A nuance event may earn at-large qualification legs only if the corresponding AFA-NIET event is not offered at the tournament in question. (Corresponding event is explained as an event with generically identical descriptions and/or titles.)

If the District Qualifying Tournament has at least ten schools participating and fulfills the entry requirements specified above the qualification procedures under #3, then it can be used as an at-large qualifying tournament under the at-large system. Therefore, students may earn at-large legs based on normal guidelines. If a finish at a district tournament results in a student earning district qualification *and* at-large qualification in the same event, the district may advance the next competitor to the NIET. Announcement of the alternate advancement will be made only after the District Chair confirms at-large results.

A student who qualified in an event by means of the at-large system shall not be eligible to compete in that event at the district qualifying tournament.

National Forensic Association National Individual Events Tournament

Contestant Eligibility

Contestants may not have received a Bachelor's Degree or its equivalent. Contestants must have been enrolled at the institution they represent in more than a course in forensics during the academic year. Students who graduate during the [current] academic year may compete in those events in which they qualified between September [of the current academic year] and their date of graduation.

Qualifying Procedures

A student qualifies for any of the events by being in a "final" round, or in the top 10% of that event, at a tournament that had at least 7 schools participating. The tournament must have had at least two preliminary rounds. In order to qualify, students must compete in all preliminary and elimination rounds at a given tournament. If an event has fewer than twelve contestants, 50% of the contestants qualify if they competed in a final round.

Novice events qualify IF they are conducted as separate events — with separate preliminary rounds — from open and/or varsity events.

In the case of state championships and similar events that arbitrarily limit entries, the "Rule of 7" may be waived by the NFA Executive Council.

Contestants may use programs or speeches that are different from those they qualified with at the National Tournament. Contestants may not switch programs or speeches during the National Tournament.

A student may enter up to two slots of Dramatic Duo if she/he has qualified with different partners. In no case may duo partners be substituted, nor may 2 students who have qualified with other partners combine to form a new partnership.

A student may enter as many events as they have qualified. The student's best five events will count toward pentathlon points.

Taken from the "Qualification Procedures for the Tournament," 1994 National Forensic Association National Individual Events Tournament Invitation, 2. Used by permission of the National Forensic Association.

Cross Examination Debate Association

Eligibility to Earn CEDA Sweepstakes Points

Tournament contestants eligible to earn points are to be officially enrolled, undergraduate students in good standing at the college or university they represent in forensics competition.

1. Contestants are considered "officially enrolled" when they are duly registered in accordance with institutional regulations as undergraduate students at the college or university they are representing in competition.
2. Contestants are considered "undergraduate" when they are registered as bachelor or associate degree seeking students at the college or university they are representing in competition and are not in possession of a bachelor's degree.
3. "Good standing" shall be determined by the rules and policies set by the institution the forensics competitor is representing in competition.

Tournament contestants are eligible to earn points for a maximum of eight time blocks over a maximum of five different, not necessarily continuous, academic years. Participation in other forms of post-secondary debate, including but not limited to NDT; non-CEDA Lincoln-Douglas; or parliamentary debate, would count toward fulfilling one of those time blocks if the conditions in subsequent subsections are met.

1. The tournament season shall be divided into two "time blocks:" July-December and January-June.
2. Students shall have used their eligibility to earn points in a given time block if they participate in three or more debate tournaments.
   a. For purposes of eligibility, a "tournament" is defined as a forensic contest involving at least four schools in which at least four rounds of debate are held and decision are rendered by judges. This definition does not include summer workshop tournaments.
   b. "Participation" in a tournament is defined as competing in at least half of the scheduled preliminary rounds of the tournament. A student's participation in individual events, with the exception of Lincoln-Douglas debate, shall not count against his/her eligibility to earn CEDA points.
3. In case of co-enrollment, a student may earn CEDA points for only one institution per time block.

Taken from CEDA Constitution and By-Laws, *Article VII, Section 11; By-Law II, Sections D, G and H; By-Law XII, Sections A-B; and By-Law XIII, Sections A-B. Used by permission of the Cross Examination Debate Association.*

Novice Team. A novice team is a team comprised of debaters, neither of whom has participated in more than two semesters of NDT, CEDA and/or high school debate. For purposes of determining novice eligibility, high school Lincoln-Douglas competition will *not* be included as counting against eligibility to participate as a novice in a CEDA sanctioned tournament.[1]

Elimination Rounds To be counted for sweepstakes points, the CEDA division of a tournament must contain at least six teams from a minimum of three schools. Only elimination rounds meeting the following specifications will be counted toward CEDA Sweepstakes:

For Quarter-finals, there must be a field of 15 teams in the division.

For Octo-finals, there must be a field of 29 teams in the division.

For Double Octo-finals, there must be a field of 58 teams in the division.

For Double-double Octo-finals, there must be a field of 115 teams in the division.

Eligibility to Participate in the National CEDA Tournament

Students who have a bachelor's degree may compete in the National CEDA Tournament only if they receive their degree in the time block during which the national tournament occurs. Students may participant in no more than four National CEDA Tournaments.

---

1 At press time, CEDA member schools were voting on a constitutional amendment which would modify the definition of a novice team, and establish the definition of a junior team. The proposed amendment to Article VIII, Section 11, reads: "A novice team is a team comprised of debaters, neither of whom has participated in more than two semesters of NDT, CEDA and/or high school debate and/or participated in three final rounds of CEDA tournaments. A junior team is comprised of debaters neither of whom has participated in more than four semesters of NDT or CEDA debate and/or who has not participated in three final rounds of a junior or open division of a CEDA tournament."

Northern California Forensics Association

NCFA Sponsored and Sanctioned Tournament Contestant Eligibility

Open Division: Any student may enter Open Division, regardless of experience. Students with four or more semesters of collegiate experience in an event or like event *must* enter Open Division.

Junior Division: A student is eligible for Junior Division only if s/he has *fewer* than four semesters of collegiate experience in an event or like event.

Novice Division: Novice Division is open *only* to those students meeting the following NCFA Novice Eligibility Requirements:

High school experience in debate and individual events. If a student has competed in high school for one year in "A" (open/varsity) division, s/he is not eligible for Novice Division in that event or like event.

College experience in debate. If a student, at *two* tournaments, wins an elimination round above the octo-final level IN ANY DEBATE FORMAT, s/he is no longer eligible for Novice Division debate.

College experience in individual events. If a student, at *two* tournaments, places first, second or third, s/he is no longer eligible for Novice Division in that event or like event.

Higher division experience. In both debate and individual events, a student who qualifies for an elimination round in a *higher* division (Junior or Open) in *one* tournament loses her/his eligibility for Novice Division in that event or like event, EXCEPT WHEN PARTNERED WITH A STUDENT WHO MUST COMPETE IN THE HIGHER DIVISION. (When a Novice student paired with an Open or Junior student in debate, dramatic duo or readers' theatre qualifies for an elimination round in Open or Junior Division, s/he does *not* automatically lose Novice eligibility.)

Like Events: Events are grouped into the following categories. Students ineligible for competition in a division for one event in a category, are likewise ineligible for competition in that division for *all* events in that category.

Prepared Public Speaking Events: Communication Analysis, Informative (Expository) Speaking, Persuasive Speaking and Speech to Entertain (After Dinner Speaking).

Limited Preparation Public Speaking Events: Argument Analysis, Extemporaneous Speaking and Impromptu Speaking.

Individual Oral Interpretation Events: Dramatic Interpretation, Poetry Interpretation, Programmed Oral Interpretation and Prose Interpretation.

Group Individual Events: Dramatic Duo and Readers' Theatre.

Debate Events: Team and Lincoln-Douglas.